A Time to Be Born

A Time to Be Born
The Feyisa Lilesa Story

Stephany Evans Steggall

THE RED SEA PRESS

TRENTON | LONDON | NEW DELHI | CAPE TOWN | NAIROBI | ADDIS ABABA | ASMARA | IBADAN

THE RED SEA PRESS
541 West Ingham Avenue | Suite B
Trenton, New Jersey 08638

Book design: Dawid Kahts
Cover design: Asharful Haq

Library of Congress Cataloging-in-Publication Data

Names: Steggall, Stephany Evans, author.
Title: A time to be born : the Feyisa Lilesa story / Stephany Evans
   Steggall.
Description: Trenton : The Red Sea Press, [2021] | Includes bibliographical
   references. | Summary: "A Time To be Born explores a young athlete's
   decision to seize an opportunity, to defy his government, to break the
   silences, to expose the hidden truths in Ethiopia, to risk death and pay
   the price of exile"-- Provided by publisher.
Identifiers: LCCN 2020048016 | ISBN 9781569027035 (hardback) | ISBN
   9781569027042 (paperback)
Subjects: LCSH: Lilesa, Feyisa, 1990- | Long distance
   runners--Ethiopia--Biography. | Sports--Political aspects--Ethiopia. |
   Marathon running--Ethiopia. | Olympics--History.
Classification: LCC GV1061.15.L55 S74 2021 | DDC 796.42/52092 [B]--dc23
LC record available at https://lccn.loc.gov/2020048016

To the Qeerroo and Qarree for whom Feyisa raised his gesture of solidarity at Rio.

Table of Contents

Preface

Feyisa Lilesa is an elite marathon runner. He is also an Oromo, a member of the largest ethnic group in Ethiopia. He was born in 1990, a year before the overthrow of dictator Mengistu Haile Mariam and his Marxist regime, the Derg. Ethiopia under Mengistu was even more oppressive than the imperial state that preceded him. The collapse of the socialist government in 1991 and the reordering of the Ethiopian state looked promising.

Political power passed to the Ethiopian People's Revolutionary Democratic Front (EPRDF), dominated by the Tigray People's Liberation Front (TPLF). Like the Oromo Liberation Front (OLF), it was a military organization dedicated to ridding the country of Mengistu. The OLF was at the forefront of the Oromo fight for self-determination. The TPLF initially gave the impression that it would accommodate the Oromos' demand for self-rule and made big promises—to create a nation state of equals and bring about an end to ethnic domination; even to democratize the Ethiopian state and society, ending centuries of authoritarian rule; and to create peace and stability.

Oromo hopes were dashed when the OLF, pushing its Oromo nationalist agenda, was forced out of the new government, although it proceeded to harass the ruling party via low-scale guerrilla warfare. Its continued armed struggle may have provided the EPRDF with a pretext to justify ongoing persecution of the Oromo people. The EPRDF, repressive and despotic, was led by Meles Zenawi and his successor, Hailemariam Desalegn. Their government was guilty of murder, torture, concealment and denial on a large scale. It used arbitrary arrest and detention, often without charges, to suppress the appearance of dissent in many parts of the country.

All resistance in Oromia, homeland of the Oromo people, was brutally crushed. Expressions of Oromo culture and heritage were taken as evidence of dissent by a government that regarded cultural expression as challenging its rule. Oromo singers, writers and poets were arrested for supposedly criticizing the government or inciting people through their work. Those wearing traditional Oromo clothing could be arrested on the pretext that such an outward show bespoke a political agenda. Hundreds were arrested at Oromo festivals.

Many long years of ethnocide, criminal abuse of human rights, and denial of social justice culminated in anti-government protests in November of 2015. Many thousands across the Oromia Region took to the streets, complaining about marginalization, demanding an end to forceful dispossession of their ancestral land, seeking the release of prisoners, and insisting on the rule of law as opposed to the rule of the gun and the torture chamber. Security forces responded with excessive and disproportionate force.

The Oromo protesters were not defeated. In times past they had rallied under political leaders; this time they responded to a young athlete. Feyisa Lilesa led the way to victory with his symbolic protest gesture at the 2016 Olympic Games in Rio de Janeiro. All he could think about as he approached the finish line in the men's marathon were his people dying back home in Ethiopia. He saw flashbacks of the enormous tragedy. He wanted the world to know and share his burden—and, hopefully, act. The symbolic gesture, the crossed wrists, pointed ahead to a better future.

A groundswell movement, orchestrated by the Qeerroo ('strong active youth'), inspired by Feyisa's fearless action, prevailed. The Qeerroo movement finally forced the outside world to pay attention to the plight of the Oromo people. They rejuvenated and energized the Oromo movement in a revolution that led to the resignation of Hailemariam Desalegn as prime minister in February of 2018.

Then, for the first time in Ethiopian history, an Oromo—Abiy Ahmed—was elected prime minister. He has initiated unprecedented reforms and encouraged many former dissidents to return home from exile. Yet bloodshed and ethnic conflict continue to disrupt the country. Unifying the various ethnic groups is just one of the many challenges facing Abiy's government. He is tasked with delivering good governance and keeping faith with the Oromo people. Abiy Ahmed has indicated his support for Feyisa Lilesa's protest gesture by meeting with the athlete for a symbolic 'unshackling' of the crossed wrists, announcing publicly his commitment to new freedoms for Ethiopia. Events in 2020 indicate that the new freedoms may be a long time coming.

Stephany Evans Steggall

When I ran in the Olympic marathon on August 21, 2016, I ran with a heavy heart. I ran with the thought of the hundreds of men and women, most of whom were of the same age as me, more or less, who were brutally murdered by the Ethiopian regime. I ran with the memory of close friends, members of family, relatives, and acquaintances who were killed, maimed, arrested, abducted, tortured, and dehumanized just because of who they are as Oromos. I ran with the memory of all the injustice, the repression, and the dehumanization I have witnessed or heard about since my childhood which coincided with the tenure of this regime. It was in memory of them who suffered, and keep suffering still, that I chose to show the sign of peaceful resistance on the Olympic track today....

Feyisa Lilesa

1

1

The villagers run to meet me, shouting my name, waving flags and sticks. Men on horseback wheel their stallions, falling in before me and behind me. They are honoring me, welcoming home their hero. The parade of thousands advances slowly. I wave and grin, shake hands and hug many people on a *buuqa birra*, a shining day.

This is one of my best dreams. In other dreams I smell home and breathe its fresh air. I see the farmland and hear the boys calling to their sheep and goats, donkeys and cows. I taste the cool water from the stream and feel the damp touch of misty morning. The earthy tang of dawn draws me out into a new day.

I start to run. I feel many good things when I run on home soil. The peace and quiet of the countryside calm my anxious thoughts. I see the road ahead and hear the regular beat of my shoes touching the ground. I run for many miles, the length of a marathon race, and I am not tired.

On the shining day of my dreams, my feelings are those of the marathon winner—relief that the race is over and elation that the day belongs to me. Such a hero's welcome is granted to few people; once in a lifetime for a person or even for a village. Instead of laurels, I wear a lion headdress and I speak to my people, standing outside the home where I was born.

'I have a great heart for you! I give you the credit for making me who I am. I am proud to belong here. I am privileged to have been born right here.'

Then my mother speaks of her wonder that she gave birth to me in this dwelling where she still lives. 'I thank God,' she says, 'for choosing me to bear this son who is making history.'

My father has his turn. 'I am like two persons on this shining day,' he declares. 'Ordinary Lelisa Gemechu Wayesa and also an extraordinary person, the father of Feyisa Lilesa Gemechu.'

He glares at the crowd, daring them to disagree. 'Feyisa has this courage in his blood. He takes it from his Grandfather Gemechu who once fought to liberate our Oromo people. He was known as the Lord of the Slave Masters.'

I am presented with a framed portrait of Colonel Alemu Qixessa, one of my boyhood heroes. Someone cries out, 'Colonel Alemu Qixessa started the battle for the Oromo! Feyisa Lilesa Gemechu finished it!'

I cannot contemplate such a huge comparison. Perhaps there is a slight physical resemblance.

I tell the crowd that I wanted to be a soldier when I was a child. Even when I was older, I still wished that I could become a soldier one day. This is hard for me or anyone to understand—a successful athlete having such a desire. When I saw the suffering of many people in my country, and yet another funeral ceremony here and there, I said to myself again, 'I wish I were a soldier.'

'I started to think that I could fight the government and die,' I explain. 'I saw a picture of one young man whom the security forces had beaten so badly that one of his eyes was gouged out. He was the only child of a widow. After seeing that and many other atrocities, in the prisons or on the streets, I stopped fearing death.'

They nod because they too have seen such horrors. I glance at the young soldiers present as 'security' on my shining day. It is the uniform, with the big boots and rifles at the ready, that attracts many of these boys. The only boots I ever wore as a child were plastic and the only weapon I held was a staff to prod the farm animals. The closest I came to being in the military was joining the Armed Forces athletics club. I stayed for a few years and I was glad to leave.

I didn't wear shoes when I was a boy, not even in the early years of running. I was about fourteen when I first wore shoes in a race, and I was scared that I would not be able to run as fast with shoes on.

'Did not Abebe Bikila win an Olympic race running barefoot?' I demanded. 'I wonder if the soles of his feet were thick and black and hard, like mine.'

Farmers in our village used to sing about Abebe Bikila, '*Yaa Abbabaa Biqilaa oduun gootaa baargama jiraa!* (Oh Abebe Bikila, the story of a hero is overseas!)' The boys sang this while caring for animals. Everyone knew about Abebe Bikila. He was a hero. To think that the same boys would one day sing about me!

My shining dream day ends and I reflect on my heroes. I didn't even think that athletes like Abebe Bikila were from our country. I thought it was some kind of *Oduu Durii* – a folk tale. He was an Ethiopian shepherd boy and the legend is told that he used to chase pheasants until they dropped exhausted.

Haile Gebresilassie was also a hero. At school, before I started running myself, I studied his picture on the cover of my mathematics exercise book. I have a talent for drawing pictures. Using a stick, I drew Haile Gebresilassie in the thick dirt on my legs. I did not dream then that one day I would be an athlete like him. The great runners were some kind of superheroes and that was why so many people admired them. Wild animals, I thought, were not as fast as these athletes.

The boys in my village were like the wild animals in National Geographic photographs, predator and prey, wrestling and kicking. I was good at the kicking game and I could compete against many opponents at one time. My feet were so strong that I could break their toes if I kicked them hard. When I saw how many of the same boys, grown up, were kicked and belted by guards or soldiers for no good reason, I was angry and I wanted to kick back—hard.

I chose a different way to protest for the cause of *Bilisummaa* (freedom and peace and independence). I still wonder where the Olympic marathon in Rio de Janeiro, 2016, really began and what it truly meant to be crossing my arms as the race ended. I was overwhelmed by the response to my sign of peaceful resistance. So many things have happened since, but one of the most amazing things was a gift from Mo Farah, the champion athlete who runs for Great Britain. He presented me with a special pair of his shoes in recognition of my protest.

'Feyisa, I was once like you, a poor African boy with no shoes to wear.' Mo had tears in his eyes as he gave me the shoes. 'I too left my troubled country behind.'

I don't know what Mo's first ambitions were. He is now one of the greatest distance runners of all time. Other than being a soldier, I thought I would be a farmer, like my father.

When I was a child on the farm, the best time of the day came in the evening, after the animals had been penned and the family had eaten. We sat around the fireplace watching the flames slowly dying and the shapes in the room fading. As the fire flickered, I closed my eyes and listened as the stories, *Oduu Durii* in my language, told by *Akaakayyuu*, grandfather, grew bigger and brighter. I became part of the story, transported by the words from the sleepy, smoky room to a place of memory and imagination.

One day my children and grandchildren will hear my story, which begins in an Oromo village. By the time it is finished, like the Olympic race, they will understand what it has cost me and what the crossed arms mean. If I tell it well, they too will feel they are part of the story and they will remember it.

2

The year 1990 was a time to be born, but it was not a good time in Ethiopia, the land of my birth. My people, the Oromo, believe that one's fate, or destiny, is influenced by the date and time of birth. Everything and everybody in the cosmos is endowed with a unique *ayyaana* (or spirit, in one of the word's various meanings). It also refers to a day, a specific day with an exclusive constellation of stars, which gives that day a distinctive aura. The newborn takes the *ayyaana* of the birthday, with much deeper significance than what you would call a horoscope.

Possibly I was born at the wrong time, even on the wrong day, but you can be the judge of that after you have heard my story. My mother would have hoped and prayed that her baby was born under an auspicious star and that there would not be a clashing of negative energies on that day.

'Like all children,' she told me solemnly when I was older, 'you were born with certain skills and knowledge. Feyisa, you are destined to develop these for good in your generation.'

I understood that, regardless of the time of my birth, I was expected to grow up and exemplify the principles of Oromia. An Oromo is born with *Oromumma*, which refers to all those elements that constitute the Oromo personality. I am Oromo. *Oromumma* also defines Oromos as one people among many other peoples and claims their right of equality with all human beings.

I was born on February 1, 1990, in my family's home, according to tradition. This home is in Tulu Bultuma village, in the *aanaa* (or district) of Jaldu, West Shoa Zone, Ethiopia. Our place is in Oromia, which extends from the highlands in the north to Ogaden and Somalia in the east, to the Sudan border in the west, and across the Kenyan border to the Tana River in the south. Our language is *Afaan Oromoo*. Sometimes I will use words from my language because it is a very big part of my story.

I am trying to remember the name of the *deessistuu* (midwife), who is dead now. *Nagaa dhaan haboqottu* (Let her rest in peace). I think it was Haadha Dhiibbbii. I shall have to ask my mother. The *deessistuu* had been to our house twice before to assist with the birth of my older sister, Lalise Lelisa, and another baby who died. My mother's name is Biritu Fulasa Sanbata and my father is called Lelisa Gemechu Wayesa. Our *Akaakayyuu* (grandfather) took pride in teaching his grandchildren about Oromo rituals, especially our naming.

'Our special way of naming children is called *Hammachiisaa*, or embracing,' *Akaakayyuu* began. 'The parents take their infant to the *mana warra Ayyaanaa* (*Ayyaantuu*'s or Prophet's House) or it's called *mana itti bulte* (The house you slept in). The *ayyaantuu* is a prophet and an astrologer. He blesses the child by embracing him or her and, after chewing green grasses cut by the mother, spits them on the baby. Spewing or spraying saliva is a form of blessing in Oromo ceremony – the wetness of saliva symbolizes the life-giving presence of water, fertility and intimate connection of persons linked as family and community in ritual practice. This sacred blessing is part of all our life celebrations.'

Grandfather's voice became more expressive as he demonstrated the embracing, the chewing, and the spitting. He was taking the role of the *ayyaantuu*, whom he had watched in wonder many times.

'The *ayyaantuu* listens for the spirits of the times, interprets the signs of the complex interrelationships among cosmic constellations, discerns the entwining of the human and the divine, and then announces the name that fits the alignment of the stars. The name-giving is called *moggaasa*.'

Grandfather stopped, in awe of the *ayyaantuu* and the mystery of it all.

My mother said that I was embraced three times by three different ritual officials.

'That is not because the *ayyaantuu* was undecided about what to call you, or unsure of what you were destined to be,' she insisted. 'Different *ayyaantuuwwan* have association with your father, your grandmother, and me so they each had a chance to name you!'

There was an *ayyantuu* who gave me the name 'Feyisa', another who named me 'Hora', and yet another who named me 'Mullata', meaning 'visible' or 'vision'.

I would have chosen Hora had my father not told me the meaning. '*Hora* is the word for a slave, or *Garbaa*,' he said. It could also mean 'lake', and other things, but I decided against Hora. I did not want to be a slave, like many Oromo in the past. Perhaps my father meant for me to be *his* slave. We did not have a happy relationship. When I started school, I chose *Feyisa*. The name means 'savior' or 'healer', a prophetic name. I accepted that my fate was to meet the expectations associated with my name. My full name is Feyisa Lelisa Gemechu.

Anyway, after all that embracing and naming, for a while they called me different names in my *qe'ee*, or village. When I was little they called me 'Bogia' because I was so fat. We were never without food in the house. The reason for this is that we were farmers, growing wheat, flaxseed, beans, corn, peas, and so on. *Teff*, the grain that is grown widely in Ethiopia to make the staple diet food, *buddeena* (fermented spongy bread; *injera* in Amharic), does not do well in our region. The crops are harvested in one season; then potatoes, onions, and green vegetables like kale are grown in the garden and harvested in another season. When one is out of season the other would be ready, so we were never hungry. But I had heard about famine in my country.

'Why is it often said there is hunger in Ethiopia?' I asked my grandfather. 'We have plenty to eat!'

'The hunger is in the dry areas of our country,' he explained. 'There was a terrible drought a few years before you were born, but it didn't happen around our village. Where we live is more than 3,000 meters above sea level. We have all the four seasons and rain falls in all of them except winter. There are times when people who live in the lowlands bring their firewood and exchange them for our potatoes.'

I must have eaten a lot of potatoes. In families like ours, the stronger ones took much of the meal when we ate together. I grew to be the strongest and I often grabbed most of the food and ran away to gobble it down. I was greedy as well as fat and I am ashamed when I remember that. I will talk more about my home and family soon, but firstly I want to tell you about our land.

The *biyyee* (soil or dirt) in *Biyyaa Oromiyaa* has a deep meaning for me because it is part of my home. The soil alone has a different meaning for non-Oromos who see it as an asset, covet it, and remove us to get access to that soil for their own purposes. They clear the people, the trees, and the animals away; then they sow that precious soil with alien, imported seeds or build cheap structures. If *Biyyaa Oromiyaa*, my Oromo homeland, were not beautiful and productive, there would be no reason for our enemies to evict us from it and kill us for it. The removal and murder of my people will be part of this story, which could also be called *Biyyaa Oromiyaa*, the saga of my father's land.

Until the early 1880s, my Oromo ancestors were the makers of their own history, when they lived beyond the military control and political influence of the medieval Christian kingdom of Abyssinia. Some were pastoral nomads, but others were practising settled agriculture and living in what is now the region of Shoa, even before the fourteenth century.

As I heard from our *haayyuu* (or elders), we moved to Jaldu from a place called Tokkee Kuttaayee, which is between Ambo and Gedo, towns further west. There are many ancestral lineage groups, or *gosas*, and I was born into the Warra Gurra section of the Mecha and Tulema *gosas*—both, because they are like brothers, unified and loyal. Throughout the years, our *gosa* grew larger and stronger.

My paternal grandfather's cousin had a story about our ancestors that he liked to tell. He lived till he was 111 years old, so he had many stories for me. His voice did not falter with age. 'Your great-grandfather, Wayesa Gika, took back this land by fighting off some Amhara family, a father and his son, from it.' He paused to look gravely at me. 'We have talked before about the Amhara, the second largest ethnic group in our country. There are also the Tigrayans, another group in the north, but not as big. You will know more about them as you get older.' As a boy I wondered about the day when Wayesa Gika took the land and what force he used. I wish I'd been there to see that. I still don't know why that Amhara family was there or where they ended up.

I now know enough about Ethiopian history to believe that during the years from the middle of the nineteenth century to about the middle of the twentieth, many Oromo in the peripheries of the country had greater freedom and more chances to assert themselves if there was a crisis in the imperial center. Power struggles there continued until the reign of Haile Selassie began with his coronation in 1930.

When the Italians invaded Ethiopia in 1935, they divided it into regions based on language and ethnicity. 'It has been claimed,' my great-uncle once said, 'that the Italians wanted to win the trust of the non-Amhara peoples through the elimination of the Amhara claim to superiority over them. Hard as it may be to believe now, Amharas could not work in government offices or use Amharic in non-Amhara territories. In Finfinne, *Afaan Oromoo* and Amharic were used. This all changed, of course.'

I think my great-grandfather saw his chance after the 1974 revolution, a class-based revolution, whose adherents marched to the tune of 'Land to the Tiller'. The Derg, the collusion of officers that came to power after Emperor Haile Selassie was deposed, were notoriously a bad lot, but they intended radical reforms to tackle the problem of land stolen under the reigns of Menelik and Haile Selassie. Some peasants took matters into their own hands and chased Amhara landlords from their holdings.

Anyway, we had our house, our *mana*, not far away from our farm, our *qonnaa*; perhaps a couple of kilometers. It had a garden where we grew vegetables and an enclosure for the animals. The harvested crops were stored at home. Our house was not exactly on the farmland or surrounded by it. If we were to live on the farmland, the animals might get out of their fences at night and destroy what we grew.

My father was proud of our big lands which yielded many quintals of grain. He sold most of the crops, but not always the animals. We had about fifteen, sometimes twenty cattle, as well as goats, horses, mules, and sheep. We had plenty of milk for 'Bogia' and his brother and sisters and plenty of oxen to plough their father's land. We would sell an animal if it was infertile. My father was also quick to sell an ox if it did not please him. 'That one,' he would say after a difficult day, 'is not willing to plough. He must go.' Sometimes these were ones I liked, but I would prefer to see them go than to see them punished for refusing to pull the plough, or for displeasing my father with bad behavior.

I started taking care of the animals alone at the age of six. At first, I went to the grazing land with my sister, who is four years older than I am. My father brought a meal for me around two o'clock and sent my sister home to help our mother. He stayed behind and watched while I cared for the animals. 'You can do this alone now,' he decided in his gruff way. 'Your sister has other work to do.'

The grazing land was around two kilometers away from our house. At first, I did not like being out in the hot sun or the pouring rain and the days wouldn't end. It was hard to stay awake and to keep watch over all the animals at once. When I drove to Jaldu from Finfinne as a young man, I saw the little shepherd boys with their animals, wielding the lightweight whips that are longer than they are. They treat the animals as companions and have special ones that know them and come to them. I remember those I liked best. 'She is my favorite,' I would tell the herd. 'I give her the best grass.' I spoiled her.

Like me, the small boys have trouble keeping control of obstinate beasts. They also play and forget to watch the animals; one of the fathers sees this and runs, shouting and waving a stick. He is upset because his hard work is ruined. Perhaps that day a lot of damage is done to the farmer's crop.

'Look at your cows eating my crop!' yelled a neighbor to me, more than once. He beat me and then told my father, who also beat me.

I constantly ran after animals. Soon I was no longer 'Bogia'. When he was old enough, my younger brother, Aduna, started to come with me. Two were better than one, but our games and chatter got us into trouble. One day we were tending horses, mules, sheep, and cattle, in the forest near a river. We could hear our father shouting our names in his big rough voice.

'Feyisa! Aduna! Feyisa! Aduna! Where are you, stupid boys?'

We shouted back but he couldn't hear us because of the noise the river was making.

'The goats!' he roared. 'Where are the goats?'

He was trying to tell us that our goats were disappearing among another herd of animals. We didn't know what we were doing wrong and started counting the animals. There were horses, mules, cattle and sheep. Two little boys had forgotten that there should also be goats under their care.

'Don't worry,' I reassured Aduna. 'We have done nothing wrong. We won't be in trouble. Abba can see that we have all the animals.'

Suddenly, our father appeared with the goats and he was very angry. We ran from him as fast as we could. The first running I did, apart from chasing animals, was to get away from my father and his heavy hand.

I was afraid of him and I kept a watchful distance from him. He would not let me plough, but I did not care. He was never satisfied with anything I did. When I was older, I had to plough if he was not around; possibly he was away for the day in another village for a funeral or something. It was tiresome to plough, more exhausting than running a marathon. Ploughing takes five or six hours a day, covering very long distances, perhaps even twenty kilometers.

The farming system has not changed. Farmers still plough land using animals and their own hard labor. It may attract the tourists' eager eyes to see the dogged oxen and the dirty farmer moving the wooden plough, but it should not be like this, a primitive way of doing things to this very day.

'The Oromo are the same as these beasts of burden,' observed Kebede Fayissa, a dear friend of mine who will come into this story. 'They strain against the yoke and bow their heads when beaten. But they do not fall to their knees easily.' Kebede was destined to bear a very heavy yoke. 'Kebede' is an Amharic name that Oromos use a lot. It probably doesn't make a lot of sense in English, but it means 'heavy' or 'severe'.

My father was rich compared to others in the village, because he owned six farm parcels. We had six *goteras*, the traditional barns in which crops are stored. Each one held as much as ten quintals of grain and we stored wheat and barley in them until they were full. We stored the remaining sacks of grain in a separate room in our home.

We reaped abundant crops without using modern fertilizers. 'We have some of the richest soil in the world!' my grandfather told me. 'If we care for it well, we do not need to improve it with fertilizer.'

In good seasons, even my father was happy when the harvest was safely stored in the *goteras* and in the house. He counted the sacks with satisfaction. I was happy too because there was no need to keep the animals from entering farmlands stripped bare of grain. Then my mother would say, 'Feyisa, come now. We will collect water from the spring.' Collecting water in the big clay pots, *hubboo*, was women's work, but I did not mind. The water from the spring was cold and clean and very good. I have tasted much water from many parts of the world, and none can compare to the water I drank there at that spring.

We did not have running water in the village, but I thought that fetching the water would be a good job to have. I loved being outside, unless it meant all day alone with the herd. The women had many rivers to choose from; on our farmlands alone, four of the farms were crossed by rivers.

I watched Hadhaa (Mother) as she emptied what was left in one *hubboo* to a smaller pot. She is beautiful to look at, with her finely shaped face, etched olive skin and far-seeing eyes. She has no need of the makeup that I see on the faces of Western women. My mother does not have to enhance her looks; she has no disfigurement to be hidden by artifice. I hoped that the wife I chose one day would be the same. My mother has a wide smile and I am happy when it is there for me.

My mother's voice could be sharp, though. 'Feyisa! I have much to do. Hurry!'

She was tired that day, just after harvest, from much cooking and serving. At harvest time, the village relied on what was known as *daboo*, a cooperative labor service when farmers worked on each other's fields in turn. This is especially needed for weeding, ploughing, clearing land, and harvesting. *Abbaaa daadoo* (the farmer) was expected to feed the group on his day. Or rather, my mother was. 'Today it is my turn,' she said proudly.

It was a good system, but hard work. My father arranged for several able-bodied men and women to help harvest and he planned how best to carry out the work. My mother and a few neighboring women prepared food and drink. Help was offered by neighbors according to the farmer's agreeable manners, love of friends, generosity, and sociability. I did not think my father had any of these qualities, but the workers would come, and the women would cook.

The workers rested under the trees in the middle of the day and *farso* (homemade beer) and *daabboo* (leavened bread) were taken to them. The oxen and horses had provided labor too and they were given water and straw from the winnowing of the barley.

In the evening, my mother supervised dinner and prepared *buna* (coffee), and everyone sang heroic songs to express their feelings of pride and longing. Some were very good at eloquent poetry. Some liked to show their appreciation of the woman's efforts: 'The *buna* is good' or 'Birutu makes the best *buddeena*.' They would say at the next house, 'Biritu did this...or that....' Such appreciation for the good food was not only gratifying to my mother; it meant more people would come to her house next time and labor for her food. The next woman at the next farm had to compete. Family pride was at stake.

The workers sang as they worked—love songs, war songs, harvest songs. At mealtime, prayers of thanksgiving and blessings were offered and more songs, unless someone in the neighborhood had died, a time when singing was prohibited.

The Oromo people have what they call *geerarsa*. A type of folk song, its name is derived from the imperative *geerar*, which means 'Sing!' As I grew older and listened to the words more carefully, I understood that some of the songs were not just about our beautiful land: *Maddii Killee Leensaa, Killee Leensaa* (Where rich, green grass is plentiful); *Dheeddi Fardeenille, Fardeenrllee* (There, horses graze).

There were also reprimands and warnings: *Namuu Gamtaanqabnee, Gamtaanqabnee* (People without unity of purpose), *Gamtaa Waliingallee, Waliingallee* (Organizations without coherence), *Jettii Jarreenillee, larreenillee* (Aliens will pick on and point fingers to exploit you). There is the belief, to this day, that the Oromo as a nation cannot achieve their goal because they lack unity. There have been many aliens who have claimed to know what is good for us and they could succeed if we did not follow the advice, *Firaaraa Infagaatinaa* (You need to band and stay close).

I always thought our people banded together well, but I had a lot to learn about our different *gosas* in different regions. I didn't know their meaning when I first heard the words of a song by Wasanu Dido that exhorts, *hin teenyu maalumatti teenyaa, tasmaamma'aa yaa nama keenyaa* (Don't be dormant, be united). I know better now.

I do understand the Oromos' love of and belief in wetness. They prayed, *irreffannaa,* on the river banks when the rain, the essential life-giving force, did not fall. They carried *gadii* (milk) and fresh grass to acknowledge the life-giving product of rain. When it pours from the sky, it makes the grasses grow, which feed the cattle which give the milk, which nourishes the people and keeps them also fertile! Such abundance is conjured up ritually with the bringing of milk and green fresh (meaning water-laden) grasses. Grasses are the ritual stand-in for water in many ceremonies, considered sacred.

The people pray, 'May you rain your blessings over our people and nation.' When the supplicants got back from prayer, they anticipated rain.

Here is a story that many will find hard to believe; I have trouble believing it myself. When the rain did not come or did not stop and threatened to destroy our crops in autumn, farmers could go to a special clan that lived in the Jaldu district. The farmers would explain the problem and pay the *maallimaa* (traditional ritual leaders) to intervene. 'If you tell them your problem today,' people would say, 'it will start or stop raining before you get home.' This amazed me. They really believe that they could attract or dismiss clouds, but they did not chase clouds as some are known to do.

The special clan was called *Warra Maallimaa*. The rumor was that the enchantment did not work if they ate sheep's flesh. Some people paid them to keep the rain away when they buried their dead, because they did not want rain to disrupt the funeral. It is difficult to believe and explain. You may ask me how does this work? You would have to experience it.

In our area we might use rivers for irrigation if there is a shortage of rainfall. Since there are many rivers around, our women sometimes struggled to decide which river to go to for water. Most of the time they went to the spring that I love for its cold water that satisfies the thirst like no other. Nobody uses irrigation much and the rivers flow peaceably without being exploited, because we have enough rainfall. Sometimes in January we irrigated potatoes on one of our lands. That is when the land is at its driest.

3

If you visit my home village in the dry season you will say it is a very brown place. The smooth skin of the villagers' feet matches the earth beneath them—earth which is so much a part of who we are. Our footprints are stamped along the well-worn lanes that serve as streets for us and our animals, and they are embedded in the dirt floors of our huts. From the doorways, faces will stare at you, the *faranjii* (foreigner; *ferenji* in Amharic), and children will crowd around you, their big dark eyes wide with curiosity.

Members of my family will be among those who stare, although they have not all stayed in Jaldu. My older sister is named Lalise Lelisa, my brother is named Aduna Lelisa; then the next sisters are named Lense Lelisa, Kabene Lelisa, and Warkitu Lelisa. Three other children died. The way they passed away, I'm told, was that their muscles were weaker, and their bodies didn't get stronger. One of my aunts couldn't have children and my parents gave her a girl child, which may seem strange to you, but Oromo tradition allows *guddifacha* (adoption). That sister adopted was one of those who got sick and died.

I am the second child of my family, because according to our tradition a child who is not alive is not counted. I was born after one baby died, which might be why my parents liked the name Feyisa. I was to heal their pain of burying one boy baby. All of us were named by the process of *Hammachisa* (embracing), which takes place five days after the birth. A festival is prepared for each one at the *ayyaantuu*'s home, when the parents take gifts and money.

Our extended family is very big. Every night we all went to my Grandfather Gemechu's house and I slept there most nights too. If I stayed at our house, my father often hit me if I spoke or annoyed him and that's why I didn't like to be there. I took the animals to their shelter and slipped away to grandfather's place.

I confided in my friend Kebede about this unhealed sore from my childhood that still causes me pain. We were in my car in Finfinne, when I was a young independent man. 'I see my father as a person who causes problems. He disturbs the family and also other people, who are not family members. When you mention the name of my father, all I recall is the way he used to chase me and cause me grief. I didn't see much of his better sides. But, the good thing about him is that he didn't make me do difficult jobs. He didn't even order me to do things that much, because he would not be satisfied with what I did anyway. He is as powerful as this car I am driving, Kebede. He disturbs me a lot and he is still so negative when I consult him.'

Kebede nodded and perhaps he understood. He came from the same district and he had seen many family conflicts. He and I shared our most secret things. I wish…No, I will not get ahead of myself in this story. All you need to know now is that Kebede was as close to me as my brother Aduna. He even appears in my dreams. I encounter mostly good things in my dreams, but there is one I sometimes have before a race that does not bode well for me. I come to a mountain while I am leading the race and I cannot climb it. This is a bad dream, but the worst dream is when Kebede is calling my name and I cannot find him. I run and run until the voice suddenly stops.

'Those are not just dreams that you have,' Kebede once said when I told him about the vivid ones. 'They are visions, especially when you think that an *Ayyaantuu* named you *Mullataa*.'

I remember Kebede's words when others scoff at dreams and visions, dismissing them as evidence of a pagan heritage, but Oromos are respectful and believing. I know of others who have powerful prophetic dreams.

Now I must return to the story. My parents' house is on the same property as my grandfather's house, about 100 meters away. According to Oromo tradition, a father does not live in the same house with his married son. That is why my grandfather built another house for my father when he married. They were neighbors. I cared for his animals too with my parents' animals. My maternal grandparents lived in a village called Kilbe in the Jaldu district, about five or six kilometers east of our village. We did not see them so often.

We loved our paternal grandmother-in-law, as we called her, more than our actual grandmother. She was my grandfather's second wife. I went to her house, not my actual grandmother's house, as my grandfather had separate houses built for his two wives. She didn't have children of her own and she loved us dearly. 'Come here to me, Feyisa!' she called when someone hit me. She loved me so much that she didn't like anyone to touch me. She glared at the person who wanted to hit me, even my father, and held me close. She brought my rain clothes to the place where I was caring for animals when heavy rain began to fall. I used to sleep with her on her bed. She was very old, and I liked her scent when I lay there beside her. Her name was Geti Bayyan.

I sat close to Geti at grandfather's house in the evenings. There was no *kuraz* (kerosene lamp) to make light. There were very few people who had *kuraz* and these were only used if they had a special event or had to work at night. We sat in a circle around the fire and listened to the stories my grandfather told us.

The fireplace was a few centimeters away from the *utuba* (main pillar) of the house. Our grandfather's seat leaned against the pillar. He was the only one who had a chair. We sat on the ground. Nobody would dare to sit on his chair. He knew about everybody's behavior in the house and nobody disturbed others when he was around. The children did not feel safe if grandfather was not there; other grown-up family members like my uncles and aunts gave us hard times. They sent us to fetch water, to do this and that while he was absent, but they wouldn't order us to do anything if he was there. He used to feed us when he ate, a practice we call *gursha*. I have a lot of good memories about him.

Best of all I remember the *mammaksaa* (proverbs) and *hibboo* (riddles) that I learned. These were presented like a game, exciting and entertaining for the young ones. *Goojjoon gamaa balballi ishii lama* (The far away hut has two doors). Answer: nose. *Re'ee daalattiin gaara gamaa keessa dheeddi* (A brown goat grazes in that far away mountain). Answer: head louse. One proverb that has stayed with me, to think about, especially now I am telling this story about myself, says *Abbaan of hin argu*, meaning 'One cannot see oneself'.

At the fireside, one of the grown-ups would reminisce about 'when I was your age….' That might be about the cost of one sheep or goat back then compared to the present. It was a happy time, listening and laughing, singing and dancing, sometimes till midnight. The next day we shared with our friends the things we were told.

I wish I could remember all the *oduu durii* that we heard. We closed our eyes and listened. I didn't always understand the message in these stories at the time. I was only listening to them because I loved the sound of them, the expressive way my grandfather told them, and the peace of the room when all was well with one another. Years later, I came to appreciate the meaning behind these stories.

I liked best the stories about heroes, such as *Mullataa Fayyisoo* (Mulata Fayiso). He was a big name, and everyone wanted to be associated with this hero. He was my relative through my mother and I take pride in the connection. To this day I hear the voice of my grandfather telling us the story of *Lola Mullataa Fayyisoo* (Mulata Fayiso's War). He told it many times and each time he added some small detail we had not heard before.

'It is 1978 (1971 according to the Ethiopian calendar) in Koftu, a village in the countryside of Jaldu,' my grandfather began, and suddenly he was back there, a witness to what took place. 'The first day of fighting is at Mulata Fayiso's house. With the assistance of another brave man, Wagi Sato, he plans to defy the Derg, who kill many who oppose them, including landowners and students. In Jaldu and many other areas, the Derg moved to systematically disarm the people, who parted with their guns extremely reluctantly and some not at all. The Derg was fearful of rebellion so they wanted to take away the means for armed fighting.'

Grandfather paused and, in the silence, we heard the harsh call of a hyena. I shivered and drew closer to Geti. She patted my head.

'Mulata Fayiso and several other men refuse to give up their guns. They meet at Mulata Fayiso's house, with their arms, and make plans. "If we give them our guns today, what will it be tomorrow? Tomorrow it might be the wives they take." Geti frowns at the thought.

'In the night 300 soldiers are deployed in Jaldu and circle the house of Mulata Fayiso. They have modern weapons, M1 and M2 carbines. The area has forest all around the house, which is fenced with tree poles. The Derg have a microphone: "Give up your guns!" The men in the house do not answer. At first light, 5.00 am, the fight begins. Within an hour the rebels destroy the Derg army, killing several soldiers and capturing ten. No one from our side is hurt. Not that day. They disarm the prisoners and set them free. This is Day 1, in October 1978.'

Men like Wagi Sato had fought in the army against the Italians. I have listened to stories about the war with the Italians many times. They killed many of our brave men, but it is harder to think of the Derg killing their own countrymen. The Derg soldiers returned and destroyed the homes of Mulata Fayiso, Wagi Sato, and others. Then Grandfather told the bit that excited me most.

'Wagi Sato has two sons and he hides them and the rest of his family. "They may kill my kids because of me," he says to Mulata Fayiso. "I must give them weapons and teach them how to use them. One boy, Tolcha Wagi, is only ten years old but he learns to fire a carbine. He joins the fight, with his brother, Dirbsa.'

I know the rest of the story. Soon people of all ages are fighting the Derg. The rebels enlist the help of the whole Jaldu community and hand out guns to fight. Mulata Fayiso himself gives my father a firearm. We all chant grandfather's line: *Yeroo waraanni nutti dhufe ni lolle, lola jabaa!* (When armies come, we fight, we fight!). Our victories are short-lived, although in one big fight we destroy twenty army trucks. The Derg deploys many armies in different directions, burning and destroying property and crops as they advance. In one awful scene they take their prisoners to a town center and gather all its inhabitants at gunpoint. The prisoners' hands are tied behind their backs, they are forced to lie down and then the soldiers shoot them in front of their families and friends. Many brave fighters die that day.

Mulata Fayiso and the remaining rebels hid for one month in the Chilimo Forest. They were finally overwhelmed by a big force. Tolcha Wagi told us years later that his father and Mulata Fayiso warn, 'If you are wounded, kill yourself. Don't give your hand.' This means don't surrender. Mulata Fayiso and his nephews were killed in battle. The body of Mulata Fayiso hung in a town of Jaldu for three days. At this point I buried my face in Geti's skirt.

Wagi Sato and his two sons escaped, but later they were captured, imprisoned, and tortured. They were taken to Maekelawi, that prison of unspeakable infamy in Finfinne. 'Some people they hang by piano rope [wire],' Tolcha Wagi tells us. 'We are tortured until we cannot stand up. We are in prison for seven years.'

I often remember those teenager boys, shut away for all those years. I know of many others now and I think about them day and night. Until April of 2018, Maekelawi continued to cruelly extract the blood of the Oromo, and others. The screams of the tortured echoed through its ghastly chambers.

My grandfather always finished the story about Mulata Fayiso with a kind of homily.

'We are all farmers—cultivating the soil and caring for our animals. We are blessed with good land and weather. For centuries our country is Oromia, our people Oromo. We have our language, our culture, our identity. King Menelik II got modern weapons from foreign countries and declared war on us. His armies killed many of our people. He attacked our language. We were forced to accept the Amharic language; we were forced to accept other names. As the years went by the Oromo were denigrated as a people without history.'

One of my young aunts always had a question to ask. 'People say Ethiopia was never colonized. What do you say to them, *Akaakayyuu?*'

'Menelik conquered Tigrayans to the north, Eritreans to the east and Oromos to the south. These people saw their black conqueror as no different from the white intruders—British, French, and Italians. We were Menelik's colonies and nothing much has changed. He gave our people and our lands to his Amhara-Tigray settlers called *neftanya*. In fact, the *neftanya* were given Oromo *gabars* (slaves) to do their work. They owned Oromos as they owned cattle and sheep.'

My grandfather sat tall and straight and he stared into the dying fire.

'In 1886, within a day 12,000 people were killed. All the time the Amhara talk about Menelik: Menelik did this, he did that. They don't like to hear another version of their history. They are Abyssinian (we call them *Habesha*) and we are Oromo. This is the reality. The Oromo economy is the backbone of Ethiopia, with its best resources of grain, animals, gold, and coffee. To get these, Menelik and others since, have committed ethnocide.

'When the Derg vanquished Menelik's descendant, Haile Selassie, they promised "Land to the Tiller". They declared land redistribution, but the grabbing of land from the Oromo continued, and still goes on in many places under this current government. We still struggle, but who knows or cares?'

I was too young to understand all this. I accepted what my grandfather said, but it was a long time, after he died—*Nagaadhaan haboqtuu* (Let him rest in peace)—before I knew more about our history and could interpret it for myself. Other boys talked about the 12,000 Oromo warriors killed during the Arsi resistance, a number that doesn't include the women, children, and old men whom the Abyssinian soldiers burned alive and massacred while looting. It's said that the Arsi campaign was the bloodiest of Menelik's reign. Arsi is Oromo country south of Finfinne. Arsi's *Abbaa Duula* (War Minister), Roobaa Butta, voiced his faith in the future independence of Oromia by declaring, 'The hour has not come but it will come; perhaps our children will see the departure of the oppressor.'

The hour had not come when I was still young—not then. It certainly did not come during the years of my father and his generation. They didn't transfer a lot of history to our generation. In such aspects, I didn't inherit anything from my father. I learned many things from my grandfather. It was my father's generation, I believed, that was responsible for the destruction of many traditions. For example, it was in their generation that children started to be named in Amharic. Only a handful of their generation did good things. There are few songs or stories about them. I hear elders talk of a lost generation, referring to those Oromo who disconnect from their roots and culture. I say that my father's generation lost its way, but this is not necessarily a viewpoint shared by others.

Kebede Fayissa also thrilled to the stories about Mulata Fayiso, a fighter short in stature but big in reputation. His name, Mulata, can mean someone who is visible, someone who towers above others, not physically but in status and significance in the community. Grandfather said it can also mean someone with a vision, someone to whom ancestral visions come. When you add *Mullataa* and *Fayyisoo*, in our language, it means someone with a vision who heals his people.

We studied sepia photographs of Mulata Fayiso on the Internet. 'Look at the furrows between his eyes,' said Kebede. 'He frowns while he plans his next strategy. Those deep lines are like yours.' Kebede stares at my face. 'Perhaps you will be another Mulata Fayiso.'

He was joking, but I started to think about my yearning to be a soldier, which started with the legends of *Lola Mullataa Fayyisoo*. My generation sings an emotional song, '*Sodaa qawwee hin qabnu* (We have no fear of bullets)'. We may die, but we still defy the weapons of the enemy.

Kebede and I argued about the best way for the Oromo to fight a corrupt government. 'I am against violence,' he insisted. 'There must be a better way.' I want peace in my land too, but back then I was an angry man.

4

In my big family we fought among ourselves, usually at mealtimes. If I think about the way we clawed at each other and called each other nasty names that the *ayyaantuu* would not approve of, I am sad. When you go through all the hard times of a poor boy and later become rich and successful, you wish that you had been kinder to your brother and sisters. Mostly we forgot our disagreements by the next day, but some words said in spite are not so easily forgotten. Later I tried to repay my siblings.

They were the ones who sold their sheep or goats to buy me clothes and the other things I needed when I started running seriously. Our parents did not help me that much, although my mother would do little things on the quiet when my father was not around. 'Feyisa,' she would whisper.

'See what I have for you.' Usually it was a few extra *birr* she had put aside after market day. In those days every *birr* was precious to me and helped me get to the next race.

We all wanted to go to the town of Gojo on market days. These were held every Saturday, with a smaller one during the week. We joined others from the village walking on the road to Gojo with their goats and sheep, eggs and vegetables to sell. Some passed us with horse and cart or on horseback. I miss the social outings of those days. Sometimes I could not go because I had to stay with the animals, but Geti or my mother made sure I got a treat. I loved the sugar canes best, sweet and juicy, better than any lollipop. I liked to meet people on market day. I think of them all as I write—the old ones especially.

We all knew Nurefssa Tujo, a spiritual leader, whom I approached deferentially with the greeting, '*Attam? Fayyaa? Nagaa?* (How are you? Are you well? Are you at peace?)'. When you ask those questions, you are also asking about the well-being of the children, the neighbors, the animals, the crops, the rivers, the valleys, etc. The individual is well only when everybody and everything around him is well and at peace. Sometimes the answer takes a long time!

I stopped and stared at men who were chewing *caatii*. It is also known as *chat* or *kat* or *qat* or *jimma*. In colloquial English, it is Abyssinian tea or African salad. I smile at these harmless names for the very addictive leaves; imagine an Englishman having *chat* for his tea or salad. The plant does not grow around our village, but I have heard it said that the *chat* plant was discovered in the Horn of Africa and the Yemen before coffee. In some places, men and boys chew all day on a wad of *chat* like people in the West chew gum. My family and friends do not like *chat*. We like *arake* (distilled alcohol) and *farso* (beer). I started drinking them with my family when I was quite young, but I have never chewed *chat* or smoked a cigarette.

We were all worn out after the long market days. We slept in traditional beds, their frames wooden and the bases of interlaced *xeepha* (strips of leather from the cow's hide, once known as *teepha*) We also had *itillee*, sheets of cow hide that we lay on. These beds are very comfortable and I slept well. I remember us at night with our animals in the same room. The cows had a fenced shelter outside—they can withstand cold weather. But sheep and horses can't; they will die if left out in the cold. I did not mind their warm presence and familiar smell, but at some point in my childhood we built a new house and separated from the animals. The house in which the animals lived became a place to cook, but we did not sleep or eat there again.

My mother often sang as she prepared our meals. I liked best the one known as *Asaabalee*, a prayer song for any time. *Asaabala* is the name of a small colorful song bird; *Asaabalee* is an endearment for *Asaabala*: 'O *Dachii* (Earth), mother of grass / Your top produces food / Your bottom produces water / We farm and eat off you / We breed and flock on you / Standing strong in your spirit / *Asaabalee….*'

I see my mother there at the fireplace using her *waciitii*, pots made from clay, to prepare our traditional foods, *caccabsaa* made from barley and thin bread, *kitta*, which is delicious mixed with butter. Food prepared in clay pots and pans tastes much better than in metal or china. The only kitchenware we bought from the market were tiny coffee cups, *sinii*, from China. There is also a traditional cup called *waancaa*, which is made from animal horns, used to drink *boka* (honey wine) and *farso* (beer). We sat at wooden tables and ate from wooden dishes.

When I was small I liked to eat breakfast. 'Bogia! Bogia! No wonder you are fat!' That's what my family would say as I shovelled in my porridge, *kinche*, an unrefined wheat, that I ate with a *fal'ana*, a horn spoon. We used our fingers for *buddena*, but not for porridge. 'He will soon be caring for our animals,' growled my father. 'There won't be time for porridge then.'

I was not pleased when I had to miss my porridge, but before long this happened often. There were times you skipped breakfast. There were times you skipped lunch or both. Some of us took animals for grazing early in the morning before breakfast was served and might return home at midday to eat lunch. Some of us only ate breakfast in the morning and missed lunch. Many days I looked in vain for Geti, who brought me food when she could slip away.

The only mealtime we were certain of was dinner, about 7:00 pm. Mostly it was *buddeena* and *itto* (*wot* in Amharic). The *itto* is a sauce, of various spices and vegetables. Other dishes are made with chickpeas, beans, and potatoes. Our national dish of *buddeena itto* (*injera wot*) is about the one and only thing on which all Ethiopians agree: it is the tastiest and most nutritious food. On holidays and special occasions, the women add chicken, lamb, beef, goat, or eggs to the main dishes. Our *buna*, (coffee), freshly roasted, is the best in the world.

When I left home, I missed those delicious cooking smells, coming from every dwelling place in the village, that drew us all home, hungry and tired, as the sun went down. I cannot understand now why we spoilt that nightly feast with our quarrels. The day came when I was homesick for the traditional meal in my own land.

We were healthy children. I was never seriously ill or injured, but I do remember the chicken pox spreading among us. Since our village is in the highlands, there is no exposures to diseases like malaria. We only catch the common cold. It's the same for me now, except sometimes when I travel, I get sick in hotels from food that is not fresh. When I eat such food, I vomit and then get well; I don't need to go to a clinic. I have never had any immunization.

I was a strong boy. Before I started school, my father sent me to the grinding machines, in Gojo, eight kilometers away from our home. I used to carry about ten kilograms of grain there and back. A lot of people went there from rural areas to have their grain ground and we waited in long queues and paid money depending on the weight of the grain. If I remember correctly, there were five grinding machines in the town. Later on, two grinding machines were installed near our village but were out of working order after two or three years, for reasons not known to me.

Other boys will tell you I was a tough kid too. I've already told you about the kicking game when I competed against many opponents at a time. We also used to wrestle. We had to be tough.

'Take the horses to the marshland,' my father commanded. I did not argue with him, but I was sullen because he ordered me about in an unkind tone. I loved the horses and once out of his sight I would ride one of them. The marshland was far from our house. There were many other boys at the marshland that day. I can say I wrestled one to one, every one of them, the whole day. I managed to defeat all of them.

I had to be strong and persistent because if one of them was to defeat me, all of them would have to come and beat me up. I wouldn't let kids from other neighborhoods pass peacefully through our neighborhood; they did the same to me. They lay in wait to hit and kick me.

'What is your full name?' they demanded if I dared to venture into their territory.

To tell them would mean defeat; you had to surrender. You said nothing; they threw rocks and their dogs chased you. You were glad then that you could run fast. Those dogs were like the jackals we sometimes saw—pack animals, small and mean and hungry; quick and ready to ambush.

Even though I didn't have an interest then to be a runner, I ran while playing games like hide and seek. The others couldn't catch me. We also used to race while we were supposed to be watching the animals, then again after taking the animals home in the evening. We were all little athletes in the making—it was our way of life, running every day in the high, thin air. We were as skittish as unbroken colts and nimble as *kuruphee* (gazelles). We often saw the graceful gazelles and we imitated their leaps and bounds. Their lustrous eyes are not unlike our own.

We were children still and, if we got the chance, we played games at the places where we cared for the animals, away from the eyes of the grown-ups. We used to jump from higher ground to lower ground, seeing who could jump the furthest distance. We took turns on a rope swing that took us out over a river and competed to jump over that river. None of us learned to swim in the proper way, but I don't remember a child drowning. During summer we used to swim in a river when it was full.

I go to beaches or proper pools now to swim, yet I don't have the same pleasure as back then in the river with my friends. Perhaps all of us, once we are adults, feel this way, because we cannot be children again. We made our own fun. Such games we played happily. We were unaware of the toys and gadgets that the rich kids in the city had.

To this day, if I see a big tree I want to climb it. Back then I climbed trees to hide from my father. He liked to hit me always, even when I was not doing anything. 'Come down!' he bellowed if he had chased me. 'I will wait here until you come down.' But he mostly gave up and walked away grumbling and muttering. If he stayed too long with his threats and taunts, I jumped from the tree and fled.

One day my cousin and I climbed up a difficult, unyielding tree in the morning and were afraid to climb down. We couldn't climb down no matter how hard we tried. We stayed in that tree the whole day. We were hungry and thirsty. My cousin started shouting. 'We are here! Can't you hear us? We don't want to be in this tree anymore! Help us!' I finally jumped out of the tree and ran away as I didn't want my father to know where I had been all day. I was truly afraid that he would kill me one day while punishing my misdemeanors. I didn't get hurt in the high jump. Other grown-ups came and helped my cousin to climb down.

Trees are very important in our culture and I have more to say about them. In the forest we found the best trees to climb. We collected berries and other wild fruits to eat. I wish I could tell you the names of all the beautiful birds I saw in the forest. I recognized the shy *urtoo* (woodpecker), but I was just a child and I did not know the names of those other flashes of color with their sweet songs. One of the longings of my heart is to go back with my children and show them the birds that I saw in the forest, if I could find them. When I went back as a young man, I did not see the birds. I don't know where they went.

I recall that there were huge trees. Ten boys could not cover the circumference of a single tree if they held hands and made a circle around it. I don't know all the English names, but *Laaftoo* is an acacia and *Ejersa* is the olive tree. They were habitats for many birds. Those trees are also gone. Today if I wanted to show you where the trees were, you would see a different place. It really upset me to look in vain for the trees of my childhood. The forest was my umbrella during rains and hot suns. It was a living, breathing place of shelter and contentment.

After I arrived in another country to live, I was asked about my own country and I told the journalists that I felt as much pain about the destruction of the forest as I did about the killing of my people. When I was selected to run at the Olympic Games, I knew there was one thing I must do before I flew away like a migrating bird, perhaps forever.

I arranged for a lot of trees to be planted on the land where I once cared for animals. I planted different kinds, a memorial for the trees and the Oromo youth cut down in their prime. I bought the trees from offices of agriculture and also from other places. I chose *Qilxuu* (oak tree) from Bishoftu, the scene of a shocking tragedy that happened just a few months later. If I had known then what would take place…no, I can't think of what I would have done. We will reach that place of many tears later in this story.

I paid people to plant around ten thousand trees on the farm. I had to convince my mother and father to allow the planting on their farmlands. By then I was a man, twenty-six years old, and I had become famous. My mother was proud of me, but she was still reluctant. None of her neighbors was doing this strange thing. I wonder now if she suspected my motives because she could usually see with a mother's eyes that there was something here she should know about.

'Feyisa, why now? Why must the planting be done so urgently? Let it wait until you return, and we will talk about it then.'

'It is the middle of June now,' I argued. 'Now is the best time to plant, while the soil is moist and the rains will water the plants.'

'What will my neighbors in the village say?'

'They have a good attitude to me. They will gladly allow this for my sake. And,' I had to clinch the argument, 'Aduna accepts the idea. He will organize his friends to plant the trees.'

My mother loved to cook for Aduna and his friends and to have them fill the house with chatter and laughter. She agreed.

I also had to convince my father to allow trees to be planted on his land. We were more reconciled when I was a man like him, but he was suspicious and grudging. I knew what would sway him. 'Abba, I will pay you and Hadhaa the income that you would have made from this land if the trees were not here.' He stared at me and I wondered if for once he could see in the request something bigger than himself. He nodded, yes. I have at least reforested the area of the land that was once a natural forest. Then I left my village, willing myself not to weep and not to look back. I have been informed that the trees were growing. I would like to go back and plant one of his favorite trees especially for Kebede.

As I thought about my forest, I was glad that most days I ran in another forest in a foreign land. I make too many unfair comparisons, but I must say it: this other forest was not as good as mine. I saw the horses grazing in this other country and I slowed my pace to admire their cared-for coats, sleek bodies, and long legs. We had horses in Oromia, mainly small and wiry, and

I liked to ride them and race them, without a saddle, even before I was school age.

Gugsi fardaa is our name for horse riding. But most of the time my father would not allow me to race the horses. He alone could race them, no one else, particularly not me. I begged him to allow me to race the horses in some events. Our neighbors used to buy horses for their children to ride in competitions we call *Gugsi*.

My father was very selfish. He didn't want me to go; he always wanted to go there alone. He ordered me to take care of the animals on the days when there were *Gugsis*. I wonder now if he was jealous of my horsemanship. I had to start begging my father a whole year before *Gugsi*. On the rare occasions, three or four times, that I persuaded him, I took the horses and had the opportunity to compete with adults. I could ride and racehorses very well, even without a saddle. Only once did I have a saddle and it felt like the first time I wore shoes to run—I did not think I could race as well as I could without them.

I didn't have the money to buy a horse of my own. This was one of the few things that made me cry, but never in front of my father. It is true to say that as a boy I was suppressed by my parents; at times my father even expelled me from the house when I was a teenager and I stayed at my aunt's home in Gojo. No longer did I have Geti's comfort nor grandfather's, because they had died. *Nagaa dhaan haboqotnn* (Let them rest in peace). They were the first of many people I have mourned. Perhaps one day I will own a horse, when I am too old to run well, and I will gallop him across the land of Jaldu. This is a dream I have when I am awake.

My love of riding comes back to me in dreams. I know I am going to win a race if I dream the night before of galloping on a horse. I have been compared to an Oromo horse, strong and willing. I like the image of the horses, surefooted and agile, and as I run, I picture them, an ancient breed that roamed free on these plains for centuries. I am sturdy and stocky, built for distance and endurance. I am free when I run, no bridle or bit to curb me.

I am a racehorse, and my feet hit the ground in a sure rhythm, edging away from the pack. I can hear others on my heels, but I surge ahead, no blinkers needed to keep me focused on the finish line. I want to win by several lengths. I am a thoroughbred. I see myself now as a warrior runner, a cavalry horse that scents the battle and will do his part to defeat the enemy as he has in the past.

My friends used to go to *Gugsi* always. I asked them to lend me their horses. 'Just once,' I pleaded. 'I will take good care of him.' They occasionally let me have a turn. All the boys were keen to compete and they did not readily share. 'Get your own horse. Would you lend him to us if we asked?' That was a good question and I know I would have been reluctant to slide off the back of my own special beast. I have always been a fierce competitor and I ride or run with one goal: to win.

The game of *Gugsi* is very entertaining and dangerous. The word *Gugsi* means to unhorse your opponent. The riders throw sticks at each other that could kill and there are persons who are blinded because of it. The ability to ride a horse alone is not enough; you must have a brave heart to participate. A competitor asks if you will chase him and you do and throw a stick at him. If he is hurt, he asks his group to help chase you and hit you by throwing a stick. The stick is thrown like a javelin. If they start to chase you, they throw as many sticks as they have until you cross a finishing line. No one touches you once you cross the finishing line. Anyone can throw a stick at you once you are in the game. You cannot complain.

One day I took a big, strong horse to *Gugsi*, but the horse didn't have speed. He was slow compared to other horses. My brother was with me on a small horse. 'Aduna!' I called when we were well away from our home. 'Let me use your horse.' The smaller horse is easier to manage. You must jump on the moment you want to ride, otherwise you cannot control the horse. I am the older brother; Aduna mostly does what I ask. We exchanged horses.

I held the small horse tight and jumped on it when it was time for the competition. I threw my stick at a man who was riding behind me. He managed to catch the stick and forcefully threw it back at me. He hit me in the back. He did not unhorse me, but it was the end of the game for me. My wound was very painful and I rode slowly home. It must be what it feels like to be stabbed with a knife.

It hurts badly when you are hit by a bullet, or so I was told by men I visited in prison. They showed me their wounds, untreated like mine on that long-ago day at the *Gugsi*. Too many young men were being hit by bullets in my country and too often they were hit in the back. That should shame the man with the gun because he shot at an opponent with no weapons, no means of defending himself and no way of escaping. I do not ride horses now; I am afraid of injuring my legs and bringing my career to an end. I would fire bullets, though, like I threw those sticks, and the thought frightened me. I told myself that I would never hit anyone in the back.

I can remember the boys chasing the *gogorrii* (wild chickens) and flinging sticks as the creatures ran away in fear. I don't like to see an animal afraid, trembling, and wanting to flee, because I know what that is like. Yet, despite my dread of my father, most of what happened when I was a young boy brings happy memories.

5

I wonder what happened to Aberu Beka? Today I am thinking about her, the teacher I loved like my mother or Geti. Aberu Beka taught me from first to fourth grade at the school in Gojo. I felt very bad when I proceeded to fifth grade without her. I looked for her in the playground and in the streets, hoping to meet her and hear her voice again. She had a special smile for me always. She liked me as her favorite student.

Before I went to the Gojo school though, my father took me to the *Qes Timirt* (Orthodox Religious School), in 1996, I think. The *qes* were the Amhara priests, who taught only the Sabean or Geez alphabet. This writing system is mostly known now as the 'Amharic' alphabet, used in religious books. I didn't want to go to that school. I only had one exercise notebook and I knew that the boys at the formal school in Gojo had many. I wanted to go there the next year.

My father took me to the Qes School because that's where he and men of his generation went. He did not learn much; both my parents were illiterate. They didn't understand the importance of formal education. One man told my father that the current education system cannot be called an education compared to the previous one; children wouldn't bring any change by learning in *Afaan Oromoo*. 'For example,' he said, as if this proved him right, 'there is picture of a cat on one of their textbooks and they teach the students that the picture represents a cat. Our children already knew what a cat looks like.' He convinced my father with such a foolish argument.

Many Amhara said that Oromo did not have the ability to learn and called them *galla*, an Amharic term of insult and abuse. You might compare the use of the word *galla* to the word Negro or nigger, inflicted upon Africans enslaved and taken to America. The names of indigenous peoples in America were changed to 'Indian' with their colonization and destruction; I have seen remnants of their tribes in this other country. The term *galla* has been used to try to destroy *Oromumma* and to devalue our culture.

It made me sad to see how my parents' era admired anyone who could write by saying, 'He writes well as *Sidama*'s son.' They referred to anyone who is not an Oromo as *Sidama*. I have heard it said that a common belief was that Oromos should not be educated beyond third grade. The Amhara claimed, '*Oromoon Gidiraa baraa*' (Oromo will learn trouble), if educated beyond third grade.

We knew landlords who were half Amhara and half Oromo; it was the children of such people who were given the opportunity to go further in school. Oromos had to change the names of their children to Amhara Christian names to get them in to the school. When my grandfather took one of his sons, Ittisaa, to the formal school, the school rejected him because of his name, Ittisaa (an Oromoo name). Grandfather took him again the next day, changing his name from Ittisaa to Haile-Mariam (an Amhara name). In such a way his son got a formal education and a job in the Derg military. He was not actually a soldier but worked for them in a different role. His name is now Haile-Mariam Gemechu. He married an Amhara woman.

'Do you know what the Amhara have done to the Oromo?' I asked his son, my cousin. He didn't want to believe the things I told him, as his mother is Amhara. I went further. 'Your father had to change his name to get a proper education.' He was so surprised he started laughing. 'I don't believe any of this!' Finding people to believe our story is always like this.

No one else in my older family received a formal education and reached a higher level; there was no one in our home who could read. There were very few older people in the whole area who knew how to read or write. Before I could read, I had to walk and run a long way to their homes, needing them to read papers like wedding and funeral invitations that my parents received. My mother and father could not always identify the names of deceased persons on the funeral invitation cards. It was really very difficult for them.

Anyway, I knew if I stayed in the Qes school the next year, my father would probably let me go there permanently, even though he had a poor opinion of schooling of any kind. My heart was set on the formal school, not because at the age of six I thought that I would get a better education, but because I knew that children played football there. I loved playing football, but I did not have the money to buy a ball.

I thought that I was cleverer than my father and from a young age I learnt the tricks of manipulation. In the autumn, after I had been at the Qes school for about four months, I approached him when he was in a rare good mood. 'Abba,' I began cautiously. 'There is no one to protect the potato crop from the animals. Lalise is needed in the house and the others are too young.'

He scratched his head, wondering what I was up to this time, but any threat to the crops always held his attention. 'I will drop out of the school and protect the crop from animals if you will allow me to go to the formal school next year. Please, Abba.'

He would not give ground so readily. 'Why do you need to go there?' He looked me up and down, from the knotty curls on my head to my small dirty feet. 'You will be a farmer like me. You will work this land.'

'Please, Abba.'

In the end he accepted my proposal. As it happened, I did not play much football for years because there were too many older and stronger students.

Then, when I felt such love for Aberu Beka, I wished that I could be a teacher someday and I would decide who could play football.

I loved going to school so much that I used to be restless on the weekends. The five weekdays were too short for me; they seemed like two days. I would have liked to stay in class every day. After joining high school, it was different.

We went to school without eating breakfast and we didn't eat anything at school either. My father would beat me if I asked for breakfast. 'You don't need breakfast!' he shouted. 'You are not working! Go on your way!' He was a hard man and my mother did not dare to plead my case. I quickly learned not to ask. I left home for school at 6:00 am, as we had to be in class at 8:00 am. I had eight kilometers ahead of me and the same distance back. All the students who went to that school from our village did the same. We ran back and forth between school and home as if it were the most natural thing in the world.

Journalists and others interested in the East Africa running culture make much of schoolboys running to school. They dwell on the image of the barefoot peasants, carefree athletes in the making. We didn't run for the sake of running; we did it because we had to be at school on time. It was not that we had an interest in running, although I always loved it; if we hadn't arrived at school on time teachers punished us. Beatings were an accepted part of life too, but later I cringed when I heard of the beatings in prisons and saw the limp and bloodied victims in the cells.

I was good in classes and proud to be first or second in tests. I remember one of my father's friends asking me what I would like to be when I grew up, as if village kids had options and opportunities. Many of them never got as far as Finfinne, let alone ever seeing the ocean or marvelling at snow-covered mountains.

'I would like to be a sports teacher,' I answered. Those were the days when I loved Aberu Beka.

He shook his head. 'It is better to be a traffic policeman and take bribes than becoming a teacher.' There was the corrupt culture coming through already, even to a child.

I didn't know of any better job than teaching, but the profession was often undermined. One teacher told us that the top three students in the class could become doctors if they worked hard and had good results. Then, as kids do, I changed my plan and wanted to be a doctor. When I started watching television, I saw doctors and nurses in uniforms; they looked important.

Before Jaldu got electricity, teachers showed us a fake television made from a cardboard carton. I thought all televisions were like that and what was the use of them? The first day I saw a real television, I was in the Gojo market and there were people lining up to watch television. I couldn't get into the shop and watch up close, as I had already spent the few *birr* I had to buy sugar cane. But through the window I saw someone moving in the television. I was so amazed that when I got home I took some coins hidden under my bed and went back the next morning.

When I got there, the *Afaan Oromoo* programme that was on the previous day was not showing; instead, it was an Amharic programme. I had to wait from early morning to the evening for the Oromo programme. I had enough *birr* for just one cup of *farso*, but I waited and watched. I was soon hooked on television. Every weekend I disobeyed my parents to watch television and slept somewhere else at night. There was an entertaining show called '*Dhangaa*' (meaning feast or extensive meal) every Saturday. I liked the programme so much that I just could not miss it.

My watching of television began about the time when the Olympic Games were held in Sydney, Australia. So that was in the year 2000. For the very first time I saw men and women competing in races and the whole show was a marvelous spectacle to me. I watched in amazement as an Ethiopian won a very long race and had a gold medal placed around his neck.

'How can they run like that in a television?' I asked the friend who was watching with me.

'Feyisa,' he promised me, 'if you train for even a week you will fly like the birds.'

I ran home like I always did, although I was wearing plastic boots that day. I was running sixteen kilometers a day—I was already training! My friend was right. I could fly like the birds in the forest that I loved so much. I already enjoyed gymnastics at school but running became my passion.

'Come with me to see the runners in the television!' I called to my friends. The television station was showing replays of the races, but that didn't matter. It was all new to us. After that about ten students from my village joined me in a training schedule.

One of them, a boy whom we envied because he had been to the capital city, Finfinne, told us a story that we could not believe.

'I saw Haile Gebresilassie driving a beautiful car!' he boasted.

'How could you?' I retorted. 'Haile Gebresilassie is in Arsi! So is Derartu Tulu!'

I was airing my new knowledge, as I had seen Derartu win a long women's race in the Sydney Games. Haile Gebresilassie had also won a long race in Sydney. I knew all this, but in my limited existence I didn't know that you could live in Finfinne even if you were born somewhere else. I was thinking that I would return to where I was born after becoming a teacher or a doctor or a soldier or after winning a race.

'Haile does so live and work in Finfinne,' insisted my informer.

'Where does he get the money to buy such a fancy car?' I demanded, unconvinced.

'Prize money. The money Haile gets from a single race could buy fifty cars. He is one of the richest men in Ethiopia.'

My mind was on the wealth to be made from running. To think that running in Ethiopia once had no social status! It was associated with servitude—masters rode horses while their slaves and servants ran along behind them.

Haile Gebresilassie told interviewers after his race that he had run ten kilometers to school every morning, and the same back home every evening. This was more than I did, so I reviewed my training anxiously. His distinctive running posture, commentators speculated, with his left arm crooked, looked as if he were still holding his schoolbooks. 'I wanted to be famous,' he told them. 'I wanted people to talk about me.'

I wanted to be rich and famous like him. I started focusing on running, but less focused on education. Today, though, I am proud to be numbered among the *Qubee* generation.

6

Generations come, and generations go. Perhaps they linger in our memory as the silent, or the stolen, or the suffering; we even talk about younger generations as X, Y, and Z. I said before that my father's generation was lost, but when I thought about it more, I saw them as disoriented and displaced rather than vanished or of no account. They were defeated in their thinking by the thug Mengistu Haile Mariam and his henchmen, the Derg.

In Oromia, the *Qubee* generation refers to those of us who first learnt to read and write in our own language, *Afaan Oromoo*. *Qubee* is the Oromo lettering system; *fidel* are the Amharic letters. *Afaan Oromoo* means 'mouth of the Oromo' and you may also hear of it called *Oromigna* in Amharic or *Oromiffa*. The Oromo prefer *Afaan Oromoo* or the Oromo language over the other two variations.

Our language was a favorite topic at the *daboo* when I was growing up, because the older villagers regarded the *Qubee* generation with admiration, envy, or delight; perhaps all three. I think they saw the hard-won literacy in our own language as the best victory of the Oromo in recent times. I was home from school one day to help with the harvest and the workers wanted to hear me talk about what I was learning at school.

'You cannot separate the history of an ancient race from its spoken language,' insisted one of the most vocal men at the midday rest under the trees. 'That is like separating us from our land and some of us here today know what that is like.'

That was enough to get one of our elders started on his knowledge of *Afaan Oromoo*. He had often talked about our language at the *daboo*. 'It is right up there at the top of many, many languages used in Africa. It is the third largest indigenous language in Africa, after Hausa in Nigeria and Kiswahili in eastern Africa. It is one of the Cushitic languages.'

He paused to take a gulp of *farso*. Then he fixed his eyes on me as if he wanted to impress this truth on the closest beneficiary of the *Qubee* revolution. 'The people who speak it are spread over a wide area, not only here in Ethiopia, but also in Kenya and Somalia. But we lacked a written literature. We still do, but it is growing.'

I was drifting off to sleep as he talked on, but I was thinking of Geti, who told me stories when I shared the warmth and comfort of her bed as a younger boy.

'In the time of the Emperor Menelik,' she began, 'there was an ex-slave named Onesimos Nasib who did much for Oromo literature.'

Geti stroked my cheek. 'What was the most significant contribution made to our literature by Onesimos?' This was her favorite question.

'The complete translation of the Christian Bible to *Afaan Oromoo*,' I murmured sleepily. I didn't know then what a Bible was and Geti probably didn't know either. I liked to hear about Oromos freed from slavery and I remember how Geti warmed to her subject as she told me yet again about Aster Ganno, enslaved while still a child. When she was liberated from slavery and sheltered at a Swedish mission station near Asmara, she helped Onesimos, but her major work was compiling an Oromo dictionary. The two of them, Aster and Onesimos, provided education to the Oromo, including girls, in their own language.

'Imagine that!' exclaimed Geti, who had never had the benefit of an education other than the stories she had heard and the traditions she handed down. 'Women and girls learned to read and write!' She poked me gently, but I protested grumpily and burrowed deeper into the bedclothes.

Depending on what record of Ethiopian history is accepted, there is disagreement about the gradual demise of our language, with only occasional glimpses of its revival. Oromo believe that the underdeveloped status of literacy is mostly because of the Amharization policy of consecutive Ethiopian governments over the past 100 years, at least. Their purpose, we contend, was to create a homogeneous Ethiopian society and identity through the medium of Amharic, the language of the dominant ethnic group in the country.

My father told me that *Janhoy* (the Emperor) used to pass through Jaldu, going to Gende Beret, north of our district.

'People worshiped him like a god.' My father spat the words in disgust. 'I didn't like that. They bowed down and kissed the ground to show respect. Why should we honor a mere man, and the one who took away our culture? All people were his subjects, not citizens.'

My father was equally scathing of Mengistu. 'He did many bad things after coming to power. Call him *Garbchaa*.' Since Mengistu was of a very dark complexion, many used this epithet to revile him. It means 'like a slave'. I can't remember now all the things that my father told us about Mengistu, but you would think that he might have taken more interest in me, the son born just one year before the collapse of the dictator's rule and his escape to the land of another tyrant, Robert Mugabe. I was the future, me and my brother and sisters.

When Mengistu's regime came to power in 1974, the ban on our language was lifted, but in reality, the teaching of *Afaan Oromoo* at any level in our school system was substandard. In its 1987 constitution, the Derg declared Amharic as the sole official language of Ethiopia. The Oromo Liberation Front (OLF) was determined to reverse this injustice and many others, by adopting the Latin script instead of *Geez* (the language of high culture in Abyssinia) used by previous writers of our language.

Then at last came the historic convention in November of 1991, attended by over 1,000 men and women—scholars, intellectuals, politicians, and organizations—at the parliament building in Finfinne. They unanimously decided to continue the OLF use of the Latin script as the most suitable, universally useful choice. There are various reasons for choosing Latin for developing an Oromo orthography: essentially, it has been adapted to many languages, especially English, and it has simple letters, so an Oromo child who has learned his or her own alphabet can learn the English script in a relatively short time.

Afaan Oromoo became the medium of instruction for education and administration in Oromia. In September of 1993, school instruction in *Afaan Oromoo* was legally launched for the first time since Oromia was occupied by Abyssinia, over 100 years ago. Yet Amhara rulers and elites still believed that the Oromo and other non-Amhara peoples, if taught to speak Amharic, would absorb Ethiopian nationalism, become Ethiopian patriots, and discard their ethnic identity. My people were told, under duress, to accept one culture

(Amhara-Tigre, known as Habesha or Abyssinian), one language (Amhara), and one nationality (Ethiopians).

The *Qubee* generation is inquisitive and it is our proud boast that we know all about the past that has led to the present. We are also keenly aware of our basic rights, enshrined in the country's little-practiced constitution; we have been taught civic education from an early age.

We grew up singing the anthems of our various regions, rather than the national anthem. Few, if any of us, can recite Ethiopia's national anthem by heart. In Oromia, because of our long-standing grievances towards the central state, the *Qubee* generation swears allegiance to Oromia; we demand an end to the Oromo people's marginalization in the Ethiopian state.

Under Menelik, Oromos and others were driven from our land; our territory was occupied and declared to be 'owned' by the settlers who distributed the land and people among themselves depending on rank and status. This was land that the indigenous population had cultivated and grazed with their herds for generations. Menelik was the first name I associated with the wrongs inflicted on my people.

It is true to say that children like me, three years old at the time of that 1993 decree, were the ones who benefited from the sacrifices of the early freedom fighters. We became the educated youth who dared to take the battle to an oppressive government. Our families and some of us have suffered gross injustices; no longer could we tolerate suppression. We were the *Qubee* generation.

We were not the only ones in the world seeking a new order. June 4, 1996 was the time to be born for Skip Marley, a Jamaican voice of protest. His song, 'Lions', is the catch cry of his and my generation. 'We are the Lions!' he sings. 'We are the Chosen, we are the Movement, this Generation, we gonna shine outta dark…You better know who we are….'

This generation. We will reverse the perception of the Oromo as a people without culture, history, and heroes. An Amhara saying I have heard goes like this: *Ye Galla chewaa ye gomen choomaa yelem* (It is as impossible to find a civilized Galla as it is to find fat in cabbage). We are not the first to challenge such an affront. There have been many before us, including a man often talked about in our district, Colonel Alemu Qixessa, an official during Haile Selassie's reign.

'You must know who Alemu Qixessa is!' I exclaimed once at a lively debate in Finfinne about our heroes. 'No account of the Oromo struggle is complete without mentioning him.'

I know about him because of his association with the Jaldu High School, a couple of kilometers away from the elementary school I went to. He built the high school on his own land, wanting Oromo youth to have the chance to better themselves. This was in the 1960s, when he and other visionaries founded the Macha Tulama Association. They aimed at providing better education and health and social welfare for the Oromo. The leaders even dared to address mass meetings in *Afaan Oromoo*, although it was banned at that time.

I attended Jaldu High School in my teenage years. It was very big because for a long time it was the only one in the district. When I was in 9th grade I was in 9G section and the letters went beyond G, although I can't recall just how many more sections there were. We had about ninety students in a single classroom. The teachers had a hard time promoting participation and evaluating each student's weaknesses and strengths. It was also difficult for them to assess homework and assignments. They didn't have time.

By the time I was in 10th grade, I had lost interest in school. I skipped classes for three weeks straight. On one of the days when I went back to class, the teacher looked around the packed room trying to put names to faces and finding one that he had not seen for a while. We were indifferent, mostly tired after early morning farm work, hungry with no breakfast to see us through the long day and subdued after our long walk or run to school.

'A certain student,' he announced, 'has been absent for many days. Please stand and let me know the reason why.'

No one stood and no one spoke. Most of them knew it was me, but they did not let me down. When I was there, I usually slept or took no interest in the class. It was a useless attempt by our English teacher. I can still see his face, uncertain what to do about it and knowing that it was hopeless anyway.

It's a shame to me now that I became so lazy and defiant as a teenager. The high school was as good as any in Finfinne. The teachers were very skilled and knowledgeable; they were educated Oromo who returned to their place of birth to teach because it was difficult for them to get employed anywhere else.

We were learning in *Afaan Oromoo* when we started elementary school, but we also had to learn Amharic. We didn't understand it very well and there are many now the same age as I am who don't know how to read or write—let alone properly speak—Amharic. I would not have managed at all if it hadn't been for another student, Dereje, a footballer and a friend of mine.

Dereje had connections with some town girls, including Zewde. The girls admired footballers. One of them, Zewde, knew more Amharic than we did and she and Dereje had a good relationship. 'Zewde,' he said in his most charming way, 'can you help me with the Amharic questions?' He boldly copied her answers and I copied them from him. Even though I cheated, I only scored 37 out of 100. I am always in a hurry when it comes to tests and examinations.

It was the same in Mathematics, a subject I liked, but I was no good on examination days due to my haste. Multiple-choice questions are tricky. I just picked the answers randomly, rushing to finish as usual. It is a tendency I had to curb when running a long race. I scored better results in subjects like Geography, when you could read and memorize the facts beforehand.

Something happened while I was in 7th or 8th grade that demoralized me. There was a teacher who used to teach us Biology and Chemistry. My grade was high at that time and I was still enjoying tests and challenges. I knew how much others had scored because we compared answers after class.

'I did well today,' I told Aduna as we jogged home. I was tired but happy that day and the evening run always invigorated me. 'I will get the first prize.' I found out the next day that students who lived in town begged the teacher to change marks and he did. He actually added marks for many students, and I came 8th instead of 1st.

'How could he do that?' I raged all the way home, with Aduna murmuring sympathy. 'He has encouraged students to cheat and he is dishonest.' I overlooked my own dishonesty when I cheated and handed in the work done by others. Somehow it was worse when a grown-up, a teacher, was guilty.

The prize for each of the top three students was not something special—a 50-page notebook—but the one you got as a prize encouraged you to achieve. When I told Kebede about this during one of our long talks, he asked gently, 'Is this your first experience of injustice?' I think it was my first, at least the first away from home.

I did not want to go to that teacher's class again. I found out also that some teachers gave exam papers to their own children to mark and they added points for their friends. Only national exams were marked by external examiners. Anyway, I vowed that I would be the one awarded in the next year and I was.

I was good at sketching things. There were assignments that required pictures of anatomy in Biology. I connived with another friend, called Fayera, who also completed assignments for me. After I had drawn some pictures for him, I thought that others less competent at drawing might like my help. I bought a stack of paper canvases for seven *birr* and drew the pictures for the students in the class. Then I collected one *birr* from each of them; sometimes I could make as much as eighty or ninety *birr* for one assignment. It didn't matter that I was doing my share of cheating; I thought those students were lucky to have me in the class and I needed the money.

'I could have been successful if I continued with drawing,' I mused after telling the story to Kebede, who went to the same school. He was laughing and I like to remember his laughter. 'I started drawing even before I went to school, while I was caring for animals. I did not wear trousers then and I did not wash my body that much. My skin was dirty, dry, and dark. I drew pictures of lions, birds, runners, on my legs using thin sticks. I could make things too, out of wood or clay or paper, and later I took these to school to show my friends.'

'What else are you good at?' Kebede asked. 'So far you could be an artist or a sculptor or a businessman!'

'Sport!' I said at once. 'Sports teachers liked me because I was good in sport. You have seen me run, Kebede.'

Thinking back to that time, I didn't give much attention to education after 8th grade, as I concentrated on sports. Education started to become boring to me. I wasn't meeting the expectations of the *Qubee* generation at this point. My results dramatically dropped after the first semester of 9th grade. Then I became one of the lazy students. I left school for a year, but I returned to finish Grade 10. I will tell you about my year of absence, but for now I'll continue with my school days.

Outside the classroom I soon became known. I won races there because there were no other good runners, but I had hard times when I went to other places representing Jaldu. Then came a memorable race when I was fourteen years old. Barefooted, I finished 4th in a race in Ambo, competing against very good athletes who were already training in sports clubs. I didn't have much confidence before that and had been eliminated from competitions two or three times because I was not talented. That's what I thought. I was in a rush to go home and tell my family that I got 4th place, even though the people who took us to Ambo wanted me to stay until the tournament was over.

'I placed 4th!' I yelled as soon as I reached the house. 'I can run! I am going to be a runner!'

I don't think they were very impressed, but I say now that getting 4th place in Ambo was my first real success and I knew that I could be a good runner after that. I won the race the next year. Then I started to win cross-country races and entered races to the distance of 5,000 meters. I thought I was invincible. I represented the West Shoa Zone and participated in Oromia competitions.

In the 10th grade, after I had been away from school, a year became longer than usual to me. I took the national examinations without studying or knowing anything much. Some papers, like History and Geography, were not challenging as they were what we studied in 7th and 8th grades, but it was different in the other subjects. My average grade always dropped because of Amharic. There were long passages to read in the Amharic examination. I couldn't have finished reading even the first paragraph before the time allocated for the examination ended.

'What shall I do?' I sat at my desk, scrunching my tangled curls and staring at the paper. I have never been one to panic and I thought I saw a way to at least answer some of the questions. I didn't have Dereje beside me; I could see him, head down, concentrating hard. Zewde had probably finished her paper already. I started answering the questions randomly, following different patterns, without reading anything. I knew that I wouldn't score much.

I always thought that if someone is rated 'F" for Failure on an exam, that the letter 'F' is written on the final certificate. But it was not like that in our system. When my certificate came it didn't have the name of the course on which I scored "F" at all. So, the name 'Amharic' was not written on my certificate.

'I was so happy to see that,' I told Kebede when we compared our ability to understand Amharic. 'I'm proud that the name "Amharic" is not on my certificate.' He wasn't much good at Amharic either.

I got a 'B' on every subject except for Geography, for which I scored 'C'. I think that I could have been successful in education if I hadn't been so determined to run. It's easier to blame others too, like my parents, who didn't help me much when I was a schoolboy. We had homework and the teachers encouraged us to study for tests and examinations. Most of my classmates were competitive and determined, but I was falling behind just about from the start, a feeling that I know in races when you want to catch up, but you don't have the strength. My father scolded me if I stayed up late at night to do my homework. 'Why are you wasting the kerosene? Do you think it is water?'

He didn't like it either when I went to school on Saturdays, which happened sometimes if teachers arranged classes to catch up on lessons and finish the courses they were teaching. By 10th grade I didn't want to go on Saturdays anyway. The school week was hard enough with classes starting at 8:30 in the morning and ending at 12:30 pm. Then there was the afternoon shift which started at 2 and finished at 4.00. Some students had work to do on their farms in the afternoon and hurried there and back in the break, returning to school to attend what they could before the day ended and trying to get back there on Saturdays.

I paid for everything to go to school. My father sometimes gave me some money when he sold animals. I used to beg him to help me, especially when he was drunk. 'Abba, I need money for a schoolbook. Can you give me some money?'

'Wasted money,' he grumbled, but he would part with two *birr*. For that he would make me do many things, like chopping wood for the fire and cutting branches from trees for the animals. I did this the whole day. He made me skip classes for two *birr* and that was not enough for what I needed. I didn't ask him for money unless I was desperate.

I helped my parents when they harvested crops and many other jobs, which was not easy, but it was expected, and I worked without complaint. They didn't buy books and shoes for me. I went to school barefooted. I wanted to help my brother too, sparing him some of the deprivation of my life. One way to make money was to go to the lowlands to buy sugar cane stalks and then sell them. With the money I bought exercise books, even textbooks for school, saving the humiliation of always asking others to lend their books.

I had chickens and I sold their eggs to cover other expenses. I was somehow self-sufficient. Then I changed to sheep and I bought clothes after selling those sheep. I faced problems when my clothes and shoes wore out at the same time. My school uniform was shabby, but that did not worry me so much as looking decent when I travelled to different towns for races.

I remember clearly the time I went to a competition in Walliso and our team was defeated in the first round.

'You can go home early,' we were told. 'Get the bus back to Jaldu. You'll have enough money for a meal and the bus.'

They gave us fifteen *birr* for the meal and twenty-one *birr* for the bus. We had to go through Finfinne and I saw a pair of very white trousers for sale. They were dazzling, shiny and clean like the tracksuit pants worn by some of the best runners. I wanted them. Instead of food I bought those white trousers.

I could hardly wait to get home to try them on. They were so tight and skinny that they would not fit, no matter how hard I squirmed. Somehow, I struggled into them and wore them awkwardly, parading around my village— for just one day. I could barely walk in them and I could not sit down. My sisters laughed at the sight of me. 'Why are you wearing women's trousers? No wonder they don't fit!'

In shame I took them off, with great difficulty, twisting and turning and wriggling. They were discarded, soiled from my grubby hands and feet. I regret very much that I didn't buy the meal because I was hungry. Anyway, I was able to sell the trousers to a relative in Finfinne some time later. They fit her very well and looked much better on her than they did on me. The only good thing about that experience is that I bought the trousers for fifteen *birr* and sold them for sixteen.

I was still just a kid, but I was always finding ways to earn some money. I was thinking that I didn't have enough means to go to school the next year to finish Grade 10 and I was desperate. I had a ram that was born from one of my previous sheep. I took the ram to market, sold him for seventy-four *birr* and bought a pregnant sheep for sixty-four *birr*. The person who sold me the sheep was one of our relatives; now he has passed away. *Nagaa dhaan haboqtuu* (Let him rest in peace).

I had no idea that he had sold me a sick sheep. I was thinking she would give birth in six months' time and I would buy myself clothes and books for next year with the proceeds from selling her lamb. On my way home from the market, the sheep was reluctant to move, no matter how hard I tried to force her. As we approached my village she fell to the ground. She was about to die, but I was so angry and frustrated that I started hitting her as if she was the one that had wronged me.

The sheep was big and she didn't look sick. I remember thinking that she looked hungry, but I trusted the man because he was my relative. He told me the sheep was healthy and fine. I could have used that sheep for a lot of things—my clothes were worn out; my last exercise book was full. I wouldn't have sold my ram and bought the sheep if I hadn't bought those silly pair of trousers. I was frustrated and I even thought the sheep was dying knowingly, deliberately.

I can hardly bear to remember how I killed that poor sheep and had no compassion for her as she lay dying. I have seen young men and women treated like this in the streets of Finfinne and I am so ashamed when I think about that poor harmless ewe.

'Nothing could have made me unhappier than this.' This is how I described my feelings to Aduna, the only one who has heard me tell this story. I was too ashamed to tell Kebede, although we shared most of our most private joys and sorrows. 'I couldn't be sadder if one of my close friends or family died.' I felt like that back then. Since then, much greater sorrow than the innocent sheep has filled me with despair. Still, her death is the saddest childhood memory I have.

I dropped out of school for a whole year and disappeared to Finfinne. I was very miserable and angry. I worked as a daily laborer, a boy still, and I did every imaginable job except for slaughtering sheep. I will never slaughter a sheep. I refused to go to the funeral of the relative who wronged me.

II

I

In some of my dreams, I am back in Ethiopia, running on the slopes of Mount Entoto, the high peak that looks over the city of Finfinne. The mountain is thickly covered with eucalyptus trees, pungent in the early morning. It is exhilarating to run there, looking below to the city where wood from the same trees is burning, as fires are lit to cook breakfast in the homes of the poor. I could smell the smoke from where I was in a foreign land. I could smell it in my dreams.

I woke, realized where I was with a mixture of regret and relief, and lay there thinking about Finfinne. It is known as Addis Ababa, because it has been called that since the late nineteenth century. Emperor Menelik and his wife, Taytu, had health problems and they were attracted to this area because it was close to natural hot springs. Apart from the promise of curatives, Menelik wanted to build his empire's capital in the middle of Oromia for effective colonial control. He named the settlement Addis Ababa, meaning 'new flower'. It will always be Finfinne—spring waters—to me and my people.

Every now and then, after I finished training sessions on Mount Entoto, I paused to look down at a city scape that is like many others around the world, from a distance. Close up, you will remark upon its many walls of mud brick, wattle, or corrugated iron; its high stone walls and armed guards preventing a proper look at the places of officialdom, concealing their many secrets and deceptions. Taking photographs of such places was forbidden.

The streets that I have walked teem with dark faces, the people of the burnt faces as the name Ethiopian supposedly means. It is a huge shanty town, Finfinne, not especially attractive except in secluded places. I know it well and love it, because it became my home and the place where I made many friends. Some of them I visited in Finfinne prisons; or rather, in this case, Addis Ababa prisons.

On one occasion, when I jogged down the mountain, I saw an old man, silent and still beside a boy, guarding their small herd of black goats. The nanny goat looked up and bleated an anxious warning to her kid. I was back in time, grandfather occasionally at my side with the animals on our farm. When I brought to mind the man and the boy, in a familiar rural scene, I was homesick and sad, remembering the day I left my family and friends in Jaldu.

The killing of the sheep caused some long-suffered, unhealed hurt to break open. My parents were wealthy by our village standard, yet they would not support my education. I knew I could do well at school, but I was always struggling to have enough money to buy school needs and to dress decently. I look down at the brand-new tracksuit and the expensive joggers I am wearing now and I think about that shabby boy about to leave home.

After the sheep died, I stuffed my few possessions in a cotton bag. I had just thirty-five *birr* to put in my pocket and I made sure there was no hole in that pocket. I had less than a couple of dollars to begin a new life.

I left without speaking to anyone, but Aduna ran after me.

'Feyisa! Wait! Where are you going?'

'Away!' I growled without slowing down. 'As far away as I can walk from here.'

'Why?' Aduna was trotting beside me.

I stopped then and glared at him, the brother who had done me no harm. That day everyone was my enemy.

'Our family owns a lot of land. They are not *gebbari*, slaves to others. Our grandparents have all owned much land. But I am of less worth to my parents than one of the *chisegna*, the peasants who work some of that land. They give my father a share of what they earn from the crops they cultivate. Why can't he share a small portion of his wealth with me, his firstborn son? Why does he hate me?'

Aduna looked down, swiping at tears with grubby fingers and scratching at the dirt with stubbed toes. He had no answer. 'Where will you go?'

I refused to tell him, but I hugged him and wished him well.

'Will you come back?' he called after me.

I did not turn around and I did not answer him. I do not cry often, but I cried that day as I strode away from Aduna.

I was going to a town called Mogor, more than forty kilometers away, trudging along, hungry and unhappy, for ten hours or so. The idea was to get work at the town's cement factory and to continue my running at its athletics club.

'Can I join the club?' I asked one of the coaches I recognized from competitions. He knew I was a good runner.

He gave it some thought. 'You can eat and train with us,' he said slowly. 'But you will have to look for somewhere nearby to live.'

I tried to find a place to live in Mogor, but I did not know anyone, and I had already spent six *birr* on one night at a shabby hotel. Perhaps I could have persevered, but I was running away and I was impatient. The coach felt sorry for me, one of the many hopeful boys who came looking for refuge, but he could not offer more, except a lift with someone going to Finfinne.

I stared out the window of the shabby old vehicle, not caring about the scenery, but silently making plans. I will work, I told myself, save some money and go back to school, even if it means living in Gojo and not going back to my village. I was fourteen years old and I had twenty-nine *birr*. In my bag were the despised white trousers that I would sell to my girl cousin for sixteen *birr*. It was a start.

You may have heard of Sentayehu Eshetu, known to many athletes simply as Coach, in Bekoji, the town of runners, south of Finfinne. He has trained some of the world's best-known distance runners and he has had much to say about them. 'Runners need to go through hardship to be successful. Here the athletes have difficulty getting regular food, with owning shoes. They must sew their shoes and manage with little food, train hard and long, but I believe this makes them stronger and more likely to be successful.' I learnt the truth of these words in the desperate months after I fled from my home.

Ethiopians have big extended families and they can call on one or other family member to help them out. One of my relatives, a family man called Regassa Badhadha (Bedada), gave me a place to sleep in Finfinne. It was in Kaliti, an industrial part of the city, where you could get a job at one of the factories or mills, even if you were a rough-looking teenager, too young to be in the workforce. I was strong and I thought I could do anything, but the work I was doing was tough, the area was hot, and the days were long.

I remember when a few of us underage laborers worked at repairing a wall. We broke up big stones with mallets and lifted them, in makeshift stretchers, fashioned from sheets of corrugated iron between eucalyptus poles. We carted heavy loads of stones and sand, climbing up and down shaky wooden ladders. At midday we rested under a tree, exhausted, and shared any food we had scrounged.

Most of the boys napped, but I talked to a boy from Ambo who had dropped out of school like me. 'Not quite the same as you,' he said softly. 'I had to disappear. The police are hunting down many of us kids, beating us up; some of us taken by force and never seen again. I can't go home.' I met others like him in Finfinne and I am sure the name he used in the city was not his real name. He slipped a banana to me—a small, sweet and delicious treat. Finfinne is the best place in the world for bananas.

He stayed with an uncle who had one of the many fruit stores in the city. Often the boy workers had nothing to eat from dawn till dusk. I didn't have a good diet at all and I was training in the evenings. Without proper shorts for training, I wore jeans, and leather shoes. I always bought second-hand clothes, but they were torn and ragged in no time. The trousers were heavy, yet I managed to run one way in them on the route I had chosen at the edge of town. I couldn't manage the return run. I was hot and restricted and I was hungry. Always hungry.

On the way back to the place where I lived, I took off jeans and shoes and carried them, resting a couple of times. It was dark by then, with no lighting, and a poor street kid without trousers is a common sight in Finfinne. Out of pride I put them back on before I reached my relative's house. I lay down, worn out and discouraged.

'Feyisa!' Regassa was shaking me awake. 'Do you know what time it is? Eleven o'clock and you have not eaten. Get up now and have your meal.'

I don't know if Regassa told my parents where I was, but the instinctive care of relatives would not permit him to treat me badly. I am grateful to him. *Baayyeen isa galateffadha.*

I decided to take a break from training for two weeks until I was paid by my employer and could buy more food. Then I went back to training, but it was too much. I took another break for about a month, hoping that I would recover my strength. Those are the only times I discontinued training in all my years as an athlete, except for a couple of times after I fled my country.

On the day that we finished that wall, one of the boys stood on the top of it and danced, slender hips swaying, arms flailing, face grinning. We all applauded. Razor wire and glass shards embedded in cement would be the finishing touch for the wall, but we didn't stay around for that. We collected the money owed to us and drifted away. I decided to go back to Jaldu to finish my schooling. I was destined to return to Kaliti, because one of the city's awful prisons is located there.

2

'Feyisa is back! Feyisa is back!' Aduna pranced ahead of me when word got out that I was approaching the village. Other boys tagged along, exclaiming over my new clothes and shoes. I was like one of the public servants you see in office buildings; I didn't look like a day laborer. I had saved money too and I could buy everything Aduna and I needed for school. He would not go without as long as I had *birr* to share.

'Feyisa!' My mother's greeting was reproachful, but she hugged me hard and brought *farso* and *kitta*. She was glad to have me home and showed it in many small ways. As far as my father was concerned, it was as if I had never been away. He was still surly and short-tempered. My sisters avoided him and Aduna admitted that he had borne many beatings in my absence.

'Have you come back to work on the farm?' This was the only question from my father. He did not ask about Finfinne or the life I had there. All he ever wanted was my labor.

'No, Abba.' I had determined on the walk home from Gojo, where the bus left me, that I would not argue or get angry with him. 'I am going back to finish school.'

Silence followed me to my room that I made nice with a few things bought in the city. I had a rug for the floor that I had paid too much for in the Merkato, the market. I had a box to store my exercise books and pens and a backpack to carry books to school. Over the next couple of years, I went back to work in Finfinne in the summer and brought home other simple adornments for my room. My mother even asked if my room could be used when guests came, because it was the nicest in the house.

My friends at school welcomed me back, but there was a charged atmosphere on the campus. What had happened in my absence? Had I been too young before I went away to notice problems? We had always been wary of the head teacher, whose first name I remember as Bandira. Bad things were happening under him in that big, well-known and historic Jaldu High School in Gojo. He was a huge and intimidating man; a member of the ruling party, the Ethiopian People's Revolutionary Democratic Front (EPRDF), in power since taking over the government of the country just one year after my birth. The EPRDF has an ill-fated genealogy, dating right back into Ethiopia's past, and always dominated by the Tigrayan People's Liberation Front (TPLF).

Before I tell you about the bad things happening at school, I must try to explain the background to the ruling party, the EPRDF. A teacher once described the importance of history, good and bad: if we don't know it, we are like a person without a name, a church without a god, a book without a story, or a screen without data.

I know my own genealogy, explained to me by grandfather's cousin (my father's uncle), the one who died at the age of 111. He told me many things, a lot of history, the genealogy of my family, which goes as follows: Feyisa, Lelisa, Gemechu, Wayesa, Gika, Garedo, Imiyu, Bichilu, Homa, Bura, Gelan, Kutaye, Liban, Macha, Raya. Many Oromo children grow up recounting their genealogy back to fourteen generations of ancestors; I have found the names of my ancestors beyond Raya from different books written on Oromo genealogy.

I can continue listing up to Orma, believed to be the original father of all Oromo, the progenitor of all Oromo. Some say he is a legend only, but to be Oromo you must descend from him. Our mythology and history inform us that all Oromo groups are *ilmaan Orma*—the children of Orma.

Grandfather's cousin would be dubious of my findings. 'I don't believe anyone can trace their genealogy back to Orma,' he had said, 'but I'm sure Oromos believe they are descended from him, although their genealogy may have been broken along the way.'

One day I will teach our genealogy to my children as a way of identifying them as Oromo. The first thing Oromo children back home know about themselves is their genealogy; beside the hearth they learn their names, repeated through songs, riddles, plays, and games.

We were taught Ethiopian history too and, while I cannot claim to have a full knowledge of it, I wondered if it is a book with some blank pages. Who was controlling the narrative? Around which evening fireplaces had the story been interpreted and pages erased or written over? I bristled when I remembered my grandfather saying that the Oromo were despised as a people without history and I wonder where this falsehood originated.

We never willingly bowed the knee to the long line of emperors who claimed the Solomonic line, the 'elect of God', among them Menelik and Haile Selassie. They were the leaders of the Empire of Ethiopia, replaced by Socialist Ethiopia, more oppressive than the imperial state. We have fought hard to resist the dictators who followed the emperors. The crimes against humanity committed by Mengistu Haile Mariam and Meles Zenawi will never be erased from the record books. Then Hailemariam Desalegn, who succeeded Meles Zenawi, added his quota to the tally of murder, concealment, and denial. Desalegn may yet have his day in court, unable to flee like Mengistu or die like Zenawi before justice is served.

The organizations associated with the EPRDF resemble many tributaries that flow into a river longer and wider than any on my father's land; a river flowing with blood; a cursed river like the Nile River when Moses inflicted the first plague on Egypt. The names of the various tributaries are confusing until you become familiar with them and their acronyms.

Opposition to the Derg briefly united three rebel groups: the TPLF, the OLF, and the Eritrean People's Liberation Front (EPLF). The last group broke free from Ethiopian control and formed an independent state. Numerous attempts to form an alliance between the OLF and TPLF, both left-wing movements, always failed. Whereas the TPLF was zealously communist, the OLF gave priority to Oromo nationalist ideology.

The EPRDF, led by the TLF, initially gave the impression that it would accommodate the Oromos' demand for self-rule and made big promises to create a nation state of equals and an end to ethnic domination; even to democratize the Ethiopian state and society, ending centuries of authoritarian rule; and, best of all, to create peace and stability.

There was a transitional government at first, arranged at a conference in July of 1991, attended by a few Oromo-based groups. The EPRDF controlled proceedings, although guaranteeing the right to self-determination—including secession—to our country's diverse communities. The TPLF dominated the newly formed Council of Representatives and it soon became apparent that it had no intention of going with the flow of the rising tide of Oromo nationalism.

It is astonishing to me that the TPLF gained so much power over the others. Like the OLF, it was a military organization, determined to rid the country of Mengistu Haile Mariam and the Derg. Tigray was at the heart of the terrible famine in 1984-1985 which killed one million people; it was also strategically placed to the killing fields of Eritrea where war dragged on relentlessly for decades. The TPLF asserted that it was 'better to die by bullet than hunger' and their guerilla fighters had impressive victories against the Derg forces; victories which they intended to repeat against any opposition to their claim for superiority and seniority in the new order of things.

The TPLF leaders were confident that they could destroy the OLF, the main Oromo military group active in the overthrow of the Derg and at the forefront of our fight for self-determination. The TPLF thought it could subdue Oromo nationalism under the leadership of its puppet, the Oromo People's Democratic Organization (OPDO), presumably one of the four-member ruling coalition, the EPRDF; until recently only a piddling group that never effectively joined the mainstream.

If the TPLF believed it could redirect and control Oromo nationalism through the OPDO, it was badly mistaken. The OLF was equally mistaken in thinking it could mobilize the giant Oromo population against the TPLF-led minority party. The OLF was forced out of the transitional government by the end of 1992 and had limited success in low-scale guerrilla warfare against the ruling party. Some say that its continued armed struggle provided the TPLF with a pretext to justify ongoing persecution of the Oromo people. Whether or not that was true, the change of government in 1991 had not altered the reality of Ethiopian colonialism in Oromia.

'Oromo want to be set free from colonial rule,' Kebede repeated when our talk inevitably turned to the woes of our country. 'This lot of Ethiopian rulers assumes that because the monopoly of power has shifted from the Amhara elites to the Tigrayan elites, colonialism in Oromia does not exist. Wrong! Oromia is *still* a colony.'

We debated this matter for many long hours and we agreed that our goal is self-determination and independence from the current occupation of Oromia by the EPRDF. The EPRDF planned from the outset to keep the imperial state of Ethiopia (except for Eritrea) intact; the Oromo resolutely refuse to accept domination.

We have listened to our elders and betters discussing at length the Oromo question. The main problem has always been a lack of agreement on the shape that self-rule should take. There have been so many Oromo political groups over the years since the Revolution of 1974 first held out the hope of change. I can still hear my relatives talking about the various merits of the Ethiopian National Liberation Front (ENLF), the Organization for Oromo People's Liberation (OOPLS), and the Revolutionary Struggle of Ethiopia's Oppressed (ECHA'AT)—all fine sounding names, but just tributaries nevertheless, all adding blood and tears to a river with no outlet, a river so blocked with bodies that one day it would burst its banks.

I have asked myself and others: are we fighting to liberate all the peoples of Ethiopia from all kinds of injustices, regardless of race, religion or class, the nationalist cause; or are we fighting just for the Oromo ethno-nationalist cause, a separate state within the country? These are two strong currents that control the ebb and flow of Oromia and not one party has built a bridge across them.

I have deviated a long way from my return to school. I was glad to be back with my friends, yet the school had become a minor war zone and I wondered about our destiny. The youth of Oromia are a chosen generation, taught to read and write in our own language; but we were also a despised generation, taught by the military government to know fear, brutality, and injustice.

Men like the head teacher belonged to a vast network of party members who acted as the government's eyes and ears; an army of on-the-ground operatives who supported the government's policies, spread its propaganda, and acted as lookouts. They were spies, informers, agents of the state. Our head teacher was one of many traitors planted in schools and colleges and universities everywhere, even in Finfinne itself.

'Watch out for him,' my friend Dereje whispered as Bandira harangued us at assembly. 'He is not a good man.'

Later Dereje told me about students killed by security forces and before long I was a witness to what happened if Bandira informed on 'rebels'. I saw my classmates arrested and I saw them badly beaten. These students didn't commit any crime, but some excuse had been found to abuse them. They were charged as 'terrorists'. I didn't think you could be punished like this even if you had committed murder. I admired the courage of those older students who protested the harsh treatment, chanting '*Mirgi Keenya nuuf haa eegamu* (Let our rights be respected)'.

The provocation for such daring came from various incidents in our area. Long before I went away to Finfinne, there was something that I was involved in, with the bravado of a boy. A huge fire was burning out of control in the Bale Forest, south of the capital city, the place where an armed Oromo uprising occurred in 1963, triggered by conflict with government officials over land use. The guerilla war that ensued was similar to *Lola Mullataa Fayyisoo* (Mullata Fayiso's War), nearly twenty years later.

The fire that concerned us in 2000 was threatening the Bale Mountains National Park.

'That's home to some of the world's rarest species,' our Geography teacher said anxiously. 'I have talked to you about some of them—the Simien Fox, the Mountain Nyala, and Menelik's Bushbuck.'

That disturbed us; then we heard rumours, spreading like another wildfire, that the Bale blaze had been deliberately lit by government forces who believed that OLF guerrilla fighters were living in the forest. Hundreds of students from Addis Ababa University had travelled to the region to assist those attempting to control the inferno.

'We will go too!' one of our senior students suggested. 'We will meet here tomorrow morning, outside the school, and go, even if we have to walk there.'

Local officers heard about the plan and it seemed unlikely they would allow it. But they gave their permission. 'Assemble outside the police station.'

Then I remembered the day when the OPDO celebrated their establishment on *Bitootessa* 17 (March 17th); a holiday atmosphere prevailed while they chanted promising slogans. I went home to share the good news with the family.

'They are going to chase the solders away!' I announced jubilantly. 'Oromo has risen!'

'Don't believe them!' snapped my father. 'They are betrayers that live for the belly.'

I wasn't so sure about the intentions of the OPDO after that. Would they really permit us to leave Jaldu?

'It's OK. They are angry about the fire too,' the student leaders decided. 'They are Oromo like us.'

A great many students from the high school and some elementary schools gathered, excited at the adventure ahead. We were all too young to be there or to really understand what was going on. I was just ten years old. The officers eyed us suspiciously and muttered among themselves.

They shooed us away. 'You can go and put out the fire tomorrow.' We grumbled and murmured, but slowly dispersed.

'They were going to arrest you!' exclaimed my mother later when I described what happened. She had been worrying all day about her two sons, as Aduna had stuck to me faithfully. 'You were spared, because there were just too many of you.'

I didn't tell her that when we returned to school after our dismissal, we were reluctant to enter our classes. We were agitated, disappointed, and, as usual, tired and hungry. Then two policemen, brandishing AK47 rifles and sticks, came and made us enter our classes.

'You have just two minutes to go to your rooms!' shouted one, waving his gun around.

We were scared when we saw their weapons, but afterwards I started to feel angry. Why should we fear them? Perhaps the weapons weren't even loaded and all of us were used to beatings with sticks. I had much to learn. There is a big difference between then and now. Two policemen would never dare to order students to do things now. Even the soldiers whom we fear and hate wouldn't go among students these days if they were not heavily armed.

We never did go to fight the Bale fire. Word came through that 150 people were arrested and charged with causing the fires. Another pack of lies for us to sort, young as we were, and deal out among ourselves. It seemed that anyone accused of supporting the outlawed OLF was suspect. I was not to know that another fire, many years later, would affect me more intensely than the Bale fire.

In early 2001, according to news filtering through to us in the rural outposts, Oromo students at Addis Ababa University began protesting after authorities blocked their efforts to publish a student newspaper and organize a student union. The students also opposed stationing of uniformed police and undercover security agents on college and university campuses. High school and university students around the country joined the strike calling for academic freedom. More than 3,000 Oromo students were arrested

Other incidents caused unrest, including one that I know more about because I was older and more tuned in to what was happening while I lived in Finfinne. In 2004 tensions were running high when Oromo students protested the government's attempt to relocate Oromia's capital from Finfinne to Adama, ninety kilometers south-east of Finfinne.

The boy I talked to when we rebuilt the wall knew all about that. 'About 350 Oromo students were expelled from Addis Ababa University alone,' he told me. 'Hundreds of students, teachers, and Oromo intellectuals were arrested throughout Oromia, as if they wanted to eliminate our educated and politically conscious men and women. My school has been closed for most of the year. Has yours?'

I didn't know, but I listened to the rumours on the street about the terrible things done to those in detention. I heard that they were forced to run and crawl barefoot over sharp gravel for several hours at a time. Stories of mistreatment in custody circulated endlessly. Family members were threatened if they tried to visit those imprisoned.

When preparations were underway for the 2005 national elections, the ruling party voiced its confidence in re-election. There did not appear to be the same restrictions on voters as in the previous election in 2000 and in local elections in 2001. My mother, Hadhaa, has told me stories about them.

'The officials at the polling booths grabbed the hands of farmers and made them check the boxes on election slips for the ruling party! Men were afraid and voted for the government.' Hadhaa chuckled at the memory. 'I voted for the opposition and disregarded the warnings. Other women did the same.'

I stared at her in disbelief. 'Hadhaa! What happened?'

'Nothing happened. There was no privacy when you vote. They told you where you must check on the election slip. If you vote for the opposition party, security forces often come to your home at night. *Na barbaacha hin dhufne.* They didn't come for me.'

My family had a big wish for this government to go away, but like everyone else they didn't know how to make it happen.

'I despise them!' How many times have I heard my father say that? I listened to the sharp outbursts from him and other farmers when they met at the Jaldu markets and the warning reprimands of others trying to silence them, fearful of lurking informers. I now know more about all this, too young at the time to understand about local officials who threatened to withhold vital agricultural products such as fertilizer from impoverished farmers if they spoke out against government policies. These same officials selectively enforced harsh penalties for the non-repayment of debts to justify the imprisonment of their critics or the seizure of their property.

In the months prior to the May, 2005 elections, OPDO officials in Oromia created new quasi-governmental structures to subject the rural population to intense levels of surveillance and to impose restrictions on farmers' freedoms of movement, association and speech.

There would always be serious irregularities at election time; nevertheless, many people saw a chance in the 2005 election. Those who knew about these things talked of openness and real political competition unprecedented in Ethiopia's history. Voters in large numbers were seeking the election of a new government.

Official tallies in the weeks following the May 15th voting indicated that opposition parties had made enormous gains in parliament but had fallen well short of obtaining a majority. The largest opposition coalition, the Coalition for Unity and Democracy (CUD), refused to accept those results, alleging that it had been robbed of outright victory by widespread government fraud. The government, in turn, accused the CUD of conspiring to overthrow the government. The government prevailed.

The post-election period was riddled with blame and bullets. My parents and their friends muttered about many deaths at the hands of security forces when protesters dared to make accusations of election dishonesty. Tensions grew in June, when protests broke out in in defiance of a government ban on public assemblies. Opposition politicians, journalists, editors, and civil society activists were arrested. Some, we heard, would be charged with treason.

Students, with their zeal for a cause, often marched to the forefront in unequal confrontations. I remember hearing about a student called Jegema Bedane in Ambo, who had already been arrested many times. When he heard that students were about to start a protest, he tried to escape from school as he knew that he was already targeted. Then the head teacher of the school reported to police that Jegema was agitating students. The police shot and killed him. The protest spread to Jaldu, where three students and three policemen were killed. We didn't go to school for about three months after that, fearing for our lives.

There was a certain boy in our village. He didn't go to school on a day when students protested; he was at his farm. They arrested him and started beating him and shouting, 'Didn't we see you when you were throwing rocks?' The boy was crying, 'I swear to Gabriel, I swear to Mary, I was sowing potato seed on that day!' (Orthodox Christians make their pledges that way.) He was correct, he was sowing potatoes. As the beating intensified, he screamed, 'Yes, I threw rocks on people's houses!' He had no other option. Making kids self-incriminate was a favored method of forcing confessions for something they did not do. They admit, 'Yes! I did this, I did that', to stop the beating.

'Run, Feyisa, run!' How often had I heeded that warning when the police charged into our village? I did run, and I crouched low in the barley crop, hearing the threats of the police, the squeals of those who had not escaped and the anguished objections of family members.

'Were you very afraid?' Kebede asked me. '*I* was.'

'Yes, I was afraid. I am still scared that I might be arrested. I am a runner, Kebede. I couldn't recover from the torture. What if they broke one of my legs? That would be the end of my career. Look at my veins!' I pulled up my trousers to show him. Even then my veins were big and prominent. 'They are wider than yours and could be easily torn if I were beaten.'

'It's a good thing,' Kebede said thoughtfully, 'that you lived in a village away from the town. Students living there were the ones more easily arrested.'

I used to imagine where they could hit me if they arrested me and whether I would scream and beg for mercy. I feel ashamed of my fear and my fleeing, but I dreaded the consequences of a bad beating.

When students disappeared, we hoped that perhaps they had been released and had then stealthily moved to another place and a different school.

Some returned with shaved heads and downcast eyes. Many talented students dropped out of school and went to Finfinne to escape the harsh treatment. Some of them worked as day laborers and I saw them in the streets. They could have become much more than that if they had not left school in fear for their lives. There were others sentenced to death; then the punishment was reduced to life imprisonment, and later to release from jail after ten years. Too many students disappeared without trace while hundreds were forced into exile; some abandoned in refugee camps across our neighboring East African countries.

These were the bad things happening in my country and in my school. Kebede and I wondered about Colonel Alemu Qixessa, whose heroic story we had both heard sitting around the fireside at night. He was a founding father of the Macha-Tulama Association, a civilian self-help organization in the 1960s. What would he think if he could see how the school he established in Jaldu had become a place of violence? Perhaps he foreknew what lay ahead for those who followed. I want to tell you about the Association because I think it gave birth to Oromo nationalism.

3

'The Macha-Tulama Association was the first all-Oromo movement,' I can still hear my grandfather's proud assertion. 'Since their time in the 1960s no force has been able to kill the spirit of freedom, self-respect, and human dignity which it planted in our mind and soul.'

Akaakayyuu, Grandfather, sang the praises of Alemu Qixessa because of the work he did in our district. He gave 10,000 hectares of his own land for the association's development activities. He was one of the small class of educated Oromos motivated to stand up for their people as they observed firsthand the discriminatory policies of Haile Selassie. He had been in the imperial bodyguard and fought against the Italians and had been a loyal subject. 'Even so, he had a deep understanding of our language. I knew a man who had heard him speak. He said he spoke so well that he made you laugh and feel proud one moment and cry and feel sad the next.'

I longed to have such a gift and I liked to hear about Alemu Qixessa. He had not participated in the attempted coup against the Emperor in 1960; not a single high-ranking officer of Oromo origin supported it. Yet, after it failed, Haile Selassie's regime followed a secret policy of limiting the number of high-ranking military officers of Oromo origin and controlling their promotion. This angered Alemu Qixessa.

'What about General Taddesse Birru? He is one of my favorite heroes!' I never tired of hearing Akaakayyuu talk about him. Back then, Taddesse Birru was the most powerful officer of Oromo origin, a rising star in Ethiopian politics.

'Yes, he was popular and fearless,' Grandfather agreed.

'Tell us about what happened with Aklilu Habte Wolde.'

'Aklilu Habte Wolde was the country's prime minister then and he didn't like the way that Taddesse Birru supported the spread of Oromo literacy. He thought Taddesse Birru, who spoke Amharic and had an Amharic wife, was himself Amharic. Aklilu Habte Wolde confided in him the educational policy of Haile Selassie in these words: "Taddesse! After leading the literacy campaign, you talk a lot about learning. It is good to say learn. However, you must know whom we have to teach. We are leading the country by leaving behind the Oromo at least by a century. If you think you can educate them, they are an ocean whose wave can engulf you."'

'Taddesse Birru, shocked at this declaration that revealed the Amharic elites' fear of an educated Oromo people, determined to make all his military skills and inside knowledge available to the Macha-Tulama Association. He had earned fame and respect for his mastery of military science. President Nelson Mandela of South Africa acknowledged Taddesse Birru as the army officer who provided him with his first military training on the art and science of soldiering.

'In the end, Taddesse Birru was impetuous and impatient.' Grandfather used the example of Taddesse Birru to advise caution and restraint. 'When the Emperor refused to stop government attacks on the association, Taddesse Birru planned to assassinate him and seize state power. The plot was a failure.'

I drew closer to hear the end. Taddesse Birru was pardoned but, later, when arrested on another charge, he fought his way out of a battle in the same way that Mullata Fayiso had. He was a brave soldier, but too trusting. He was betrayed by an Oromo peasant called Abba Jifar Waqayo, whose infamous name and treacherous deed, Grandfather declared, stains a page in Oromo history.

'Like all the other leaders, Taddesse Birru was cruelly tortured, but not one of them agreed to testify against the others. Taddesse Birru was a militant Oromo nationalist, a symbol of courage and a martyr to our cause. *Nagaa dhaan haboqtuu* (Let him rest in peace).'

Always after hearing the story of Taddesse Birru, I reviewed my ambition to be a soldier, a leader in the fight against the government. The idea persisted, although the thought of torture always put an end to such daydreaming. When I was able to read and find information for myself, I discovered more about Nelson Mandela. He was sentenced to life imprisonment by the apartheid regime of his country; Taddesse Birru was sentenced to life imprisonment by the regime of Emperor Haile Selassie. Nelson Mandela was freed and lived to make history in South Africa; Taddesse Birru was executed without due process of law and buried in a mass grave. Not that Haile Selassie fared any better, but that's another story.

Kebede always heard me out when I extolled the name of Taddesse Birru, but his hero was Lieutenant Mamo Mazamir, another leader in the Macha-Taluma Association and a martyr to the cause of Oromia. Mamo Mazamir wrote poems that brought tears of joy to the audience and short plays that were shown during Macha-Taluma Association gatherings. These plays were about the way Oromo labor and Oromo wealth sustained the Amhara ruling elites and they made the Oromo conscious of their deprivation and the distortion of their history. Mamo urged them to be the agents of their own liberation.

'He was a great orator too,' Kebede told me. 'Elders in my village say he spoke so convincingly that he attracted many Oromo youth to the movement. The elders told me about a letter he wrote to the leaders of the Oromo armed struggle in Bale. He urged them to keep up the heroic armed struggle "defending every inch of the Oromo Nation to the last drop of your blood."'

As I have told you, Kebede was not one for bloodshed, but he knew off by heart the last words of Mamo Mazamir before he was hung in an Addis Ababa prison: 'I do not die in vain. My blood will water the freedom struggle of the Oromo people. I am certain that those who sentenced me to death for things I did not do, including the emperor and his officials, will receive their punishment from the Ethiopian people. It may be delayed, but the inalienable rights of the Oromo people will be restored by the blood of their children.'

I am sad now as I remember Kebede quoting those words to me. 'The blood of their children….' Did he ever think that he would one day give his blood? I believe so. We both vowed that we would not remain silent, but in this time of hate, when we were teenagers, we were watchful observers only.

I am telling you all this, so you know the background to the Oromo struggle for freedom from oppression. One of my teachers called it an irony of history that the officials who watched the hanging of Mamo Mazamir in 1969 were killed in the same prison in 1974 and buried in a mass grave. They received their punishment, as Mamo predicted. Haile Selassie was murdered a year later.

Those men of the Macha-Tulama Association are our heroes and I am reminded of another, Haile Mariam Gamada, as I touch a tattoo on my right shoulder. It is the *odaa*, or sycamore tree, the Oromo symbol of freedom and self-administration. The *odaa* is the most sacred of trees and its shade is the place of peace and the center of religion. I will tell you more about all this and why I chose it for this tattoo.

The *odaa* tree was designed as a logo for the Macha-Tulama Association by Haile Mariam Gamada, a lawyer and a staunch advocate for Oromo history, which he knew better than most. Accused by Haile Selassie as the organizing genius behind the Association, he was tortured and crippled. It is said that he was taken to his trial on a stretcher. His last words are known and quoted to this day: 'I am exhausted. I feel I am on the verge of death. I do not expect to recover. So this is my last farewell to you. Whether we die or not, our ideas about the freedom of the Oromo will be realized by our children or grandchildren.'

These stories are being told to the children and grandchildren. My generation may well be the one to celebrate *bilissumaa* (freedom and independence). This is my hope and prayer, but even as I tell you what I know, surrounded as I am by a crowd of witnesses, Oromo leaders and the young ones who followed them were still imprisoned, tortured, and killed. They have often been accused of connections with the OLF.

Survivors of the Association were the founding members of the OLF in the 1970s, at first an underground movement that kept the spirit of resistance alive. They played their part in the overthrow of Haile Selassie's regime, but their plans for the future of Oromia were thwarted by the Derg just as surely as they were two decades later by the TLF.

The OLF did not leave the Jaldu area as quickly as it did from other areas after being defeated by the TLF in the 1990s and the current regime didn't have full control of us right away. For this reason, farmers were accustomed to OLF soldiers and loved them. Their office was there for some time. Tolcha Wagi, the boy soldier who fought side-by-side with his father and Mullata Fayiso in their battles against the Derg, had joined the OLF after serving his prison sentence. He represented its interests in Jaldu when the Derg was finally defeated. I met Tolcha many years later when I competed in a race in Washington DC. He had fled his own country, like so many others. He was thrilled to see me and he hugged me hard in the warm and wonderful way we have when greeting one another.

'Feyisa! I know your parents well! The last time I saw you, you were just a kid! Not much more than a baby.' He indicated with his hand how small I was then. 'I went to every place in your village, educating the people about self-determination. We needed to organize and struggle against the TLF. We were defeated.'

My father had told me that some outlawed OLF members lived in our house even after this regime took control, but I don't remember that. Tolcha was not one of them. He told me what happened on the night of June 21, 1992.

'The TLF surrounded my office, just like the Derg surrounded Mullata Fayiso's house all those years before. At daylight they opened fire.' Tolcha paused and stared into the distance. 'They killed my friend, Tamana Bushu, who had been beside me in many other fights. I don't know how I escaped, but I did. I will fight until I die for the Oromo, even in this city such a long way from home.'

Tolcha is proud of what the *Qubee* generation is achieving. I owe my identity to men like him and the heroes of the Macha-Taluma Association who sacrificed a lot for the cause of *Oromumma*.

'I am grateful to you,' I told Tolcha as we said our goodbyes. 'You and many other *Goota*, brave men, gave us the opportunity to learn our language and to be really aware of who we are.'

Tolcha shrugged, but I could see that he was pleased.

'Being one of the *Qubee* generation does not only mean learning in *Afaan Oromoo*,' he counselled. 'You have a big responsibility to be loyal to Oromia and to follow the politics of our country. You are one of Oromia's sons, Feyisa. Never forget that.'

I was sorry that I could not talk more with Tolcha. I promised to keep in contact with him.

'You know my history,' he said. 'You can follow me on the Facebook. And "like" me!'

This brave man no longer holds a gun, but he is a sentinel for our cause on Facebook, posting the information and the pictures that Aduna and I and many others send to him. He is no longer leading OLF soldiers, but he has many followers on Facebook. I was destined to meet Tolcha again in Washington DC, but that came later when much more had happened in our country and we were both exiles.

When I heard about the EPRDF disarming the Oromo in the 1990s, I thought of Tolcha and how his father and Mullata Fayiso rebelled against the Derg when its officers disarmed the people. My father was furious and repeated the EPRDF outrage story many times.

'We bought those guns by selling our precious animals. I sold one of my favorite horses to get an AK47. We should have defied them. *Abboomamuu diduu.*'

These were his words of contempt. Abba was so proud of that gun. He cleaned and polished it lovingly and if he was in a good mood, he would let me, little as I was, hold it. He laughed loudly at the sight of me, a tot weighed down but determined not to drop the precious weapon.

'Those soldiers who came for our guns didn't show any regard,' Abba ground one big fist into the palm of his other hand. 'They were beating respected men, women, and elders, all because of the firearms they rightfully owned. They were even beating those farmers who had already sold their guns. They didn't believe them.'

Oromos didn't protest their rights at that time like they did later. I saw with my own eyes what happened when one man refused to part with his weapon. It was a big gun, a *faali*. Now this man was highly respected, and people listened to his opinions. But they were afraid to hide their guns like he did. The soldiers beat him mercilessly until his wife ran out and thrust the *faali* at her husband's tormentors She could not bear to see him beaten to death.

Our hope was the OLF at that time. We were sure they would regroup, and we waited for them to come and liberate us. 'Perhaps ABO will come this year.' We said this every year as the reality of life under the EPRDF worsened. ABO is the *Afaan Oromoo* abbreviation for OLF. I first heard the word ABO in 5th or 6th grade, but the front was also referred to as ONEG, the Amharic abbreviation for OLF. Strangely, this was the term my father used, so I was ignorant of ABO.

'Do you know what ABO stands for, Feyisa?' I can't recall the name of the boy at high school who asked the question, but I had to shake my head. 'It stands for *Adda Bilisummaa Oromoo* (Freedom and Peace for the Oromo).'

I liked the name. I said to my father, pleased to be airing my knowledge, 'I want to join the *Adda Bilisummaa Oromoo!*' He roared with cynical laughter. The words mean Oromo Liberation Front.

Then I went to Shashamanne, a city south of Finfinne, for a running competition which was held on an OPDO holiday. I saw on TV my high school's students chanting '*ABOn ha gubatu, Adda Bilisummaa Oromoo ha gubatu!* (Let OLF be burned, let Oromo Liberation Front be burned!).'

I was upset that they cursed *Adda Bilisummaa Oromoo*, because I love the name. For once I was eager to get back to school to question the students I had seen and heard.

'Why did you chant that slogan, "*ABOn ha gubatu, Adda Bilisummaa Oromoo ha gubatu*"?' I demanded.

'Where have you been, Feyisa? Don't you know we could have been killed if we sang *Adda Bilisummaa Oromoo*?'

I soon learned that people could be cruel with words, and even kill you for using the wrong ones.

4

When I was in the Armed Forces Club in Finfinne, there were many runners and leaders who came from different districts and my Amharic was inadequate for talking to them. They made fun of me. I have heard it said that even my hero, Abebe Bikila, was looked down upon by the snobbish elite of Finfinne, because of his thick Oromo accent. They thought of him and all Oromos as backward peasants.

Everyone laughed when my name was called, and I was angry. That made matters worse. If I challenged the decision of a club manager or dared to offer a different opinion, he would mock me. One of them said to me in Amharic,

'*Ye ONEG amelekaket aleh*', which means, 'You have the attitude or ideology of OLF'. The employers, the non-Oromo, seemed to know more about the OLF than I did.

Another taunt went like this: '*Yihe lij jerbaw ye tena ONEG sayhon ay kerim!* (This guy has to be investigated; he could be OLF!)'. Sometimes I retorted, 'I don't even know what the OLF looks like; I don't know if they eat grass or food.' This was a traditional expression. They jeered.

I burned with hate and I vowed that I would beat them all, not with my fists but with my legs on the running track, just like Abebe Bikila, who was mocked when he told people that he would go abroad one day to compete. The ridicule and humiliation made him even more determined and he became the first black African ever to win a gold medal at the Olympics.

When journalists asked me about the best moments of my career, I told them about that race in Ambo in 2004 when I ran barefoot and came in 4th. 'I was happier than an Olympic champion that day!' They jotted down the details and waited expectantly. What else, they said, dissatisfied with my answer. There have been many other highlights, but not one as exhilarating as that new knowledge that I could run, and I would do whatever it took to become an elite athlete.

The next race that made me very happy was the Great Ethiopian Run of 2007. Before this race became popular there was an annual Armed Forces championship, a prestigious event attended by the Emperor, who wanted to develop an athletics training programme. The Great Ethiopian Run in Finfinne is now the biggest road race in Africa and was on the runners' calendar for a few years before I took part. It offers a chance for new athletes to emerge and have the opportunity to compete on the international stage. By the time I ran that race I had been 'spotted' by an Olympic runner called Mulugeta Wondimu, who was scouting for promising athletes to join the Armed Forces Club.

This is how it works in Ethiopia: promising athletes start running at school and are selected from the local community for regional races. Then the best are selected for clubs. If they perform well, they are chosen for the national team and other coaches take on their training. Those who are most successful are on their way, to an international race, with high hopes for Olympic selection.

Mulugeta Wondimu saw me run in an *Oromiyaa* competition held in Bale, when I was representing my zone, West Shoa. I came in 3rd in the race and Mulugeta approached me afterwards to talk about the club. He chose me and four others to join the club in Finfinne.

'Feyisa!' he called out to me one day after club training. 'You are in good condition. You should enter the Great Ethiopian Run this year. It's ten kilometers long and you are ready for it.'

I was thrilled to be picked out but there were obstacles. 'I have not registered for the race, Mulugeta. Anyway, I am registered to race at Hawassa. Only seven athletes can compete from each club in the Great Ethiopian Run and seven others have already registered.'

'Your performance is better than some of them. I will speak to your coach.'

I knew the Great Ethiopian Race offered better chances for recognition, but I thought Hawassa, a city in southern Ethiopia, offered bigger prize money. As usual, I was desperate for money. I earned a small salary, 520 *birr* a month, from the Armed Forces Club, but I was sending some of it home to my mother. She had divorced my father and she was living with the younger children on her share of our farm. Farming is a man's job, requiring more strength than a woman has to plough the land.

Aduna was finishing school in Ginchi because at that time Jaldu high school did not go beyond Grade 10. This meant he boarded in Ginchi and could not always help my mother when she most needed him. I was sending nearly half of my salary to support him, but I still had to pay for transport and clothes and shoes. Always shoes, but only for competition. They cost more than 300 *birr* a pair and I didn't have shoes for training apart from the one pair a year issued by the club. My salary may have been enough for me alone, but not when I was supporting my family as well.

'Why don't you explain your problems to them? Can't your father pay for Aduna?' asked Kebede, who heard about my financial difficulties when we met in Finfinne. He was working long hours in his own business, renting houses, not earning much himself. Any spare time I had from training I liked to share with him.

I found it hard to explain my mixture of pride and sense of responsibility, especially for Aduna. He was a good student and he wanted to go on to university.

'You and I and maybe one other can start an Ekub,' suggested Kebede. 'It's a kind of saving, where we pool our money and then pay it to each member in turn. Let's start with 300 birr each this month.'

I agreed to the idea and we asked another trusted friend, Tolessa, to join in. We had our first 900 *birr*.

'Kebede, I need the money first. Can you and Tolessa manage? If I win the race in Hawassa I can pay it back into our account immediately.'

I had two good friends who helped me out in many ways. This was one of them, when they handed over the birr without question. Looking back now I can see that I was like a punter at the horse races, gambling my friends' money on a win that I might not have. I sent 200 *birr* for my brother, 400 for my mother, and spent the last 300 for shoes.

Then, for reasons I never knew, I was scratched from the Hawassa race. I was frantic. I searched for Mulugeta, who was always kind to me, unlike other Amharic or Tigrayan leaders in the club.

'I am no longer in the Hawassa race! Is it too late for me to register for the Great Ethiopian Race?'

'You will be in that race. Leave it to me.'

He put my case to our coach. 'Feyisa should participate in the competition,' he argued. 'He has the potential to win.'

I had experienced many problems with the coaches favoring other boys, but not on this occasion. I would be on the starting line.

Well, that is not quite true. The traffic in the city was very bad that day and I was tempted to get off the bus and run the rest of the way. Donkeys, goats, sheep, beggars, blue and white Fiat taxis, packed dusty vans, and ineffectual traffic policemen—the scene was familiar to me now, but I wanted it all to go away. I had a race to run.

I arrived late at the starting place, the Ghion Hotel, a landmark in the city, a place where many VIPs have stayed, in the heart of downtown. I had to start from the back as runners already occupied the front lines. I lagged behind for many meters, but I had too much at stake to lose.

This is a 10,000-meter race with a generous purse—10,000 *birr* at that time for the winner! I was in 7th place with three kilometers to go to the finish. I was feeling better now, because a person who finishes in a 10th place wins 350 *birr* and I was sure I could make at least 10th place.

I am often asked if I really enjoy running or is it just a job like any other job. I love running. You will have heard that 'run, jump, throw' are the natural and universal forms of human physical expression. The Oromo child engages in all of them, gleefully throwing javelin (*darboo*), participating in high and long jump (*utaalchoo*), and wrestling (*waldhaansso*). Running (*fiigicha*) is the most popular form of sport for us.

I am at my happiest when in my stride, loping along, but it takes a strong will, a competitive spirit, and a self-confidence to succeed. Experts talk of the Ethiopian runners' advantages of training in high altitude with thin air, existing on a lean diet, and running in mountainous terrain. Perhaps this is so, but there was another element that favored me in the Great Ethiopian Race and has favored me in many races since.

I enter a race with full confidence if I dream beforehand about that race. I have already told you that I know I will win if I gallop racehorses in my dream. This is the best dream. If I take a shower with clean water in my dreams, I won't win anything; clean water means there is nothing in it, and I go home with empty hands. The night before the Great Ethiopian Race I dreamed that people were pouring dirty water on my head while I was running. The dirty water has something in it and it means I will win. Usually I do win after this dream, but I did not win the Great Ethiopian Race. I believe I would have won if I had arrived early and started closer to the front of the pack of about 35,000 runners.

I finished in 3rd place and won 6,000 *birr*. I was so surprised and delighted that I was hardly aware of the congratulations all around for the boy of seventeen who had performed very well against some of the best athletes in the country.

'I have never held this much money in my hands before!' I exclaimed to Kebede when we met to celebrate my victory. He had watched the race and was as happy for me as he would have been had he won the race himself. 'But it's a cheque, not cash.'

'You are holding it too tightly!' He lightly tapped my closed fist. 'The bank may not accept such a crumpled cheque!

'I am afraid I will lose it on my way to home!'

'We will take it to a bank right now. Feyisa, I am proud of you! An Oromo son performing so well in Finfinne!'

I counted and recounted the cash they gave me at the bank.

'Here!' I instructed Kebede. 'You take half of it so that I will at least have that half if I am robbed on the way home!'

Laughing and teasing, we divided the money and put it in different pockets and in our socks. I paid the Ekub back and the rest went into my newly opened bank account. Then I started winning races every week, or every two weeks, and so on. The money then kept on coming in: 3,000 *birr*, 5,000 *birr*, and so on. Soon I would be paid 200,000 US dollars to participate in a single race, but that didn't make me any happier when I compared it with the 6,000 *birr* I got on that earlier occasion. Because I have enough money today, it doesn't surprise me if money comes.

I could have faced a lot of problems if I hadn't performed well in that race. Because I did so well against stiff competition, the Adidas company offered sponsorship. That was a special moment, signing up with my first sponsor! They paid me 3,000 US dollars for a year. I didn't know much about sponsorship then, but that was a lot of money when converted to the Ethiopian currency. Then, after a year, I signed a contract with Nike for 20,000 US dollars a year.

Everything changed after that race. I could buy any clothes and shoes I liked, and I could help my family with ease. The Great Ethiopian Race! I will always think of it with joy. I have Mulugeta to thank for giving me that first big break.

'Do you know, Mulugeta,' I said as the successes multiplied, 'I was not that happy when I started to win big prizes as I was after the Great Ethiopian Race. It wouldn't give as much joy as that one if they pay me a million US dollars today!'

He was thrilled for his protege. 'You won that prize at a very critical time when you faced many challenges.'

He and I both knew that some of the hardest challenges were in the Armed Forces Club. I am always keen to find out more about people and places and I wanted to know how the club came about. My ambition to be a soldier never really faded and there I was training in a military club!

'The running culture in Ethiopia began in the armed forces,' Mulugeta explained. 'It is while serving in the army that most potential athletes are introduced to competitive running. Beginning with Wami Biratu, our first Olympian in 1956, the armed forces have been a source of financial and moral support for our best athletes.'

'What about Abebe Bikila?' I asked, because he was the first object of my hero worship.

'Yes, his talents were first discovered shortly after he joined the Imperial Army. Onni Niskanen, a Swedish sports instructor, noticed him and began training him for the marathon. His 1960 Olympic marathon win stunned the world. Mamo Wolde, the 1968 Olympic champion, was a soldier too.'

The lives of both those runners ended badly and I trotted off to start the day's training with thoughts of them. I thrilled to the stories about Abebe Bikila, who ran the marathon, barefoot, on the cobblestones of the Appian Way in Rome. Now that I am able to see film clips of that great run, I watch in awe as he broke ahead in the last 1,000 meters and crossed the finish line at the Arch of Constantine in 2 hours, 15 minutes, and 16.2 seconds. His kinsmen like to quote an Italian journalist's comment, 'It took one million Italian soldiers to conquer Addis Ababa, but only one Ethiopian soldier to conquer Rome!'

Perhaps my desire to be a soldier began with hearing about these runners. Abebe Bikila told one journalist about the day he came upon a squad of Imperial Bodyguards training in the streets of Finfinne. 'They were sharply uniformed; they had precision, discipline, polish,' he said. 'I was very much moved.' Abebe Bikila joined the Imperial Bodyguard, the most prestigious section of the armed forces; for a young man like him, from a humble background, it provided a way of escape from an impoverished life. The Bodyguard was never sent away from the capital to guard the country's borders—it was a relatively safe role in the defense of the Emperor.

Certainly, my decision to run the marathon was made because I admire Abebe Bikila so much. A short distance runner only runs with ten or fifteen runners, but in a marathon the number is usually at least 200 or 300, sometimes thousands, and I get a lot of joy competing with many runners, passing them all, one after the other, and coming in first.

Athletics is a popular spectator sport and I am exhilarated by the crowded sidewalks and packed stadiums, cheering me on. The thought of TV audiences in their billions, especially for the Olympic Games, is a heady incentive to the elite athlete. Such a huge international audience was uppermost in my mind in Rio de Janeiro and we will come to that momentous event by and by. I grin when I think of the boys back in Jaldu watching the runner in the television set, exclaiming, is that not Feyisa, whom we chased in the forest and threw sticks at in the *gugsi*?

I imagined the older ones in my village, shaking their heads in wonder, remembering Bogia, the fat little boy they scolded for his greed! Trainers have questioned my weight, and this is another factor in favor of the marathon. 'You weigh too much for track running,' I was told when I complained of back pain. 'This is due to the intensity of the short distance track running. You are having to push your body too hard for this kind of race.'

My weight, at sixty-eight kilograms, is still high. One criticism I have heard is that I chose marathon running too early; I should have started running marathon later. I started running marathons in 2009 when I was nineteen and you will hear more about my races as the story progresses. For now, I want to talk about the club, which was situated in Arat Kilo, near the national palace.

We were given clothes, but only one complete sports suit, shoddily made, and shoes that fell apart after about three months. I was glad to have a real trainer for the first time, because until then my training was not scientific or programmed. I can remember saying to myself, covering many kilometers because I thought that's all I had to do, 'I have to run up to that mountain and back!' Then I did that regardless of how long it took me. I only trained seriously when I was approaching a race. I was like a lazy student who studies when the exam approaches. I was improving on my performance every year though, as much as thirty to forty seconds for a ten-kilometer race.

My first trainer at the club was Megersa Hunde and he was out there on the track three days a week to advise me and the team I was with. For the rest of the week we trained on our own, youngsters with one common goal: victory on the race track. Some of the friends I made there come into my story later, in unexpected ways. I stayed in the club for a few years, but I left as unhappily and as angrily as I left my home after the death of the sheep.

Let me tell you why I left that club. The director of the club was from the Tigrayan ethnic group and I am not exaggerating when I say that he discriminated against me in his decisions. I won thirty-one medals for the club; the first person in its history to bring back so many medals from competitions. Because this is an Armed Forces club, there are ranks of promotion with military names which go as high as General and Colonel. My rank was *Ajajaa Shantamaa*, the equivalent of commander of 50 soldiers! Your salary increased as your rank increased.

'I don't have any love for this ranking system,' I confided in Teklu, one of my friends at the club, 'and it really annoys me when the ranks are not assigned fairly and I am not promoted as I should be.'

'What has happened now?' he asked.

'Look at Yemane Tsegaye, the Tigrayan athlete!' I was getting ready for training and I pulled the lace on my shoe so viciously that it snapped. 'He has not won any medals for the club. He had not one rank, yet he was chosen to go to a competition in Germany, representing Ethiopia, and finished in 4th place. Then they promoted him four ranks!'

I pulled on my other shoe, tying the lace with less vengeance. Teklu was ready to go, dancing up and down lightly on his toes. He waited for me to finish.

'I went to Korea, Teklu, representing Ethiopia, finished in 3rd place and won a medal for the country! I got only one rank promotion.'

We jogged out into the cool air of early morning and I calmed down as I started the day's programme. Running always soothes me and reassures me. I couldn't let the matter drop though. I was the one winning medals for the club inside and outside the country. I confronted the director.

'Why are you treating me like this?' I demanded, trying to keep calm. My Amharic deteriorates quickly when I am upset. 'Why am I not promoted fairly?'

He resented my questioning his decisions and instead of giving me an answer, he blustered about my car. Yes, I had a car to drive then and I drove it to the club for a few months. I drew the colors of the Oromo Liberation Front flag on the side of it in defiance of my tormentors at the club. Red, green and yellow; in the middle, the *odaa*, the sycamore tree, Oromo symbol of freedom.

'You are a rebel, Feyisa,' he countered. 'In this club we are loyal to the government. Remember that next time you dare to defy me.'

'You are tribalist! I am only asking for my rights to be respected.'

I marched out of his office, as straight-backed as any soldier, and went to the offending car. My hands were trembling as I fumbled for the keys and I sat behind the wheel for a while, deciding on my next move. I drove away and stayed away until Mulugeta came to talk to me.

'You are right to be upset,' he began. 'I have seen the way you stand up for others when they are mistreated. You are a leader among the athletes, Feyisa, and they miss you. I beg you to come back.'

I agreed, reluctantly, and returned because I had a special request for the director. He had influence and I needed his help. The ink on my car had started to fade so my first step was to change the color to a neutral shade that would give no offense. I trained quietly for a couple of weeks, careful not to get into arguments with anyone. Then I returned to the director's office. He acknowledged me coldly.

'My cousin who is studying in Nekemte has been arrested,' I said. Nekemte is about 300 kilometers west of Finfinne. My cousin was a third-year engineering student at university. He spent every summer with me. 'He has been arrested by mistake; he doesn't get involved in politics. My cousin is innocent. Can you please help my family arrange for his release from prison?'

The flag on the car had not been easily forgotten. 'How dare you ask?' he shouted. 'What were you doing coming to this camp with an OLF flag on your car? Now you want my help for your cousin. Troublemakers, all of you.'

I strode out of his office as angry as I had been on the previous occasion. To my surprise, he relented. I don't know why. He went with me to the dreaded Maekelawi prison, but he did not have any power or influence there. Four months later my cousin was released. It could have been much worse.

I was still determined to leave the club for good. You could leave by giving notification, but according to the rules the leaders could make you continue there if they decided this in a meeting. They rejected my application. I was despised by management, but they wanted the many medals I brought to the club.

I had a very smart friend in the club called Hirko Yada, whose home was in Holeta, a few hundred kilometers north-west of Finfinne. He lives in Canada now. Hirko was also keen to leave the club and to start his own coaching business, confident that he would earn more that way. The club wanted a pretext to discharge him, as they did not make any profit from his coaching.

'This is what we will do,' he suggested, keen to conspire against a corrupt administration. 'I will take your application form to the director. I reckon he'll sign it without looking at it properly, thinking it's my application. He's wanted me to leave for a long time.'

It was a bold move, but it worked! The director did not even read what he had signed. Then, with extra cheek, Hirko took his own application to be signed, pretending that the other one had been lost. Again, the director signed without question.

In such a way we both left that club. Many others left soon after, including Mulugeta. The leaders called me, claiming that I could not leave, I had a financial obligation to them, they had not agreed to my leaving, etc. I returned once more to that loathsome office and slapped my signed form down in front of the director.

'You have tricked us!' His face and voice were full of hatred. 'I will see that you are punished for this.'

I marched out again, head high, but anxiously wondering if he would call the police. For days I expected a visit from them, but the director must have known that his signature was clearly on the document and that it would bring shame on him when others knew that he had fallen for the deception.

In the time that I was in the club I didn't compete for a couple of years due to injury. The leaders decided on a layover claiming that I was not fit. This was another frustration for me and I was glad to leave in 2013. By then I was enjoying success and recognition, 'living the dream' as the young ones say.

5

I have experienced many great races; for now, I will talk about just one of the best, the marathon race in Daegu, South Korea, at the World Championships in 2011. It was after this race that I complained most bitterly about the ranking system at the Armed Forces Club. The World Championships are organized by the International Association of Athletics Federations (IAAF), the governing body for athletics.

I was twenty-one years old, the youngest of the Ethiopian distance competitors who boarded the plane. Always when the plane took off and I saw Finfinne spread out below me, I was overwhelmed by a feeling of love and loyalty for the city and my country. I never gave up hope that Ethiopia will be a place of peace and freedom and independence: *bilissumaa*! That was my prayer a few years later when the plane I boarded in August of 2016 left the runway and carried me away.

The atmosphere at the major competitions is charged with tension and anticipation, but I am not intimidated by the venues or the crowds or the competitors. Another question often asked of me is, 'Feyisa, do you get nervous before a race?'

'No, not at all!' I am quick to respond to this one. 'I am not worried or sleepless beforehand either.'

I find it hard to explain that for me the race is a game, like the ones I played at home in Jaldu with my boyhood friends. You play games with a relaxed spirit and childlike joy. Running, or in my language, *fiigicha*, is a competition, which I compare to jumping rivers, climbing trees, horseback riding (*gugsaa*), and outrunning neighborhood bullies. The packs, like the Ethiopians or Kenyans who run tactically together before one or other breaks away, are reminiscent of the packs we played in as kids. This much is easy enough to understand for most enquirers; I find it harder to explain my peculiar dreams, which affect me with an inexplicable fatalism.

We know that our main competitors in the long-distance races will be the Kenyans. While we have just left a city that many describe as drab and ugly, they will have flown out of Nairobi, which is comparable in its order and beauty to any European metropolis. Like most of us, the Kenyan athletes have come from farms and villages. The lush Rift Valley, 200 miles from Nairobi, has been their first training ground. Some commentators agree that the Kenyans understand the sport of running much better than the Ethiopians.

There is no denying that they outclassed us in the women's races in Daegu. The men's events were closely contested with Mo Farah of Great Britain winning the 5,000 meters ahead of an American runner and our teammate, Dejen Gebremeskel. There is often controversy in the events and in this case Imane Merga, also on our side, was awarded the bronze medal, but he was later disqualified for having run inside the curb of the running track for some ten to fifteen meters.

'Bad luck, Imane.' We all crowded around and commiserated. Imane took comfort in winning the bronze in the 10,000 meters. The spectators were on their feet, screaming, as Ibrahim Jeilan, one of us, snatched victory from Mo Farah by the narrowest of margins.

I saw Mo Farah run for the first time in Daegu. Like his fans the world over, I am charmed by his wide grin and the 'mobot' pose he adopted. This is the man who honored me in Rio de Janeiro and we became good friends. We talked about our best performances, and our worst.

'I remember watching you run the marathon in Daegu,' he said. 'You did well against the Kenyans.'

I relived the race. Abel Kirui, the Kenyan, was defending champion and reporters claimed that the story of this encounter was all about him. After we ran in casual style to fifteen kilometers, with the Moroccan contingent testing the field, the pace picked up and the field opened out. After twenty-five kilometers, the race came down to Kirui, Vincent Kipruto, Eliud Kiptanui, Abderrahime Bouramdane, and me. Then Kirui accelerated, running 14:18 between the twenty-five and thirty-kilometer marks. Nobody could go with him and he ran all alone, extending his lead for the remainder of the race to finish in 2 hours, 7 minutes, and 38 seconds. I finished third, in 2 hours, 10 minutes, and 32 seconds. Distance: 42.195 kilometers or 26.2 miles.

I like to study the statistics, pondering how I might improve upon strategy and pace. The race against Kirui was special because he became one of my closest friends in the running community. I always want him to win, provided of course that I am not in the competition myself! I support him more than I support other Ethiopian athletes.

'You know what, Feyisa?' he asked when we discussed the race. 'I was not even picked to be in the team for these championships! A couple of runners withdrew with injuries and I was recalled.'

'If you hadn't been here I might have won!' I grumbled, half in jest. 'None of us stood a chance against you.'

'You did OK. I heard that your time of 2:05:23 in Rotterdam last year was the fastest ever by a 20-year-old. You must have been one of the youngest competing here too. You've got a big future, Feyisa.'

The race in Daegu was my season's best and I went home happy. I used to childishly hate the Kenyans when they competed so well against Ethiopian athletes. I didn't like it when my country lost. Then I started to admire their talent, asking myself how can they run like this, why are they this dark, why are they taller, why are they thinner? I envied their body shape when I watched them on TV. I was not thin or even slim at that time. My body is not like other marathon runners and this has been pointed out to me more than once.

You hear of intense rivalry and jealousy among elite athletes, but I don't see anyone as my enemy. It pained me when other Ethiopian athletes chose to speak against the action I took at the Rio de Janeiro Olympics, even though they knew about the atrocities committed daily in our country.

Kenenisa Bekele, the winner of many gold medals, considered by many to be the greatest distance runner of all time, is also my fellow Oromo. We have never been close, but I was stung by a statement he made before a race in Berlin.

'Anyone has the right to protest anything,' he pronounced, 'but you need to maybe choose how to protest and solve things.'

Then the journalist asked him specifically about my protest. 'It would be better to get your answer from Feyisa himself.'

'What about other Ethiopian runners who have made similar crossed-arm gestures?'

'Sport should be separate from politics,' Kenenisa replied. 'Everyone has a right to protest in Ethiopia and the government is trying to solve things in a democratic way.'

How could he say that? Kenenisa has received some criticism from others for such untruth, not just from me; on social media in Ethiopia there was a split between supporters of the two of us.

'Many people are being killed for protesting,' I said publicly when Kenenisa made those remarks. 'How can you say that's democratic? I'm very angry when he says that.'

There was no Oromo whose friend or family member was not in prison. I knew some athletes whose relatives were in prison. Hiding and bending the truth is not good. I felt betrayed when Kenenisa said that. He was not chosen for the Ethiopian marathon team for the Olympics Games in Rio de Janeiro. Perhaps that is a factor.

The biggest hurt was the answer given by Haile Gebresilassie, my boyhood hero, when asked about me.

'I don't involve myself in politics,' he said. 'If I were involved in politics, I would leave athletics. I am now competing to become the Ethiopian Athletics Federation (EAF) president.'

He distanced himself from the cries of his Oromo countrymen and women and he succeeded in his aim of becoming president of the Ethiopian Athletics Federation following an election in Addis Ababa. Kebede, who understood these things, would have said that it was 'politically expedient' for Haile to remain silent about human rights abuse.

When I was asked by a journalist about Haile's remarks, I replied, 'I admire Haile as a runner, and as a champion. But on the other hand, rich people are generally charitable and they give back to their people and they help the poor. In Ethiopia, most of the rich people we have are selfish and greedy and they live a parasitic life where they attach themselves to the government.'

I know that Haile has done good things for benevolent causes and for athletics; he was a founder of the Great Ethiopian Run, from which I benefited. I know too that he established a chain of Haile Hotels and Resorts, expensive tourist destinations in Ethiopia. He is a very wealthy man.

In their defense, a representative of Haile and Kenenisa responded to my words by saying that such criticisms did not take account of the complicated and volatile political situation in Ethiopia, where they both still live. Their supporters and other disinterested observers contend that many public figures run a fine line between resisting oppression and staying in the country where they may still do some good.

Let us see what good Haile does as President of the EAF, which has its critics too and will come into my story again. He says he wants to bring Ethiopian athletics to a higher level. 'Athletics changed my life completely and I am thankful for that,' he told the media after his election. 'I have gained a lot of experience throughout my athletics career and now it is time to give back to my country and sport.'

In my time of hate, as I was entering adulthood, I still loved these two athletes. I cut their photographs from newspapers and pasted them in my exercise books and pinned them to the walls of our house with thorns. It was a source of amazement to me that I later competed on the same running tracks and roads as they did. They were my role models and I learned many things from them. They inspired and raised my confidence; I am grateful to them for that. We have not had personal disagreements, but I regarded them as enemies of the people, no different in their self-interest and self-protection to those who propped up the Ethiopian government.

When I first started running and saw Haile and other victorious athletes carrying the national flag or wrapping it around their bodies with such glowing pride, I wanted to be like them, flourishing that symbol of patriotism and honor. What a moment of glory! But the Ethiopian flag was splattered with blood. How could I hold aloft the blood of the murdered Oromo? I was offered an Ethiopian flag after the race in Rio de Janeiro, but I refused to accept it.

I also bought the uniform of Ethiopian athletes from the Addis Merkato, Africa's biggest open-air market, where you can buy just about anything. This purchase was made in the first flush of excitement when I started winning races. I kept the uniforms, but I didn't like to wear them. How could you love the trademarks of your country when you saw so many hurt and humiliated in the name of that country? The hatred of Oromo people by those in power, as well as the attitude of others who denied or ignored the wrongs committed against them, worked against loyalty and love.

I saw a Tweet from Haile exclaiming, 'What a beautiful day for a run! No matter how far you go, no matter how quick you run, today just enjoy.' This was on June 7, 2017, Global Running Day. He received many responses, greeting him as a hero and a legend. He was running on Mount Entoto; I was running beside strangely shaped mesas in a foreign land. Our paths had diverged. Instead of his picture drawn on my leg with a twig I had an *odaa* tree tattooed on my shoulder.

'*Waaqaa!*' I cry out aloud. 'Why is it up to me? What have I accomplished?'

6

My call was to the god of the Oromo, known in our tradition and culture as the creator of the universe and the source of all life. Although many of my people have become followers of Christian or Muslim religions, there is still widespread belief that only *Waaqaa* can give life, send rain, and provide for our every need.

I like to talk about religion with others, especially the elders, whose knowledge of all our beliefs should be written down for safekeeping. *Waaqeffannaa*, the beliefs of Oromo religion (*Amanti Oromo*), has no written holy text; it has relied on oral transmission. Sometimes as an older boy I thought about Geti telling me that the Christian Bible had been translated to *Afaan Oromoo* and I wondered why we had no sacred writings in one book. I raised this with Nurefssa Tujo, the spiritual leader in Gojo.

'Our beliefs are not written on paper,' Nurefssa agreed. 'They are written in people's hearts, minds, oral histories, rituals, shrines and special functions. Priests, rainmakers and elders like me know our beliefs and pass them on. Everybody, including you, Feyisa, is a carrier of our religion.'

As I moved in wider circles and told others about my belief in *Waaqaa*, I was accused of being pagan and superstitious. I cannot always find the words to defend my faith, but I know from my talks with elders that *Waaqeffannaa* is one of the ancient indigenous African religions. It is the faith of Cushitic people, including the Oromo, who lead their life according to the law and will of *Waaqaa*.

I am glad that they did not force the people in the place where I was born to take another religion as they did elsewhere. Under imperial rule the Oromo traditional religion was actively suppressed; in addition to land dispossession, the imperial powers made Orthodox Christianity the official religion. The Oromo in various places were forcibly baptized into the Orthodox faith. Sometimes they responded by converting to Islam in protest, or to Protestant Christianity in defiance, because they associated the Orthodox Church with the oppressor. You would have to say that their conversion was not always because of conviction, but as a reaction to colonization.

There were no Muslims where I was born. Since it is in central Shoa and is bordered by Amhara country (predominantly Orthodox Christians), no Muslims attempted to convert people to their religion. I was puzzled by my parents' seeming uncertainty about their beliefs. For instance, they seemed to accept Orthodox Christianity, but they did not have a deep knowledge about the faith and they didn't know its secrets.

'We only need to go to church to bury our dead,' my father said when I questioned him.

'We respect the ancient values,' my mother claimed. '*Safuu*, being ashamed for wrongdoing, is important, Feyisa. Never forget that.'

I agree with my mother about *safuu*, a moral code based on Oromo notions of respect for all things, directing each of us on the right way to live. *Safuu* is much more than being ashamed of wrongdoing. *Safuu* refers to something regarded as sacred, inviolable, not to be tampered with, fixed and respected. The line that you don't cross.

In fairness to them, my parents did not have the advantage of much education and they had known so much disruption in their early lives. It was safer to stay within the simple day-to-day concerns of the farm and the village. But they esteemed the traditional norms and used those as guides to action, instructing their children to adopt the same sort of respect.

We were not threatened by the Orthodox priest who came to our village. He even went to the *Ayyaanaa's* house—the *Waaqeffannaa* priest's house—to eat and drink. When leaving he sprayed *tsebel* (holy water) on the house! We accommodated him and the Orthodox believers without losing our traditions, but for a long time *Afaan Oromoo* was not spoken in their church and we did not understand why. More recently, people start to understand after Protestant believers came and started preaching the Gospel in *Afaan Oromoo*. Then, almost all people became *Pente*, converted to Protestant beliefs. As a result, the Orthodox priests started to preach in *Afaan Oromoo* to compete with Protestants. Overall, my family is predominantly *Waqeffataa*.

I think the appeal of our religion is that it promotes peace (*nagar*), reconciliation (*araara*), love (*jaalala*), and harmony (*walin jireenya*). These qualities are not unique; they are similar to Christian virtues. Just another example, of interest to you perhaps, is our belief in ten truths, in a way like the Ten Commandments. Some of these sound like a Christian creed: we believe in one God (*Waaqaa Tokkicha*); we believe only in the power and wisdom of *Waaqaa*; we believe in the meaningfulness of all creatures created by *Waaqaa*.

I celebrate any festival that I am invited to by friends who are Christians and Muslims. I participate with love, but most of the time I like to celebrate traditional festivals related to my identity. One of my favorite celebrations is called *daddarbaa* (throwing), which we enjoy at the time the crops become ripe. The celebration is before you eat any of the produce from the crops. This was something unknown to most of my friends, including Kebede.

'We make *Marqaa* (porridge),' I explained. 'It is prepared on the farmland and eaten at that time. The reasoning behind *daddarbaa* is that we can eat, drink, and become full once our crops are ripe.'

'Where does the throwing come into it?' he asked.

'There are animals and birds that do not have shelter and provisions. Part of the food prepared for the celebration is thrown out for these animals so that they can eat and become full too. This practice is in keeping with our truth about the meaningfulness of all creatures.'

Kebede, and others to whom I have described *daddarbaa*, were charmed by the idea of food put out in different parts of the farm for the animals to find. On the day of celebration our family and our animals ate very well and were full. Even the wild birds that I loved so much might get some of the provender.

'However, people who follow other religions regard this celebration as a ritual to worship demons,' I finished my explanation. 'It is a kind of animist practice in their view.'

'I suppose,' reflected Kebede, 'they say that to undermine our culture. Now that different religions have come to Oromia, some of our people are embarrassed to follow such traditions.'

'That is true. There is more to it than that, don't you think?' I paused, collecting my thoughts. 'Some of us are afraid, with good reason. Grandfather often talked about the promises of democracy made in the earliest phase of the Revolution in 1974. When we tried to reclaim our land, and our political and cultural rights, the Amhara military officers who dominated the Derg massacred many Oromo, especially the educated ones. Nothing much has changed.'

'I was told that the government in 1974 officially declared that Oromo people worshipped idols, lakes, and trees,' Kebede said. 'They wanted us to be seen as backward heathens. Every Ethiopian regime has suppressed us, even though it has been a longstanding tradition in our country that religion is a private matter.'

'When I go to the Addis Merkato,' I told him, 'I pass the Orthodox Christian Church of Georgis. It was once called *Birbirsa Hill*, where Oromo celebrated *Irreecha Arfaasaa* (Autumn Thanksgiving); now it is Arada Georgis. Many of our places have been condemned as pagan relics, destroyed, and replaced by institutions linked with Amhara culture, such as religious buildings and practices, and labelled or referred to in the Amharic language.'

I am glad to know that some of us are returning to our old ways and celebrating festivals like the *daddarbaa*. You will hear more about them, especially *Irreecha*, a Thanksgiving Day, when the Oromo gather in places that have symbolic meanings, such as a hilltop, a riverside, a lake, or under a big sacred tree. We are not worshipping these places; only honoring the creator in his creation. I have celebrated *Irreecha* with Kebede and I wished that he could see for himself the places where I ran and called out aloud to *Waaqaa*. He would agree that the yellow roadside flowers look similar to our own *kello* flowers, which the Amhara call *meskel*. When the summer months came to an end in this other country, just the same as in our country, the fields and meadows turned yellow with wildflowers like the ones at home.

My cry to *Waaqaa* is a prayer, as I believe that he can intervene in the cosmos, created and sustained by him. I believe that somehow my running is a gift given by him, part of my destiny to heal the hurts of my countrymen.

This god name, *Waaqaa*, was unheard of in my place of exile. I often hear men and women exclaim, 'Oh my God!' or similar words. It seems to me that most of us, regardless of our country or our language or our beliefs, call out to that Other Presence within or beyond us—whatever we conceive him to be—when we are confronted with the unexpected.

I don't wear any symbol like a Christian cross or a Muslim skullcap that identifies me and sets me apart as Oromo or *Waaqeffataa*, but people who see my bare arms at the gymnasium or the swimming pool or out on the running tracks notice the *odaa* tattoo on my right shoulder. 'What is it?' they ask. The *odaa* tree is one of the richest Oromo symbols, representing the relations between the past, the present, and the future. It features as the logo for various Oromo organizations and it gained in significance even in the forbidding political climate.

The Oromo national flag, the *faajjii*, has three symbolic colors: *adii* (white), the past, the skeleton remains of our ancestors; *diimaa* (red), the present, the fire and energy of the living and the spilt blood of the dead; and *gurraacha* (black), the future, the unknown, the uncertainty, and the vulnerability.

You are hearing about my past, my present and my future, all part of this story, which I think about when I sit down and when I lie down, when I walk and when I run.

III

I

often run twenty miles daily, nearly the length of a marathon. One day I recall sitting for a while under a stand of tall thin trees, thinking about home. These trees are not like the big leafy ones I climbed as a boy to hide from my father. At home, though, such trees could be a sacred place, offering peace and protection. Any tree that throws a shadow is safe. One of the beliefs of my people is that a sacred tree offers asylum for anyone in danger of being killed because of some serious transgression of our laws.

I was aware of the possibility that I could be killed by those who said that I was guilty of breaking the law. Whose law? Theirs or those of my people? I could not go home because of the accusations. After Rio de Janeiro, a government spokesman in Addis Ababa, Getachew Reda, claimed that I would receive a 'hero's welcome' if I returned to Ethiopia. I told journalists that I was not fooled.

'The state-run Oromia TV posted on Facebook just after the race, "Feyisa Lilesa successfully sent the terrorists' message to the international community"', I said. 'They quickly took down that message, however, and changed their narrative to a more positive one echoing spokesman Reda's statement. But I saw the original accusation posted and I do not trust them.'

Sometimes I wondered if I was a runner or a runaway, but I felt strangely calm and safe, beneath a living tree. It is a tree of truth and I have told the truth. For that I chose to be uprooted from the place where I was planted and transplanted in foreign soil. I am a champion runner, but I am not what they call here a champion tree. Sometimes I quiver like the aspen under which I sat that day.

It trembled when the wind blew and the leaves shivered. A tree seems to me like a race of people, its branches the many *gosas* and sub-groups, and lineages and families. Its fruits are our children. I have learnt that aspens reproduce by seeds and spread when the roots of one tree sprout additional trees, called clones. The intermingled roots can form an entire grove—one organism—a single root colony of many skyward-reaching trees. This describes my people well.

But the aspen communities were dying because of fire suppression, conifer encroachment, and browsing pressure from the elk, the deer, and the livestock. These words—suppression, encroachment, and pressure—were familiar words. My people were dying for similar reasons.

We should never take even one single leaf from a holy tree. We have a high regard for all trees. On some Oromia land the farmers will not cut the leaves or branches; instead, they use long hooks to draw the branches low enough for their animals to eat. Some of the aspen leaves dropped, natural in the fall, but it bothered me. I saw black scars on the white skin of the tree, where branches have broken and fallen away. One of the stories I heard as a child was about a holy tree—a *qiltu* sycamore—that was damaged by the blows of an axe. Someone had violently expressed contempt for our beliefs by hurting the tree.

I chose to live in another place because my people had been held in contempt—hated, mocked, abused, deprived, killed. We have dark skin, not white, but so do our tormentors....

I should go now. Till tomorrow morning then.

Libaan, the soft light of the morning, gave way to the brightness of day. The light in this place was harsher than in my land and it burned. I must tell you more. *Gaaddisa*, meaning shelter or shade that protects from the heat of the sun, is significant for us. We have the *gadaa* system, explained to me by one of our elders as a link in a chain of Oromo socioeconomic, political, and religious practices, but it is complicated. Let me just say for now that in times past our *gadaa* leaders met under the shelter of special *odaa* trees to review *seera* (law) and uphold *aadaa* (custom).

There are five major ceremonial centers named after *odaas*. These are the regional centers where people met to deliberate and make laws: *Odaa Nabee*, in central Oromia; *Odaa Bisil*, in western Oromia; *Odaa Bulluq*, in north-western Oromia; *Odaa Roobaa*, in south-eastern Oromia; and *Odaa Bultum*, in eastern Oromia. *Odaa Bisil* is the one closest to my village, and I remember the excitement when our *ayyaantuus* and *hayyuu* set out on horseback to attend a meeting there. A few villagers went on foot, but they had a long journey ahead of them, at least thirty miles. My family did not go because of the remoteness of the place, but we prayed to *Waaqaa* under our own special tree in our *qeʼee* (village).

'Hadhaa, why don't we plant an *odaa*?' I asked my mother when I was still a small boy. 'Our tree is not as big as the *odaa* Grandfather has described or as leafy and mysterious as the *gurra* I like to climb.'

'You don't pray or celebrate under a tree planted by human beings,' Hadhaa's voice was muffled as she wrapped her shawl around her head and neck, her face buried in the folds. 'The tree should be one that sprouts naturally; its location determined by *Waaqaa* alone. We have the acacia for our place of prayer.'

Like the aspen, the acacia's leaves fall in winter and it flourishes with new foliage in the spring. Its high branches spread out, a benediction over the villagers gathered below, praying for long life, good grass, healthy animals, and abundant harvest.

As I thought about these things, I started running back to my home among conifer tress, facing the east and the risen sun. The Oromo traditional religious belief is that we come from the east and sometime in the unknown future we will go back there, to a place beyond the dawn. Early in the morning, across Oromia, the head of each household comes out of his house, turns his face towards the sunrise and says prayers of thanksgiving to God for the new day. He worships, sometimes with his wife, offering praise. Then at night, in the dark, as they make ready for bed, they may pray again.

There is no limit to the time or place for prayer—anywhere, anytime, alone or with others. Real peace, we believe, is found in silent concentration on the past to see the way one must go. My mind flitted from place to place, like the pretty little green, black-winged lovebird that I often saw in the Jaldu forest.

I was shocked to see similar birds in cages in my city of exile. I had the urge to set them free, to watch them spread their wings and fly. The thought saddened me as I slowed down near my home and looked up to see my wife, Iftu, at the window, watching for my return. She became a captive because of my choices and I yearned to see her smiling and dancing freely again. Not so many years ago, on a day when there was no wind at all, the leaves on a big tree in her village were *sirbite* (dancing). This was a good omen for our future.

2

There was a time when I did not think I would marry, because of Bilisse. She was the only girl friend before Iftu and it hurts even now to speak of her. We first met at school when I was only in seventh grade. I wrote her name and sketched her face in my exercise books. I was very young, but I loved her. She lived in Gojo and I loitered after school to talk to her. I followed her when she went to the stream to collect water and we talked of many things. I told her how I felt.

'I love you, Bilisse. Will you marry me one day?'

She promised me that yes, she would marry me after we had finished our education. I daydreamed of her and longed for the day we would marry. It was more than what you would call a crush; I was obsessed, and I couldn't handle the strength of my teenage feelings. There was no intimacy, but Bilisse was in my mind, day and night. I left school and joined the sports club in Finfinne; I telephoned her on a landline and she waited for my calls at a shop where there was a telephone. We had a regular time for these calls and I lived for them each week. She missed two calls and I was frantic. I thought she must be ill. I left the club after the second time and went to Gojo.

I saw her leave the classroom, but she must have spotted me and somehow avoided me when I waited at the school gate. I confronted her near the stream where we once chatted so freely and happily.

'What is wrong, Bilisse? Why won't you talk to me? What have I done wrong?'

She just shrugged, avoiding my eyes and making some excuse to leave with her friends. One of them turned back and bluntly told me that Bilisse had started a relationship with another boy. Her words hurt just as badly as that stab in the back at the *gugsi*. I would have fought that boy off, whoever he was, but the pain was crippling and all I wanted to do was go away again where I could not see her. This was worse than the tight white pants; for a while even worse than the dead sheep.

'*Yoo ana bukkeen orma ilaaltu. Maalan balleesse hiriyaa koo?*' I muttered as I run from the scene. 'You look past me to another one. What wrong have I done, my friend?'

I returned to Finfinne and the club, glad to be training, running until I was exhausted.

'No more girls,' I vowed to Kebede who was the only person I told about Bilisse. 'From now on my life is about running, nothing else.'

He studied my frowning face and wisely said nothing. He had a girlfriend of his own and I was rather jealous of her because often he wanted to be with her instead of me, or she would be there with him when we arranged to meet at coffee shops. Bilisse and Kebede are among those people in my life I dearly loved and keenly missed.

Do you know what is like when you run into a spider's web and you desperately claw at your face to pull away the sticky threads? When Bilisse comes into my thoughts I try to rid myself of those memories that persistently cling, just like the spider's web.

I was in the habit of calling my mother every Saturday after I moved to Finfinne, using a landline telephone like I did for Bilisse, as there was no mobile network coverage in our village then. Hadhaa went to a house where there was a telephone to wait for my call. I didn't call my mother for about three or four months after I broke up with Bilisse. I am ashamed now to think of Hadhaa sitting there, patiently expecting my calls. I knew what that was like, waiting in vain. Not once did she rebuke me for this, so perhaps somehow she knew about my sorrow.

I am now acquainted with grief, a doleful companion who comes and goes, returning at unexpected and unwanted times to upset my life. The unwelcome presence went out of my life for a while, after I met Iftu.

3

I think of Iftu as *Washaawwashee*, my lovely spirited one. I first saw her at the Jaldu High School, but she was just another face in the crowd of grey uniforms. I wasted too much time looking for Bilisse's face in the throng of students before I joined the Armed Forces Club. After my last meeting with her, it was a long time before I walked the streets of Gojo again.

Then one day I went with Aduna to the spring where many of the girls in Gojo collect water. Aduna was talking and laughing with one of them and I stood back, watching the scene. I felt older, wiser, even superior to these boys and girls. I watched one girl crouch to fill her *hubboo* (clay pot) and then a smaller vessel. She sat back to drink from it and I was reminded of the spring water I loved in my own *qeʾee* (village). She wiped her mouth with the back of her hand and turned towards me. It was Iftu. She smiled, not at all self-conscious, and I went down to sit beside her.

'Are you thirsty?' she asked, and she dipped the *wantsha*, cup, back into the spring. 'Here you are. It is cold and good.'

I described the spring near Tulu Bultuma, my village, and she nodded.

'I live in a village near there. Chilimo. Do you know it? I was born in Ademsa Galani, in West Shoa, but I didn't stay there. I live with my *Akkoo*, grandmother, mostly, but I rent a house here in Gojo during the week, to go to high school. I dropped out of school for a while when I was in ninth grade, but I came back and now I am in Grade 12.'

After that our conversation went on naturally, as I told her about Geti and my grandfather and about the year I left school to live in Finfinne.

Aduna was signaling me to go and I stood, watching Iftu smooth her skirt, brush herself down and lift the *hubboo*. She was a solitary figure, walking away, petite and graceful. Most of our people are small of build, with a few exceptions. People thought Abebe Bikila was tall because he was so thin, and his legs were so long, but he was only five feet, ten inches tall. I am just over five feet, seven inches.

I had a friend who knew Iftu and I asked him about her. He was from Iftu's village and he was the one who gradually brought us together. There is no 'going out' or 'dating' in our culture like couples do in other societies. You find the place where the girl you like is fetching water, feeding animals, or watching over them. The next time I visited my home I went with my friend to Iftu's village, Chilimo, knowing she returned there on weekends to help her grandmother. I hoped she would be out of doors, where we could talk and walk together. I was lucky. She was with a group of teenagers, following the antics of two boys racing their ponies.

'Do you like to ride?' she asked, with the slow, shy smile I came to love.

'I like riding very much,' I said, 'but I do not ride anymore, because I am afraid of injuring myself and spoiling my chances as a runner.'

'I have heard that you are a very good runner.' Iftu was plaiting stalks of grass, her long slim fingers nimble and nice to watch.

'Can you run?' I asked.

'We used to run when I was very small in the village.' She laughed, and I had my first glimpse of her playfulness. 'Grandmother admires the athlete, Derartu Tulu! She had this dream that I would be famous like Derartu and run for our country!'

Derartu Tulu grew up tending cattle in the village of Bekoji in the highlands of Arsi, the same village as Kenenisa Bekele. I have mentioned both these names already. I admired Derartu very much myself, especially after watching her race on television, the 10,000-meter race at the Sydney Olympic Games.

'Derartu is grandmother's hero,' Iftu went on. '"The first Ethiopian woman and the first black African woman to win an Olympic gold medal!" She must have told me that 100 times. I was refusing to drink milk and Grandmother insisted that I must. "You will become like Derartu if you drink milk!"'

'Can you run after drinking all that milk?' I asked, matching her cheeky grin.

'We used to run of an evening after six o'clock, out here in the wide spaces, competing two by two. Then we started to run on the streets, but I began to feel pain, cramp, after running. Grandmother said, "I just want you to be like Derartu; I don't want you to be sick." I stopped running and didn't return. I didn't like running at all; I was running to please Grandmother.'

She looked at me with that steady gaze, half-defiant. 'I play volleyball though, against other district school teams. And,' she added in a kind of hurry, 'I like to watch people running. I have seen you running and winning a race at school.'

I nodded and told her about my running and my own dreams of winning an Olympic medal. Little did we know then that when I won the medal I would be introducing Iftu to the miserable presence of grief. After we got to know each other better, she told me that when her grandmother heard about me, she was delighted to think that there might be someone in the family like Derartu!

'Do you know what she did?' Iftu's big brown eyes were shining. 'She put some barley seed in water, covered it, and waited to see if it sprouted. If it sprouts, it's a sign of good luck and a favorable indication of the boy's character. If the seed does not sprout, it is not a good sign and the girl's family does not want to give her to that boy. Grandmother says that the seed sprouted for you! She even did it twice to be sure!'

Such traditional practices are still common in our rural areas. So are the rituals for the young man and woman attracted to each other. We study each other from a distance and do not express our feelings in a hurry like I did with Bilisse. Sometimes we had the chance to talk, but we were given little time together. I had my racing commitments, and my visits to Jaldu were not frequent. Iftu and I were attracted to each other, but I was building my career, race by race, and I was not quite ready for the changes and responsibilities of marriage.

4

I smile when I think of Iftu drinking all that milk to improve her athletic abilities. Abebe Bikila's coach, Onni Niskannen, was also a great believer in milk and extra vitamins for Abebe; he introduced strange foods like rose-hip soup and pollen to the athlete's diet. Abebe preferred traditional Ethiopian food, including meat, but he ate *kinche* (porridge) for breakfast on his fasting days; still my staple in the morning. Abebe Bikila was an Orthodox Christian and often fasted in line with his church's teaching. It's not surprising, with his fat-free physique, that he recovered quickly from an appendix operation before winning a gold medal at the Tokyo Olympic Games.

Abebe reckoned he gained weight when he had a six months' rest from running to recover from a torn ligament in his leg. I gained weight too, when I first went to live in another country, because I was not in my usual training schedule. I allowed myself just one burger when I arrived, but it was tempting to have more in a country of big helpings and many food choices. Sometimes I can revert to that little fat boy, Bogia. It was easier when Iftu joined me, but here I am getting ahead of my story again.

The closest I went to Rome, scene of Abebe's greatest triumph, was to Rovereto, a northern Italian city, in January of 2008, where I ran my personal best for the 10,000-meter race, 27 minutes and 38 seconds. I also went to Pergine Valsugana, another city in northern Italy, for another 10,000-meter race in the Pergine Valsugana Meeting Internazionale, when I was still a junior. That was in July of 2008. I had won a race, 5,000 meters, the week before in Lugano, Switzerland. This was my first international win; one of many first-time reasons for gladness.

You never forget your first trip overseas or your first adventures in another country. When we were boys, my friends and I stood, heads tilted back, cows and sheep and goats forgotten, watching the white trails from jets slowly break up in the sky. The planes and the passengers on them were from another world far removed from ours. I liked geography at school, drawing maps and memorising facts about distant places, seeing pictures of castles and cathedrals, all part of an *Oduu Durii*, a fairy tale, that one day came true for the son of an Oromo farmer.

Firstly, there was the taxi ride to the Bole International Airport in Finfinne, an experience in itself, although I was soon used to it. The cars and buses compete with barefooted farmers, laughing and beating the ground with their sticks as they run behind laden donkeys and herds of sheep or goats. Horses and cows share the road. Everywhere there are people; people in everything from flimsy muslin shawls over long skirts to shiny business suits, milling and walking or standing and staring.

Our driver had one hand constantly pressing the horn, a hopeless warning to indifferent pedestrians and foolhardy drivers in their motley vehicles. In years gone by, or so it is said, the emperor's lions were sometimes transported uncaged, in open trucks. After all the other sights to be seen on the city streets, like a sheep transported on a motor bike, or goats teetering on the top of heavily laden lorries, I can believe it.

At the airport the team followed all the procedures familiar to me now: checking-in, clearing customs, boarding, fastening seat belts, taking-off. After a while all the airports, even all the cities, seem the same to a globetrotting professional athlete, intent on the race in front of him or weary when it is over.

After my race in Rovereto, I had my first taste of intense, world-class competition at the 2008 IAAF World Cross Country Championships in Edinburgh, Scotland. Edinburgh was also my first experience of what it was like to be in a really cold place, although the race was held at the end of March and there was no snow! I have never liked snow—cold and treacherous stuff.

Again I thought of Abebe Bikila, whose coach, Onni Niskannen, once defended his champion's poor performance in the Boston Marathon, way back in 1963. 'I was not with him,' Onni explained to journalists. 'It was cold, and he did not dress warmly for the race, and then he did not have his glucose. At 20 kilometers in the Olympic marathon I have fruit juice with glucose and rose hip waiting for him. I am not allowed to hand it to him, but he picks it up and I yell to him, "*Ahun hid!*" (Now go!) But in Boston he did not have the glucose. Without sugar the lactic acid builds up. Soon he and Mamo Wolde began to get cramps and they were sitting on the sidewalk massaging their legs, three or four times.'

That marathon is remembered by some because cars from the local Society for the Prevention of Cruelty to Animals were cruising ahead of the runners, with the state troopers on motorbikes, picking up stray dogs because in a previous race a runner had tripped over one of the dogs. I wonder what the Society would make of all the animals in the streets of Finfinne?

Abebe still managed to finish fifth in Boston, while I came in 14th in Holyrood Park, the place where we ran in Edinburgh. The race was 7.905 kilometers in distance through such a different landscape to what I was used to. Perhaps there was snow on the mountains; if so I didn't notice. Another first was hearing mournful bagpipes and watching in wonder as a sole player, a woman, played them, her kilt swirling in the mist.

The cold was a factor for me; it was a grey sleety day and the track was muddy. The coaches repeated, 'Keep warm. Jog around, don't stand too long on the wet ground.' Our green and yellow tracksuits were thin and inadequate compared to the heavy jackets worn by the spectators and the thicker tracksuits of our competitors.

We all finished our races spattered with mud, but it was a great day on the track for Ethiopia, with our runners winning the four main races. Ibrahim Jeilan and Ayele Abshero, first and second in my race, were both attracted to distance running after seeing Haile Gebresillassie win gold at the 2000 Sydney Olympics. Just like me. The winners of the women's elite and junior races were sisters, Tirunesh and Genzebe Dibaba, from Bekoji. Coach Sentayehu Eshetu was very proud that day. These girls are cousins of Derartu Tulu, another of his proteges, and I am sure Iftu's grandmother knew about them. We were all young and keen, sent great distances to run great lengths for Ethiopia. I feel differently about it now.

Kenenisa Bekele won the elite men's race that day. This was a great triumph for Kenenisa, whose interest in the sport wavered when his fiancée, 18-year-old Alem Techale, died of an apparent heart attack while on a training run with him a couple of years earlier. They were in Ararat, a forest in a hilly area on the outskirts of Finfinne, when she collapsed.

We heard that Kenenisa Bekele carried her to his car, but she died before they reached a hospital. The tragedy was discussed at the Armed Forces Club. According to what I heard, Kenenisa said, 'I am half the man without Alem. I honestly do not know if I can ever be the same runner again.' Yet here he was, adding another gold medal to his pile. When I thought of his grief for his girl and the horror of that death day my heart softened towards Kenenisa. He married another girl in 2007 and he was running with renewed enthusiasm the next year.

I wanted to finish 2008 running in the Obudu Ranch International Mountain Race, an annual 11.25-kilometer mountain running competition held in November in Obudu, Cross River State, Nigeria. The race offers some of the best prize money available for any mountain race; it is known as the world's richest mountain race.

I was not yet considered good enough for a full-length contract with an agent or manager, but Gianni Demadonna, principal of Demadonna Athletic Promotions (a global management agency for athletes), had taken note of my progress and he was helping me with shoes and facilities. Gianni was working to develop me and prepare me for more competitions, and I approached him about the Obudu race.

'Gianni, I have had a good season,' I began. 'I really want to be in that race. Will you arrange it for me?'

'I don't like your chances, Feyisa,' he said doubtfully. 'You are strong this year, but there are many other Ethiopian athletes who will be chosen first. You will have other chances, but not this year. Coach Gabriele Nicola agrees with me.'

I persisted and finally Gianni did ask the organizers to enter my name. He was right; they pointed out that there were better athletes to invite. I was upset about this, foolishly refusing to accept the situation and I argued with Gabriele Nicola, the coach who worked for him. This ended with me having to find another manager and coach.

'I am happy that you have performed well in Europe this year, Feyisa.' Gianni was sorry to see me go, I think. 'I have done a lot to help you get started—good work that has paid off—but if I am to be your manager, you must trust my judgement and accept the terms. Gabriele Nicola and I work in your best interests, according to your level of ability and best opportunities. We are here to guide you.'

I had a lot to learn. I have reason to be grateful to Gianni, because he helped me get started and he would not have made much from the young headstrong runner from Oromia. I found another manager, Hussein Makke. In the usual financial arrangement, 15% of an athlete's earning goes to his manager who then pays the coach.

I regard 2009 as a time to keep, a time never to be taken away from me or forgotten. When you think about this story that I am telling you, remember the beauty as well as the ugliness of what lay ahead. 'I fear the taste of *buna* that is too bitter may remain strong in you,' Iftu said to me, a few years later when she saw my anger and despair for our people. 'You have also enjoyed the good things, as sweet as the sugar cane you love so much.'

She was right. I competed in many satisfying races in 2009, feeling fit and happy, perhaps because I was getting to know Iftu and thoughts of her were replacing Bilisse. The 2009 IAAF World Cross Country Championships took place on March 28, 2009, at the Al Bisharat Golf Course in Amman, Jordan. This was an important race in my career.

'You are nineteen now, Feyisa, and in good form,' my new coach, Haji Adilo, told me after a day of hard training. 'You are ready now for senior competition.'

Haji was following on from my first coach, Megersa Hunde, at the Armed Forces Club, and Gabriele Nicola, who worked for Gianni Demadonna. Gabriele was supervising our training while teaching another coach, Gemedu Dedefo. It was Gemedu who took notice of me at one of the competitions and pointed me out to Gianni. Haji was once an Ethiopian marathon runner who represented the Assela high school, like Haile Gebresilassie, in athletics competitions.

My disagreement with coaches along the way was because I thought they undermined my potential; they wanted me to participate in small competitions that didn't cover the cost of my airplane tickets and I was paying from my own pocket. The awards I received at the small competitions were not enough. I wanted to participate in bigger competitions and earn more money. I suppose I was greedy for advancement.

'You underestimate my ability,' I argued. 'I can have good results on big competitions. You are restricting me!'

They defended their decisions and said that I was too hasty, wanting too much too soon. I planned to build my profile as far and as fast as my legs would take me, despite the coaches' warnings of overreaching my body. I was young and impetuous; they were older, but not wiser in my opinion.

'There is heavy cloud today,' our team manager warned as we prepared for the race in Amman. 'I don't like the forecast for a strong westerly wind and it is cold. The course is stony in places and muddy in other spots.'

The weather and the condition of the track have never bothered me, the barefoot farm boy who had been outdoors in all sorts of weather with the animals or on the way to school and back. I was proud to be there on the starting line for the Senior Men's 12-kilometer race in Amman with about 150 competitors. I wasn't close enough to see the last-minute tussle between the front runners, but I could hear the crowd cheering. It was one of the most thrilling finishes in the history of the IAAF World Cross Country Championships; best of all, the winner was Ethiopia's Gebre Gebremariam in a time of 35.02. I came in 12th place, at 35.22.

I went from the ancient ruins and arid country of Jordan to the capital city of the United States, Washington DC, for the Cherry Blossom Race, a distance of ten miles or just over sixteen kilometers. This was my first race with a really big number of competitors, 12,000 or so. The runners were started in what are called waves, to lessen overcrowding on the course.

Runners are assigned to their waves based on their estimated finish times, which they must specify when they register.

The organizers allocate corrals, sectioned areas at the line-up of a race that help separate athletes into different pace groups. The faster you are, the more likely you will be in one of the first few corrals. Runners are sometimes corralled about one hour before the start time. Once in the corral, you can move about, warming up and planning your race.

Sunday, April 5, 2009 was a perfect Ethiopian kind of spring day; the masses of pink cherry blossoms against the blue skies were one of the prettiest sights I have ever seen. Running beside water always makes me feel good and I surged ahead with a pack of Kenyans close on my heels. The crowd was shouting as a Moroccan, Ridouane Harroufi, and I threw ourselves at the finish line, but he beat me by the barest margin.

I cannot recall much about my first experiences of Washington DC except its clean, commanding buildings and impressive roads. After the race I met Tolcha Wagi, whose exploits as a boy in Mullata Fayiso's War have stayed with me throughout my life. In Washington, he was doing as much as he could for our people back home and working with the Oromo diaspora to continue the fight for freedom. 'You are one of Oromia's sons, Feyisa. Never forget that.' I have never forgotten that and because of his words I was destined to meet him again in several years' time, in very different circumstances.

I stayed in the US to compete in the Crescent City Classic in New Orleans, on April 11, 2009. I was runner-up again, behind a Kenyan, Mark Kiptoo. I don't always take any notice of the scenery when I'm running, but I remember thinking as we ran through the City Park that its huge oak trees were reminiscent of the big trees I loved in Oromia.

'Many trees had to be planted after the Hurricane called Katrina destroyed much of the park,' one of the other runners told me later. He was speaking in English, but I had enough understanding of the language to follow what he was saying. I was already thinking about the trees I wanted to plant in my Jaldu forest, replacing some that were hundreds of years old like the oak trees in the park.

I was ready to try out my stamina in a half-marathon race, 21.80 kilometers or 13.1 miles long, and after a couple of trial runs in Ethiopia when I managed the distance with ease, I returned to the US with a group of runners for the first International Team Challenge at the Rock 'n' Roll Virginia Beach Half Marathon on September 6th. I set a time of 1:02:15 but again I was beaten into second place by another Kenyan rival, William Chebor, whose time was 1:01:29.

We like to hear what others said about the race afterwards. Our team manager told us that a retired Olympian runner, Todd Williams, called it a no-holds-barred competition, with surges that were all-out blasts. He said it was hard to believe we were racing a half-marathon.

We began aggressively, with my teammate, Zenbaba Yigeze, and me in the lead, making 4:41 minutes for mile one, then stringing together five consecutive mid-4:30 miles. At mile four the race turned into a two-man duel, between me and William Chebor. We tried unsuccessfully to drop each other in a series of punishing surges as the route turned to the backside of the course from miles five through nine. As the course looped back along a long street just past nine miles, Chebor surged ahead for maybe the tenth time in the race, and this time I could not cover the move. With victory assured, Chebor kept his lead to the finish line on the boardwalk beside the beach.

Ethiopia won the Team Challenge, thanks to our girls coming in first, second, and third in the women's race; and Zenbaba Yigeze ran third behind me in the men's race. 'The youth of Ethiopia prevailed today,' said a TV commentator that evening. 'They ran beautifully as a team and were worthy champions.'

I told you that 2009 was my year, my time to keep. I was in a hurry to take my running up a level to the full marathon and there are those critics who say I started running marathons too young. I admit that the better prize money was a factor, as I was now seriously planning a future with Iftu and still helping my family, but it is also true that I could run further as I finished the shorter distances. I was not tired or lacking energy. I believe I was ready for the marathon when I was nineteen.

The trainers of elite runners have their own language about attitude and fitness, times and schedules, diet and weight. It is a big advantage to have a coach or trainer with whom you connect readily. Abebe Bikila called his coach *Niskanen abbat*, (*abbat* means 'father' in Amharic). When they were together, they sparred and wrestled like cubs, and there was much hugging and backslapping. Onni Niskanen was determined, though, to correct the faults he saw in Abebe's running style. He did not hold his head properly, his arms flew all over, and his balance was bad. Onni had a sauna at his house, unheard of in Ethiopia in the 1960s, and insisted on physiotherapy after each training session. I envied Abebe Bikila's close relationship with Onni, his dedicated personal trainer.

Weight was never a serious problem for Abebe, but I must be constantly aware of its importance. My weight is relatively heavier than the average marathoner, but when you weigh more you also have power. When you weigh less you can change your speed as you like, yet even though I weigh more, I can still change my speed as I want, like the athletes who weigh less. I am as flexible as they are.

'This is because your body is proportionate,' explained Gabriele Nicola, my coach in 2008. 'Your legs are long, so are your hands. The length of your body above the waist is proportionate to the length of it below your waist. If the length of the body above the waist is not proportionate to that below the waist you struggle to balance your body.'

So even though I weigh comparatively more, I am running well, and I don't feel the weight of my body; it feels lighter to me. I know some runners who weighed less and started running after I did. They were among the top athletes in a very short time because their bodies were lighter, but they were inconsistent and disappeared from competition after two years. They got tired, but I am consistent.

'If you have a body like mine,' I said to my friend Teklu Deneke from the Armed Forces Club when we trained together years later, 'you can run steadily for many years and you also have power. But it requires hard and intensive training which could injure your feet.'

We did a lot of hard and intensive training together. We understood each other's tactics and weaknesses.

'I know whether I am going to perform well or otherwise before a race starts,' I told Teklu. 'When I wake up in the morning and close my hands to form a fist, if my hands are dry and thin I know that I will run very well that day. That shows my weight is lighter, I feel strong and I can sense it. I feel confident. But if my hands are fat and full of blood I know I will not perform well that day. I sometimes feel sleepy.'

I'm not sure if Teklu believed me but, like every runner, he has his secret strategies and lucky charms, worn outside the body or inside the head. I don't just run with my legs but with my mind too. You don't always win a competition because you are physically fit, but because you are mentally engaged. You must feel your body as you run, whether it feels lighter or heavier as you go ten kilometers and then twenty kilometers and so on. If you cannot control your body in twenty or fewer kilometers, you will not perform well regardless of your tactics. If you control your body at least until you are in the thirty-kilometer zone, you will finish the race well.

Everything came together perfectly for me in the Dublin Marathon, 26 October 2009. I slept well the night before, as I always do before a race. I had my favorite dream, galloping on an Oromo pony, and I had a long shower under the strong jet of warm water, something that I enjoy at hotels after the unreliable water supply in Finfinne. At that time, I still admired the toiletries set out neatly in the bathroom, including a toothbrush for the boy who once cleaned his teeth with *rigaa*, a toothbrush made of twigs! Everything is soft and clean—the bed linen, the carpet, the towels. These were unknown in my first home, a hut with dirt floors.

I trotted to the starting line, clenching and unclenching my fists. My hands felt thin and dry and I was buoyant, light of heart and body. I wore an orange Nike singlet and grey shorts, white Nike shoes, a gold chain that Iftu had given me around my neck, a watch and, unusual for me, a grey Nike cap against the chill air. I was in the lead pack from the start, but this time I was contending with Russian competitors. In the years ahead at Dublin, more Ethiopian and Kenyan runners dominated the 26.2 miles, or 42.1 kilometers, or 138,336 feet, depending on how you like to measure it.

The course was not challenging, the conditions were good, and I was confident that I would win. I broke away from Aleksey Sokolov in an easy run, 2.09.11. I raised my arms as I crossed the finish line, a triumphant gesture that would take on a different meaning when I was an older man running a different race in 2016. I wanted to clip minutes off that time, and I would, but Dublin was my first marathon win and I was happy.

I look back at photographs of that race and think about the head-hugging cap I wore. My hair was shorter then but look at it now! Since my hair is like this, a long curly mop, it holds moisture that helps me to run many kilometers without adding water again and again. This is why I grow my hair and I don't plan to cut it. My hair doesn't have a particular style; it is not an afro, or *goofaree* in our language. You comb afro; I don't comb my hair. I am not following any hair fashion; this is my natural style and the thick black curls retain water. While others may scoff, it really helps, because I do not have to pause often to take water at aid stations during a race.

My hair style has something to do with Oromo tradition. Unmarried youth and heroes, like rebels or bandits, the OLF soldiers for instance, chose to grow their hair like I do now. Women sing, '*Goofaree goota birraa/arfaasaa roobee*' (praising a hero by describing his hair style). Unmarried youth keep their hair like I do but they comb it. After marriage, most of them cut off their locks because they do not have time to comb or treat their hair. Many responsibilities come with marriage, and they included a short hairstyle for me, out of respect for tradition… for a couple of years anyway.

5

I was going home from Dublin to prepare for my wedding and I had a cheque for €15,000 in my pocket, the prize for winning the race. This was a lot of money in *birr*, a promising start to the marathon of marriage. The elite runners rely on their earnings because the training grounds and racetracks are their workplace. It is a serious business.

Yet I am happy in the carnival atmosphere of the marathons, these major events marked prominently in the racing calendar every year. Some participants run for pleasure or leisure, a fun run, just to be part of a spectacle full of color and causes and costumes. We don't all wear basic athletic clothes! In places like New Orleans we run to the music of many street bands; we are greeted with placards, whistles, and flags at every turn. Each race has its dramas—the collapsed runner, the obstacle of an overenthusiastic spectator or escort vehicle, the unfortunate runner who takes a wrong turn. Most of us love what you call 'bling,' the shiny ribbons and medals and trophies that are tucked in the luggage for the homeward journey.

Many of the races are held to coincide with holidays in the host city. The Rock 'n' Roll Virginia Beach Half Marathon is on the Labor Day weekend in the US and the race is followed by a big concert. The concept of 'holiday' is hard for most Ethiopians to grasp. Every day is about survival, enough food to eat and a place to lie down at night. We had the occasional break from school when we were students, but we were expected to work in the fields or in the home or in the marketplace.

Virginia Beach was a marvel to me: bare bodies dashing in and out of the water or stretching out on the sand; families strolling along the boardwalk with pet dogs, ice-creams, and sodas. I never had money for soda when I was a child, but Hadhaa occasionally bought a bottle for me. I mostly drank fresh milk. The hotel where I stayed was on the beachfront and it had a balcony where I stood and watched the surf rolling in. The sea has a soothing voice, a rhythmic sound that pulsates night and day. I think of Iftu's soft, lilting voice, which always calms me.

Before I went to Dublin, she and I both went to one of the Oromo festivals, an annual pageant as vivid and as exciting as any marathon race. Oromo do have a couple of special holiday festivals that bring the community together. *Irreechaa* is one of them. This is our equivalent of the American Thanksgiving, celebrated as *Irreechaa Birraa* at the end of September and *Irreechaa Arfaasaa* in April.

'*Irreechaa Birraa* marks the end of the long rainy season.' All Oromo children learn the basics, like a creed, and they participate from the time they are born. 'We give our thanks to God because the dark days are gone for another year. The skies open no more and we come into the light.'

We gather in large crowds, especially on riverbanks and the shores of lakes to thank *Waaqaa* for all his bounty and pray for *nagaa* (peace) and *araara* (reconciliation) among humans and with God. As I have mentioned before, Oromo celebrate the *irreechaa* regardless of their religious backgrounds. This has puzzled me in the past but an elder explained it well.

'Whether they are *Waaqeffataa*, Christians or Muslims, they participate in the festival. The moral counsel and ideals officiated by the *haayyaa*— elders, wise men, the learned—do not contradict the essence of any of the three religions. In fact,' he paused to consider, 'the *haayyaa* who officiate it are now from all three on most occasions. The festival unites the Oromo and harmonizes their thoughts and voices.'

Irreechaa is a glad occasion, when all families and *gosas* are reunited. It is preceded by the *gubaa* (meaning bonfire), when we meet, usually at an elder's house, to gather around a big fire and say, 'Goodbye, Dark! See you next year. Happy New Year!' All present throw sticks and twigs into the fire that represent the errors of the past year—all the bits of wood contribute to the blaze. The misdeeds they stand for go up in smoke. Then we have prayers, blessings, dancing, and feasting.

Without *gubaa*, you don't have *irreechaa*, according to the purists of Oromo ceremony, who blame ignorance on the part of some celebrants. Perhaps the elders have *gubaa*, but they do not insist that the young participate, and such neglect weakens the significance of the occasion in some places. It is celebrated in different ways, depending on where you live, what crops you grow and what food you prepare from them. If you don't grow *teff*, then maybe you have barley to make the meal.

In our area, several villages gathered together to enjoy the *gubaa*. Iftu's village, Chilimo, and mine, Tulu Bultuma, were together and we met on a clear cool night. The head of each house came out with a torch and we all lit our own torches from his and went to the place chosen for celebration. We ate and danced and sang, all night, going from house to house. It was a big celebration, including all the houses so no one was left out. The villagers wanted everyone to sing and dance at their houses, so the celebrations often continued the next day.

If you looked closely, you saw little groups within the crowd, singing and dancing together. In one of these I was dancing with Iftu Mulisaa Lamu, a beautiful girl in a special dress that shimmered in the firelight. She wore the golden *kello* flowers entwined in her braids and a gold necklace that matched the one I was wearing. This night was our time to keep, to sing just for each other: 'See! The winter is past; the rains are over and gone. Flowers appear on the earth; the season of singing has come…. Arise, come, my darling; my beautiful one, come with me.'

Our friends and siblings and their friends were among those who danced and sang with us that night, all dressed up for the occasion, smiling knowingly at us. Aduna was growing up and I was getting to know Tokuma, Iftu's brother. All these kids were what we call *sabboontota*, proud of who they are; they all declare *Oromumma*, but at great cost to some. Tokuma, in the midst of that happy throng, had a hard destiny ahead of him.

I found it difficult to reconcile what I knew of these young rural lives with the charges brought against them. If only they could have stayed safely at home, farming the land and tending the animals so valued in our culture that they were included in the celebrations. Early in the morning after the *gubaa*, the celebrants went to the corrals where the cows and oxen, sheep, donkeys, and horses were kept.

The animals were brought back, after the rivers recede, to our farms from the pastures where they grazed in the rainy season. Oil or butter was smeared on each animal as a reward and fresh grass was spread on the ground. The ritual acknowledged the contribution made to the people: the cow gave milk, the sheep provided meat and wool, the oxen bore the yoke and tilled the soil, the donkey trudged along under heavy burdens, the horse carried his master. They were as essential as the land on which they grazed.

'Let the animals also be happy! It is our New Year and it is theirs too!' When I hear this, I mourn again the killing of my sick ewe and I am ashamed. I found it impossible to watch or participate in the slaughter of a sheep for the feasts that followed.

In my country of exile, I reminisced with other Oromos about the festival which we can still celebrate, but without the animals. 'We should have some *gubaa* for the livestock, but I cannot do this here.' Lubee Birru, one of Oromo's most respected elders in the diaspora, grinned. 'I do not have any cows! Only cats.'

Lubee was a member of the Macha Tulama Association in Oromia in the 1960s, a founder of the Union of Oromo in North America in the 1970s, and he worked closely with the OLF for many years. To think of this knowledgeable, dedicated elder, watching cats in Washington DC instead of livestock and strategizing against the TPLF in Finfinne, was almost comical, but too sad. Lubee exemplified the best that an Oromo man can be.

The *Qubee* generation understands well that the Macha Tulama Association (MTA) opened the way to take the Oromo nation into the current phase of its history. Its members, like Lubee, initiated the rescue of our people from cultural and political demise and from the depredations of conquest and colonization. The MTA was banned by Haile Selassie, but its work was resumed by the OLF. The MTA was banned, and its leaders imprisoned, for the second time in 2004 by the TPLF, but in the mid-1990s, its members took the initiative in reviving the *irreechaa* festival.

Millions of Oromos from all over the country, as well as non-Oromo visitors from other parts of the world, gather for the *Irreechaa* festival, which has no parallel in Africa. The biggest celebration is held on the shores of *Hora* (Lake) *Arsadi,* near the city of Bishoftu, central Oromia. Bishoftu is about sixty kilometers south-east of Finfinne. It is also celebrated by Oromo in exile, connecting us to a common heritage through all the symbols displayed in the huge parades and celebrating the revival of our culture in songs and dances.

'Feyisa, the harmony of these gatherings should not be a sign that all is well in Oromia.' Kebede was solemn when we parted company at the last *Irreechaa* we attended together in 2015. 'I hope we are not sending the wrong message to the journalists and tourists who attend. We are not a peaceful country and our government is not stable. One day, perhaps, *Irreechaa* will be spoiled for us, because the government doesn't like the Oromo to gather in such numbers to declare themselves.'

'The songs of the artists who entertain us now contain much anger, don't they?' I feared then that his words were prophetic; that one day we would not be celebrating unmolested.

'I heard of one federal police officer who boasted: "We are above the law. We beat and torture people to get information, whether they did anything or not.... Either they will give us info or in the future they will be too scared to oppose us. It's a win-win."'

Not long after Kebede and I talked that day, some of those boys and girls celebrating with us were gunned down in Ginchi. I knew, and he knew, that the anger would intensify. You cannot expect a nation whose youth were tortured and killed, whose peace-loving families were evicted from their homes and land, and whose innocent protesters were rounded up and jailed without due process of law to remain silent and accepting.

I was not dwelling on these matters when I was with Iftu, the girl I would marry. She was like *kalaalaa*, a luxuriant creeper that symbolizes a girl's beauty and also, a time of frivolity. *Kalaalaa* also symbolizes connection – the reaching out and connecting people as we do at the *Irreechaa*.

Iftu is every bit as lovely to look at as Hadhaa, my mother. All the women dressed in traditional clothes, various white materials richly enhanced with beading, tapestry and jewellery. I have a picture of Iftu that I treasure, in which she is showing off the soft drapes of her white dress edged with red, white and black bands, a wide fringed sash and an embroidery of an *odaa* tree prominently placed.

That year we were at *Laga Raachaa* (River Racha), closer to our villages than *Hora Arsadi*, where the biggest celebration takes place. We must gather beside water, our life-giving resource, although we are not worshiping it or any other things suggested by those who misrepresent our beliefs as pagan and superstitious. When you think about it, water is important in the rituals of other dominant religions; Christians baptize with water and Muslims use it constantly for purification.

Our festival resembles a wedding, with smiling and greeting and hugging, all participating in colorful finery, singing and dancing, following traditional practices. The elderly men carry *bokkuu*, ceremonial sticks, symbolic of the democratic principles of the *gadaa* system, representing power and justice. The men are proudly wearing Oromo attire too and some wear headdresses that distinguish them as warriors. I have a grey jacket and waistcoat, with tie and hat to match, featuring black, white, and red stripes and stippled with the *odaa* tree, for the *gubaa*; for *irreechaa* I wear plain white linen with a simple insignia of the *odaa*.

The married women carry their own sticks, *sinqqee*, symbols of the undisputed rights of Oromo women everywhere and recognition of their dignity and preeminent place as the sources of new life. Mothers are held in the highest esteem and they are honored by leading the procession with other women and children to the waterside, carrying *kello* flowers and *coqorsa* (bunches of thick, untrimmed grasses). They are followed by a phalanx of men, with Oromo flags and banners.

The pageant proceeds, slow and steady and dignified, while the women, through whom human life enters the world, carry the grasses (nourishers of cattle) to the source of life (water) and sing: 'We go for reconciliation …. We are bringing the forces together….'

The women ululate (*ililtaa*), a piercing sound, emotive and wistful. At the river's edge, the flowers and grasses are dipped in the water and the elders explain that our hearts and minds must focus on the good. This is always a tender moment of forgiveness, thanksgiving, and gratitude for the bounties of *Waaqaa*.

Irreechaa is a ceremony, a sacred event, a *booqa birra* (shining day), and I was sad when I was no longer there with my family and friends to celebrate. Iftu did not say, but I knew she missed it and all it represented to the Oromo people. I saw her looking at photographs on Facebook and watching some of the DVDs she brought with her. One day I came home from training, earlier than expected because of a storm. She was sitting alone, tears in her eyes, watching the tape of our wedding feast.

'Iftu!' I sat beside her and turned her face towards me. 'Does it make you sad to see this?'

'I like to remember what it was like then, before all the troubles.' She stopped the tape. 'Also, I can see the happy faces of people we love, sharing our wedding and our laughter. It is one way to bring them closer for a little while.'

Iftu was unhappy and I was to blame. We were young and joyous back then: the runner with the trophies, the promise of a successful career; and his bride, with her beauty, the promise of his gold band on her finger.

6

I remembered too. There is a time for everything and this was the time to love, when Iftu was *addooyyee*, and I was *dargaggeessa*, girl and boy of courting age. We are the same age, born in 1990, in the same district, with the same experiences of traditional Oromo life. Iftu's father is Mulisa Lamu and her mother's name is Tolashi Eticha. Her place of birth is the village called Ademsa Galani, but, like my village, you may have difficulty finding it on a map. She was closest to the grandmother who raised her and one of Iftu's fears in the foreign land was that she would die before her granddaughter returned to her.

You may wonder why it was her grandmother who raised Iftu. In many Oromo regions, after the mothers recover from giving birth, they return to work and their mothers (the grandmothers) assume many of the child-rearing responsibilities. The bond between children and their grandmothers is intimate and quite traditional: the mothers raise their children's children.

Iftu has told me that she dreaded an arranged marriage, still an acceptable practice in some Oromo *gosas*. 'I hated the idea of being forced to marry someone I did not know or love. I have attended weddings where this was the case and the girls were very unhappy. Even one of my cousins. There was no joy for her on her wedding day. She wanted, like me, only the *qeerroo*, the young unmarried man.'

In traditional Oromo culture, *qeerroo* is a young bachelor, but the term has taken on a different meaning in recent times, as you will soon hear.

Iftu looked at me shyly. 'Some of us feared *suubboo*, a man already married. It would be for me like eating *dhangaggoo*.'

Dhangaggoo is a bitter plant. I do not think Iftu would have shared the fate of the girls forced to marry strangers. Unlike me, she was raised in a home where the Christian religion had influence. Nevertheless, we still announced our coming together in traditional ways. We celebrated our love with songs which blended our love of the natural world with our love for one another.

One of the best memories for me was Iftu singing: '*Dargaggoon daanisa rooba / yoo daraarewoo / Ya hiyyooshee…/ Qalbii nama buta roobaa…* (Young man is a strong built beautiful tree / come o rain / If it promises blossoms / He takes your breath away…).' *Hiyyooshee* appears in many songs, symbolizing spring flowers; it is something associated with blossoming and flowering.

Part of Iftu's charm for me is her guilelessness, the charm of a girl who has never worked outside her home or travelled beyond familiar places. At just nineteen she had no exposure to a wider, different world like I had. I value her unaffected *Oromumma*, her being an Oromo daughter who loves me, an Oromo son who loves her.

In the traditional Oromo way, the elders of the villages are involved in the marriage ritual, *guduunfa*, meaning 'to tie together'; it is the common name for the Oromo negotiation process which equates with an engagement. The boy's parents choose a person, not because of his wealth but because he is highly respected, to negotiate with the girl's family. Her family must feel honored that this man has come to their home to ask for their daughter. This man may be very busy because he is going everywhere in the district as an ambassador for nuptials! He leaves early in the morning on his journey to the girl's house and when he arrives, he calls out, 'We are here to talk!' Her family puts chairs outside for the honored guests and they all discuss the weather, the crops, the town—everything but the real purpose of the visit.

After all the small talk at the house, the visitors rise to go. 'We will be back next week to ask for your daughter for our son.' They do not wait for a *yes* or *no* from the father; they just leave, knowing their intentions are understood. The whole village knows about the visit, a favorite topic that continues after the return of the boy's ambassadors, when, hopefully, the parties agree, and plans are made for the wedding. The couple is now engaged, much to the delight of everyone. Prospective brides are not allowed then to go anywhere alone—not to the markets, to wash clothes, or to be unattended with the man she will marry. She is protected: *qarree darbu geese. Qarree*, the symbolism or purity of girlhood, is about to pass.

Some Oromo choose to have a Christian ceremony because they loved the missionaries who came to our country from the American Presbyterian Church. They connected with the Oromo at a deeply cultural level, unlike others who tried to suppress our customs. They came into our homes, ate what we ate, sat where we sat, and learned our language.

Such attitudes are to be respected, but I know from our elders that there were missionaries who questioned the compatibility of the Oromo traditional life and the Christian religion. They wanted converts to shed their culture to become good Christians. Some Oromo found it impossible to live outside their culture and left the church. Over the years there have been Oromo men who became ministers themselves but refused to renounce their Oromo identity. They upheld their Oromo culture and history, by embracing, shaping, and indigenizing Christianity to make it work for them and their people. Wherever they took the gospel, they also took their *Oromumma*.

I believe it is possible to honor spiritual beliefs and observe cultural practices. I noticed this living among people of a Western nationality, and there are Oromo Christians among my friends who still look forward to *gubaa* and *irreechaa*. They also participate happily in the five days of wedding celebration such as Iftu and I enjoyed.

From childhood I have loved the excitement and social pleasure of weddings. Some families choose to have the wedding on one of the few holidays in the year, because they don't have to spend a lot, with crowds already in the village in celebratory mood and party food prepared in abundance. An Oromo wedding is a very special occasion, a festive diversion for the people.

Iftu and I were married in Ambo, on the November 5, 2009, according to the Western calendar. Ambo comes into this story again, as the scene of much unrest, but you may have heard of it already because of its famous hot springs and bottled mineral water. Our marriage was arranged simply by going to the government office responsible for administration of marriages, where we took an oath and signed a marriage agreement.

In the Oromo culture, a wedding continues for a few days. Firstly, there is the day of the nuptial ceremony and the reception, when we sing and dance and eat, much as we do at *irreechaa*. On the days that follow the groom visits his family with the bride, then her family, and then the two families all together. On the fifth day the new wife prepares food and shares it with guests, friends, and family. We do not go away for what you call a honeymoon, but at the end of the fifth day we are *Heennaan haama*, cutting *heennaa*, as one of our *seenaa* (farewell) wedding songs says. *Heennaa* is a small plant in green pastures; cutting it is symbolic of severing relationships and parting ways with our parents and, in Iftu's case, grandparent.

I sat with Iftu on the day of her tears and rewound the movie of our wedding. We watched it together. I saw again her face, her lovely profile in repose. I saw my own, which one journalist compared to the face on a coin. We both have very defined facial bone structures, a feature of our people. At this place of ceremony, we were solemn, eyes downcast. Iftu's hair was braided with white flowers; it was not long before a distinctive patch of grey appeared, where the hair is drawn back from her forehead.

We looked so small and young in our white clothes, so different to the usual athletics gear and casual clothes we both wear. Some say the Oromo are slight in build but dignified in bearing and, as I saw again the way we looked on our wedding day, I agree. I had come a long way from the boy in shabby jeans or ill-fitting white trousers.

I turned the tape off and grasped Iftu's hand, as I did that day in 2009. Iftu has beautiful slim brown hands, with shapely unpainted nails. I lifted her hand to my face and held it there. 'Iftu, our life won't always be like this. One day we may be able to go home forever. I need you with me now. You are my beloved, my friend. You are the one bringing contentment, much more so than winning races and earning big money. Talking to you, watching you, holding you makes my life bearable. We shall sing and dance again one day in Jaldu, perhaps at our daughter's wedding, or our son's.'

She nodded and smiled. 'Remember the day when there was no wind at all, but as soon as that big *Qilxuu* tree in my village saw us coming it started *sirbite*? Not just *tchotchose*, moving its branches, but dancing! I knew without a doubt then that we were destined to be together, whatever happened.'

7

Leaves dancing. I often watch the trees to see such a vision again, but I think it seemed to Iftu and I that everything danced that day because we were in love and planning our wedding day, when there would be much dancing and singing. An outsider watching an Oromo dance, *dhichissa*, will probably say the movement is more like an athletic demonstration than a dance! I suppose it does resemble a sequence of rhythmic exercises, with much stamping, jumping, and skipping. We dance in time to music which has an insistent urgency about it; shrill, repetitive, and, you might say, discordant. I have always liked *dhiichisa* (dance) music, though, and to me dancing is as natural a sequence of steps as running is.

We were encouraged from a young age to learn *mammaksaa* (songs) and I remember my sisters and brother and I singing at grandfather's place. We added to our repertoire at school, with music included in the curriculum. When I was in Grade 2 our music teacher gave us homework to listen to songs on the radio, then to choose one we liked and sing in front of the class. This presented a problem for me because we did not have a radio at home. I liked a catchy song in our music textbook, an old song called '*Ooha obbo boolee*', about the *gosa*, so I revised it as I ran to and from school, ready to sing for the class.

'Feyisa, stop!' the teacher commanded after I had sung just a couple of lines. 'This will not count because it is one we all know from the textbook.'

I wonder now why I could not explain to her that we had no radio. Pride or embarrassment, I expect, and I was close to tears. I thought I would not get a mark, but this teacher, my favorite Aberu Beka, was fond of me because I was good at sport and made her laugh when I did circus tricks. She let me finish the song and gave me a pass mark, a kindness I have never forgotten.

Later on, my father sold a bull and bought a radio. I loved it and as my interest in athletics grew, I ran home from school in time for the sports news. I followed soccer, and I had this thought that if I could not be a professional runner, I would be a soccer player, fast and daring on the field.

I saw a CD player in Finfinne, when I was a teenager, but there was no such thing where we lived. In the summer break, I walked or ran to a town eight kilometers away from our village just to listen to songs at a friend's home. He had a cassette player that held two batteries and we bought and traded tapes to play. I listened to many artists, singing along loudly and dancing to the songs that had a fast pace. My friend had a tape of music by an artist called Ali Birra, but his songs were so slow that I asked for a different tape. When Ali Birra's songs came on the radio at home, I switched it off or changed the station, even when my mother remonstrated.

'What kind of song is this?' I muttered.

'Ali Birra!' she exclaimed. 'He is a hero! His songs have a big message, Feyisa. You should listen to them.'

He sang about Oromo freedom and identity. He produced his first album in 1971, the first in the history of Oromo music, and then recorded successful hits such as '*Hin Yaadin*' (Don't Worry), '*Ammalelee*' (Have Love for Others), and '*Gamachu*' (Happiness).

Kebede and I had long discussions about Ali Birra while we listened to his music. Kebede knew more about him than I did, such as his command of many languages and his love of touring the country to sing with other well-known artists. Ali married a Swedish admirer and he became known internationally.

'He is an ambassador of Oromo people,' according to Kebede. 'He lends his mouth to us and speaks on our behalf about many topics. He is not afraid to communicate our problems.'

'He follows the public interest and expresses it very well,' I said. 'The lyrics show that he is courageous and confident, not afraid to speak his mind. He has passed through many ups and downs because of his views.'

'Artists like Ali Birra are so aware of their identity.' Kebede was looking on the playlist for his favorite song, in which Ali Birra mourns his friend, Ahmad Taqi, an Oromo nationalist revered by many of us as a true fighter and martyr of the Oromo cause.

Ahmed Taqi knew General Taddesse Birru (do you remember, one of my heroes—a founder of the Macha Tulama Association) and when the General was under house arrest they both began to teach the local people that they have rights equal to those of the landlords in the area, and that being Oromo is not a curse, but a virtue to love.

'Many of our people still don't get it!' Listening to Ali Birra made me aware of how the general population seemed to be sleeping. 'I would go crazy if I were these artists, because too many Oromos are not listening to what they are saying.'

It stressed me and made me angry when people around me chose to stay ignorant while I talked to them. I love Sayo Dendana's songs and many songs of other Oromo artists like Ababa Abishu and Dagim Mokenen. They have good voices and their songs are great, so I can't say a single artist is my favorite. Many of them sacrificed a lot to develop Oromo art without earning a single *birr*. They didn't get help and not many people bought their work to encourage them. They are among those who spoke up for our struggle. For this, I loved them all, whether their songs were good or bad.

I think the artists did not buy other work themselves as much as I did, but their resources were limited. If someone took a CD from my car, I bought another original CD. We Oromos should develop our artists by buying CDs. We number around fifty million people, so if we all buy a share, then that artist can live on his work. It is not just about the artist, but about supporting Oromo art in general.

It amazes me that Ali Birra sang about our culture in the dark times. The *Qubee* generation is the offspring of people like Ali Birra; to me he is like a father. I hope that he sat back proudly when he watched me speak up for our people in Rio de Janeiro. This is what he wished for many years—to see us challenge the regime.

'In the future,' I told Kebede, 'I hope I can sit back and watch our victorious generation reclaim its rightful place in Ethiopia.'

'I hope for that too,' Kebede replied. 'You and I, your children and my children too.'

We listened to Hirpaa Ganfure's revolutionary songs, among them '*Gubatte yaa bosona Baalee*', about the burning of the Bale forest, and memorized the lyrics. We were both hungry to know more about our country's history, to be better prepared to teach the children we did not have yet. My name was heard on the radio, which was astonishing to the boy who once listened to the sports news in his village, and later there would be songs about me. But back then I was sorry that I had not taken my schooling seriously.

When I left the Armed Forces Club, where we were treated like soldiers not to think for ourselves, I wanted to return to school. I felt demoralized by the club, and also by my results in Grade 10. I wanted to continue education to recover from that, although I knew it would not be easy for me to go to school as well as train and compete. A higher education also gives you a good profile as an athlete and I made up my mind that I could do it. I went to register at the Menelik School, near Addis Ababa University in Finfinne, but I was told that my national examination results from Jaldu High School had expired and my application was rejected.

When I told Iftu about it, soon after we were married, she understood because she had dropped out of school for a while and knew it was hard to return to study. She is articulate and intelligent and had advanced further at school than I had, to Grade 12. This was a good time as we gradually got to know more about each other. We talked about the importance of reading and language.

'I have not read enough Oromo literature, although I did read a lot of *Afaan Oromoo* books in the sports club,' I said. 'I want to learn Oromo history.'

'Do you think we should read more books in English and talk more in that language?' she asked, as I had started going abroad for competition. 'If we practice at home, you will become more fluent.'

She knew I was having difficulty speaking English and I wanted to answer questions from the press. We would have spoken English more at home, if only we had known what lay ahead. I started buying English books in the hope of improving my understanding, but that distracted me from reading *Afaan Oromoo* books.

'What a big library you have!' visitors exclaimed when they came to our house.

'I buy a lot of Oromo books from bookstores,' I explained, 'even though I do not have time to read them. I buy the books to encourage their authors. I just don't feel comfortable if I pass by a bookstore without buying an *Afaan Oromoo* book. I want to do my part for Oromo writing.'

'What were the first books you read?' Iftu wanted to know.

'The first *Afaan Oromoo* book I read was a very small book. I wish I still had a copy.' I scanned the shelves in vain. 'The title is *Abdii Duukkanoofte* (Darkened Hope). It was about a student, I think. Then I bought another book from Ambo, called *Seenaa Kabir Waadoo Gadaa* (Story of Kabir Wado Geda), a hero from Bale who participated in the Bale Rebellion.'

'I would like to read that one!' Iftu has talked of her heroes, too many to list. I said that she would find this book too distressing.

'I had already been selected by the sports club when I read it,' I said, clenching my fists at the memory. 'That book made me disagree with the leaders and want to fight with others in the camp. I got so angry after reading the book as I came to know what those people, the Amharas, did. I did not want to talk to them or eat with them after I read what they did to that hero. I finished reading the book in a couple of days, but, as I read it, I wished he would die early in the story, because of the extent of the torture he endured.'

'There is too much anger in you, Feyisa,' Iftu sat closer to me and put her head on my shoulder. 'Please do not do anything foolish. You cannot win against this government.'

I made no promises. I had been abused verbally at the club and treated unfairly there in other ways, but it was nothing compared to Kabir Wado Geda. Again, I entertained the thought of being a soldier and venting my anger against the government forces that were still as ruthless as they had been in Bale.

'Perhaps we should watch more films,' Iftu suggested. She was trying to deflect my anger. 'We might improve our English that way.'

'No, I don't like watching films.' I was being hard to get on with, but I can't focus when I watch most of them. 'The first film I saw, in Finfinne, was about wrestling. I was watching it by mistake on television. There was an *Afaan Oromoo* programme called *Do'ii Sirbaa* (Music Show) every Thursday and Sunday, which I didn't want to miss. One day someone had changed the channel to an African channel and I saw the wrestling film. Huge men were beating each other up.' The film upset me greatly, which is strange when you think about what a tough little boy wrestler I had been. 'It frightened me, Iftu. I was terrified until I arrived at my home that evening, because it was so real. I kept thinking someone was going to beat me up as I walked from the place where I saw the show to where I lived. I think it scared me away from films!'

After that I did watch other *Afaan Oromoo* films, including *Eelaa* (Burden), a romance with an underlying political meaning. Everyone talked about that film. After I started going abroad for competition, I rented my own house in Finfinne, to be independent, and I bought a television. I even went to the Mercato to buy *Eelaa*.

Iftu was unused to the world of television and movies. 'I got permission once from my family to watch you race on TV,' she told me. 'They thought it was some kind of political competition, but it wasn't! I went to town with my neighbors to watch.'

'You like TV now!' I teased her. 'But don't be bothered with races. You'll get too nervous. Watch the soccer with me.'

Iftu and I were always glad to get away from the television and the training ground and visit beautiful places. This was a novelty for her, sitting beside me in the car, exploring the wider world. One of our favorite places is a waterfall, *Fincaa Wagne*, loud and lovely in the summer when the rivers are full. It is in a remote place called Dulla and access is difficult, but that is part of its attraction, far away from city life.

I missed these places, associated with home, and I wished that I could write songs about them. Such places offer healing and refreshment. Mention the word healing and I start to think about our naming of people, *Hammachiisaa*.

There was a certain man, whose name I don't remember now, but it was a Muslim name, an actor, about the same age as I am. I had seen him in a television drama, *Filera*, and other shows. When I went to Arsi, his region, for a wedding, I saw him by the side of the road and offered him a lift. There was another person sitting in the front passenger seat, but I asked him to sit in the back, so this actor sat next to me.

'I know who you are,' I told him. 'I like your acting.'

'I thought you were picking up a stranger!' he said, looking closely at me. 'This is amazing. I recognize you too, Feyisa Lilesa, one of our best runners.'

He was thoughtful for a while and then he said, 'You have a good name. It has a special meaning. Do you know that? A child is named for a reason.'

'Yes,' I said. 'When a child is born God puts the name of that child in the mouth of the person who names him.'

'They called you *Feyisa*, "healer" or "savior"! Naming is not an easy thing. How many people have you saved?'

'I have a big responsibility,' I said. 'I think I have saved members of my family from their problems and also friends who are in trouble.'

'This is good,' he nodded. 'You have much more ahead of you.'

I often think about that actor and the chance we had to talk. Naming and fulfilling destiny are such big concerns. I wondered about the destiny of a boy born in 1990.

I have heard of Oromo who claim to have been born at the wrong time and given the wrong name. I read the story of a woman, Hawani, from Ambo, historically a center of Oromo learning and knowledge. Hawani's family was well-known and respected.

'I was born at the wrong time, maybe even on the wrong day, as the Oromo say,' she wrote. 'Now I understand what the Oromo mean when they say that one's fate is decided at birth…. I know that this suffering is the fate of the Oromo of my generation.'

Hawani was born in 1974, when Haile Selassie was deposed. I thought this would have been a good time to be born, but Hawani said no. Many Oromo people were imprisoned or killed in Mengistu's era. Her family endured murders and imprisonments, including an uncle and aunt who were in jail for nine years. Their child grew up there with them—luckier, perhaps, than some who did not see their children for the duration of their prison terms.

Hawani told her readers that the whole idea of imprisoning a person in Ethiopia was not to correct him or her. It was done to punish and terrorize. The sentence was directed not only at the prisoner, but at the whole family. It was meant to serve as a lesson and as a warning to all who sympathized with the Oromo cause.

'We were forced to speak Amharic. Oromo were treated very harshly, and women like my mother had to go long distances with food for prisoners. There were many families that just disintegrated and disappeared. In 1990, when I was sixteen, I left for England. After Mengistu fled the country in 1991, we all thought things would change. But nothing has changed for the Oromo. They continue to be persecuted by the so-called democratic government of the EPRDF….'

She is right, and I think again about the destiny of a boy born in 1990, the year before she fled our country. Her final words, written in 1996, come back to me, remembered like the refrain of a song: 'I hear from home that the Oromo people are determined to resist the present Amhara-Tigre domination…. I have no doubt that the Oromo will win in the end, but at what cost, I wonder?'

IV

I

Marathon runners know all about costs, if we want to win in the end. I paid plenty for my dreams in the 'white trousers' days, when I was poor and defeated and weary. The experiences in the Armed Forces Club were sometimes humiliating and frustrating, when my running was motivated by anger at the injustices. The highest cost of all is yet to be explained to you, but I believe I was preparing to pay it years beforehand.

Most elite athletes count the cost of injuries in time lost and races not run. I feel keenly a sense of failure when I leave the track limping, long before the finishing line is in sight. The marathons I did not finish due to injury were the World Athletic Championships in Moscow and the Frankfurt Marathon, both in 2013, and then the Chicago Marathon in 2014. In those years, though, I couldn't stop training; if I were to stop, I would gain more weight. I also competed when I should have been resting my injured leg, because my family depends on what I earn by running.

Injured athletes are beset by worries about the time wasted. We are the world's most obsessive timekeepers, ever conscious of our personal bests, our past training times, training and racing splits, and world records. We never run aimlessly, but with perseverance and purpose, eyes on the track ahead of us, ever glancing at the fancy watches on our wrists. One day, one of us will run the sub-two-hour marathon. Who will wear the crown for running the first 1:59?

Perhaps it will happen on the flat streets of Berlin, the scene of many world records in the men's marathon. On September 28, 2014, in the IAAF Gold Label Road Race, Dennis Kimetto, a Kenyan, broke the world record with a time of 2:02:57. This was 26 seconds faster than the previous time, set by his countryman, Wilson Kipsang. The record is ratified by the IAAF, the international governing body for the sport of athletics.

Eliud Kipchoge, another Kenyan, whose name has significance in my story, attempted to run a sub-two-hour marathon in the Breaking2 project, organized by Nike, at the Monza F1 track in Milan in May of 2017. He ran with Lelisa Desisa (Ethiopia) and Zersenay Tadese (Eritrea), hoping to break the barrier, exactly sixty-three years after the Englishman Roger Bannister became the first person to run under four minutes in the mile race. Eliud missed his target by 25 seconds. His time, though better than Dennis Kimetto's, was not ratified by the IAAF because it did not meet some of the strict criteria.

'This journey has been good,' Eliud said after the race. 'It's been hard. It's been a long journey...it's taken seven good months of preparation. I'm happy to have done it. With the race I felt good. Now it is just 25 seconds I need to lose. I believe in good preparation and planning and if I stick to that the 25 seconds will come.'

Eliud talks often about running as a journey—a very satisfying one for him, with many highlights.

We race to win, but only one gets the top prize. In athletics there are no spontaneous generations. In other words, we work our way up the ladder and through the competitions until we approach and hopefully reach the top, like Eliud, a brave and heroic figure in the marathon band of brothers. We are fierce competitors, but there is shared pain and glory. Sporting generations develop slowly, and I am among the elite Ethiopian athletes of my generation who have become known in the first couple of decades of the twenty-first century, after our apprenticeships on the regional, national, and international circuits. The master runners come and go, but only some are long remembered and revered.

I expect I may be remembered for the action I took in Rio de Janeiro, but there have been a couple of achievements on my running record that I treasure. The first one occurred at the Rotterdam Marathon, on April 11, 2010. It is not a Major in the racing calendar, but it is in the highest class of second-tier marathons. I went into the race feeling good after winning the Xiamen International Marathon (in China), an IAAF Gold Label Road Race, earlier in the year. Marathoners like its coastal scenic course and that day, running beside the water, belonged to me.

'You get mixed feeling from running, both pleasure and sadness,' I told a journalist after that race. 'There is fatigue, your mind sometimes wanders about, and you try to block out negative thoughts. I am not usually a front runner—that is a lonely and psychologically tiring position. When you make your move, surge ahead, cross the finishing line first, you feel very happy because you ran more than forty kilometers and took two hours to finish, without knowing till the end what your result will be. I overcame the obstacles this day and I am happy. You feel like shouting when you win!'

He asked me if I was an aggressive runner. 'I run to win,' I answered. 'I have tactics like all the others, but I never cheat.' I said that because this race was criticized for many instances of cheating, with some runners carrying multiple timing sensors or even using public transport mid-course.

The Rotterdam race is known to be a fast track, on the right day. The city is beautiful and, if I had more time, I would have liked to explore it. Most of all from that course I remember a bridge, the Erasmusbrug, which I could see from my hotel window. We started out from the bridge on a cool grey day, the sort of day most runners welcome because the conditions are favorable—no heat or humidity to overcome, no temptation to pause for drinks, no wet slippery roads.

I kept pace with the Kenyan pack, running strong and sure. I was surrounded by them all the way, even in the final result. They took the first three places, as well as fifth, sixth, seventh, and eighth. I was in the middle of them, in fourth place, ten seconds behind Vincent Kipruto and well ahead of Bernard Kipyego. Best of all, my time of 2:05:23 meant that I was the youngest runner ever to break 2:06! This time also made me the third fastest Ethiopian ever, behind Haile Gebresillassie and Tsegay Kebede.

That night I dreamed of racing against Haile Gebresillassie and winning, way beyond my wildest boyhood dreams! He was still my hero then, but events were unfolding in Ethiopia that I could not ignore; events which would lead to seeing him in a different light. A promising career as a marathon runner was about to collide with concern for my Oromo people. As I have already told you, I won the bronze medal at the 2011 World Championships in Daegu, South Korea, with my friend Abel Kirui the gold medallist. I was content—my time of 2:10:32 was my season's best—what we call our SB.

I went home happy from Daegu, anxious to be back with Iftu, who was expecting a baby, but I heard disturbing news when I got there. Kebede had talked to me often about a man called Bekele Gerba, a champion of our people, a man not afraid to speak up about the way things were, but always advocating non-violent confrontation with the government. He had met with Amnesty International delegates, who were in the country investigating reports of human rights abuse.

'While you were in Korea,' Kebede told me, 'Bekele and some other opposition party members were arrested, just days after meeting with Amnesty International. The delegates were ordered to leave the country on the same day arrests took place.'

'On what charge was Bekele arrested?' I asked.

'No charges have been made,' Kebede shrugged, 'but this is the usual pattern. We are arrested just because we are Oromo.' He had been following events as best he could and knew more than I did about the justice system. 'International law requires that anyone arrested should appear promptly before a judicial authority and criminally charged. This does not happen here.'

On my training sessions I had time to think about what was happening to Bekele Gerba and many others. I thought of him as if he were an athlete, taking the risks, counting the costs, desperately watching the time—measured in years, not minutes—in a marathon for justice and freedom, its finishing line receding in the distance, no matter how determined he was to win against oppression and abuse. Now his marathon, in one of the hardest terrains of the world, was interrupted and he was sidelined, injured, marking time in jail.

Was it possible, I wondered as I jogged, for Bekele to be victorious? Can there be any winners in this long-fought struggle? Emperor Haile Selassie famously remarked, when he met Abebe Bikila and Abebe Wakjira, the athletes chosen to run the marathon in the Rome Olympics, 'How can such thin men win?' Abebe Bikila won the race. Can the slender outsiders, like Bekele Gerba, win against the heavyweights of the EPRDF?

2

The story of Bekele Gerba will be told many times to our children and our children's children. The remarks he made in court will be repeated over and over: 'I am honored to learn that my non-violent struggles and humble sacrifices for the democratic and human rights of the Oromo people, to whom I was born without a wish on my part, but due to the will of the Almighty, have been considered a crime and to be unjustly convicted.'

We may not be sitting around fireplaces in villages telling this *Oduu Durii*. Probably, many Oromo will read it for themselves on the Internet. The *Qubee* generation has the stories of the world at our fingertips, with our Smart phones and iPads.

I first heard the word 'computer' after I joined the sports club, when people declared, 'It's the age of computers.' Aduna was in the 11th grade then, and one day he said casually, 'I am taking a course called 'IT'. Do you know what that is, Feyisa?' I shook my head and he explained about computers and Information Technology.

'We have only one computer in the school, and we line up to see how the teacher operates it. I wish I had one.'

The schools in my district never did have enough computers. I started seeing them in Internet cafes in Finfinne. Then, when I went abroad for competition, starting in 2008, I saw Kenyan athletes browsing websites, showing me pictures of different athletes. I didn't know where to touch the computer to do that. I just stood still and watched what they were doing with those magical buttons. It was like the first time I saw the runners in a television set—again, I was enthralled, an immediate fan of IT. Kenya was more advanced than our country in terms of technology.

In 2009, when I went to Jordan for a race, I bought myself a laptop. I took it to people who knew about computers and they showed me how to use it. Then I could find out so much about the world, and much more about my own country, even as I travelled to some of the other places on the globe. This was a different education to what I had planned.

I have now read much about Bekele Gerba and I understand why Kebede and many others regarded him as a heroic man who shared the agony of our people. He entered politics in 2009, joining the opposition party, the Oromo Federalist Democratic Movement (OFDM; later the Oromo Federalist Congress, when it merged with the Oromo People's Congress). That was the year the *Charities and Societies Proclamation* placed severe restrictions on the work of organizations advancing human and democratic rights. Many had to shut down, change their mandate, or reduce their work.

It was also the year when an Anti-Terrorism Proclamation with many provisions that contravened human rights, supposedly guaranteed by Ethiopia's constitution and international law, was announced. The Proclamation provided the Ethiopian government with the right to crack down on political dissent, including peaceful political demonstrations and public criticisms of government policy. It permitted long-term imprisonment and even the death penalty for 'crimes' that were not acts of terrorism at all. In some cases, defendants were deprived of the right to be presumed innocent and denied protections against use of evidence obtained through torture.

These harsh laws prompted Bekele to run for office in the May 2010 parliamentary elections, in which the EPRDF claimed more than 99% of the seats in parliament. The ruling party's win was predictable, the culmination of the government's five-year strategy of systematically reducing space for political dissent and independent criticism. European election observers said that the election fell well short of international standards. This is what I read when I could access more websites away from Ethiopia:

'Voters were pressured to join or support the ruling party through a combination of incentives, including access to seeds, fertilizers, tools, and loans.' I particularly remembered reading this because of our farm.

'That's not all,' Kebede said when we sat long and late talking about these things. 'People were threatened with being denied access to public-sector jobs, educational opportunities, and even food assistance. Officials and militia from local administrations went from house to house telling residents to register to vote and be sure to vote for the ruling party or face reprisals, such as bureaucratic harassment, even losing their homes or jobs.'

We needed men and women like Bekele to protest in the places of power. After several hundred Oromos were imprisoned, he attended court as a party member to witness proceedings against them. Shocked, he called some media that day and gave an interview about what he had seen and heard. 'I saw prosecutors organizing false evidence,' he informed them. 'They were calling upon people and they were giving them orientations to testify against others they didn't even know, people they had never seen before.'

Government officials started following Bekele. Then he was arrested and sentenced to eight years in prison, suspected of belonging to the banned OLF. This was a favorite accusation against Oromos detained for actual or suspected dissent. That organization had been largely ineffective, with leadership divisions, but it continued a low-level armed fight against the EPRDF with targeted killings, attacks on military camps, ambushes, and skirmishes.

The government seemed to equate participation in peaceful protests, membership in a political opposition party, or refusal to join the ruling party as evidence of 'OLF support'. As I understood it, the government anticipated opposition to the EPRDF in Oromia and the pretext of OLF support was frequently used to silence voices the government did not want heard and to justify the large-scale repression of all dissent in Oromia.

Bekele Gerba is a Christian man, an advocate of non-violence, a believer in the methods of Mahatma Gandhi and Martin Luther King, so he is an unlikely supporter of an armed militant group. While he was imprisoned for his public stance against injustice, he translated some of the speeches of King into *Afaan Oromo* and his work was published as *Mul'atan Qaba* (I Had A Dream). He came to believe that the power of the Oromo people is really great, given our large population and our culture of reconciliation and peace. But don't take up arms, he counselled; use civil resistance and non-violence.

Kebede studied the wrongs against prisoners. 'Under international law and the Ethiopian Constitution,' he explained when I questioned Bekele's arrest, 'the rights to freedom of expression, association, and cultural participation are guaranteed. No one can be arrested based on their actual or alleged political opinion, participation in peaceful protests, lawful exercise of their right to freedom of expression, or expression of their cultural identity. Such arrests are arbitrary and contrary to international and Ethiopian law.'

Many of my people will testify that these rights were denied them. Think of Bekele taken to Maekelawi, that place known to us all as a torture chamber, and then Kaliti prison. He witnessed the truth that 'the prisons in Ethiopia speak *Afaan Oromoo*.' Most of the inmates were Oromo. Bekele was kept in maximum security for more than a year, in a den of thieves and thugs who fought among themselves—even the police and guards feared them. Then he was taken to Ziway, filled with Oromo from the countryside; suspected, like him, of links with the OLF.

A statement that Bekele made after his release in 2015 stayed with me and motivated me to take action of my own. 'In one way I was very glad to be there in prison,' he said, 'because I felt myself sharing the agony of my own people. How am I different from those people? Those people went to prison because they demanded their rights. I was also there because I demanded my rights. In this country I think that the Oromos are being excluded from the political and economic spheres or meaningful participation, something to which I always object. Therefore, I had to share their pain and I am glad of that.'

Bekele wanted us to appreciate our diversity. Let people sing in their own way, speak in their own language, celebrate their own culture, and wear different kinds of clothing. He believed that things could be put on the right track, and wrongs could be righted.

He travelled the country talking about how to make the democratic principles of the Constitution work for the Oromo, who were being dominated by one small group. He won a lot of respect for his integrity and eloquence and his devotion to the Oromo cause. When he was a younger man, he was suspected of supporting a students' riot at Adama Teachers' College, where he taught English and *Afaan Oromoo,* and was dismissed by the college. He went to Finfinne where he continued to teach at Addis Ababa University as a lecturer in Foreign Languages.

'I had never been involved in politics,' he told his audience. 'I was simply an academic and I thought that politics was not a job for everyone—I am a teacher and, if I am a good teacher, I think that will do and that was that. But gradually I found out that my peoples' grievances were not addressed in a way they should be. I got involved in politics to contribute my share. I don't know whether I have done anything or have made any changes. Before I could do anything substantial, I was taken to prison.'

He drew crowds, who listened with understanding to the story of his past.

'Surprisingly, the place in the West Wollega region where I was born and raised is a typical monolingual area. All the people around, all the shop owners, all the government employees, and all the school staff speak only one single language, *Afaan Oromoo*. It is a very special place I can say, even by Oromia standards. Therefore, I didn't know whether there was any kind of difference between one ethnic group and the other or if there was oppression elsewhere.

'But when I went away to university, I began to realize there are different ethnic groups and there are various things you will find difficult to tolerate.

When I went to the big towns like Finfinne and I spoke my own language in a taxi or in a bus, people turned around and took a look at me. I was surprised by their reaction. And then the consciousness happened—the social consciousness—not so much political. It was the knowledge of difference.

'I like speaking languages. I am an outgoing person. I have no problem living with other ethnic group members. But I came to understand that there is something wrong going on against the ethnic group I come from.'

Bekele talked about the circumstances that led to turmoil and instability. In 1991, the military regime was defeated by the ethnic fronts whose identity it had suppressed. It lost control over the peoples represented by these fronts and the country seemed close to disintegration. Observers pointed to Eritrea, which won its independence at great cost. Would other states follow? Would Oromia be given back its territory, redeemed from the internal colonialism inflicted by past regimes? Our ethno-national struggle continued, against imperial and military governments.

The fall of the military government in 1991 and the reordering of the Ethiopian state that followed looked promising. The Constitution established Ethiopia as a multicultural federation based on ethno-national representation and provided for nine ethnic-based regional states. The creation of the Oromia state has greatly helped in the revival of *Oromumma*, our national identity.

But the regional state governments were weak compared to the federal government. The OPDO was created by the TPLF and not by Oromos. Many Oromos distrusted it. It was an inadequate force within the ruling coalition. The new regime, with an ethnicity-based federal setup intended to lead the country towards liberal democracy, did not deliver. Democratization that allows self-rule and shared rule failed.

'Constitutionally, this is a federal country,' declared Bekele, 'but this is not a gift from the ruling EPRDF. Federalism came out of the situation that existed in 1991. Then there were about seventeen armed groups actively engaged in rebellion, with all their weapons and strongholds. When the Derg collapsed there was no way out of the political deadlock except to go for federalism because everyone could have gone home on his own way—the Oromos had the OLF, the Ogadens have the ONLF, and so on. No other kind of government was possible.'

'How do you evaluate the years since?' called someone in the crowd.

'Federalism was dictated by the situation at the time,' Bekele repeated. 'But since then its practice is being eroded on a daily basis. If you look at some regions, I don't think they are even electing their own rulers. Practically, I think the country is as unitary and as centralized as it has been before.'

'Who is to blame for that?'

'There was one big man, the late Prime Minister Meles Zenawi, who used to appoint regional officials without the consent of the people of those regions, who used to transfer them to the federal government as he liked. That was what was happening and continues to this day.

'In federalism you plan your own way, levy taxes in your own way, you execute it in your own way. Your priority is different from the federal government or other regions. That is not what's happening now. If you take Finfinne, for example, which is also the seat of the Oromia regional state, EPRDF officials singlehandedly decide on the fate of the city and its areas in the name of a "self-administered city". As things are happening now, the federal government makes plans by itself and executes them by its own finance. That is not true federalism.'

Bekele told us about what happened in March of 2011 when about one thousand Oromos were taken to the Maekelawi prison without the knowledge of the Oromia regional state officials.

'They didn't know; they didn't have any knowledge of the Oromos taken by federal security agents from every corner of Oromia. Here is when one should ask, what is this regional government doing? Did the regional government invite the federal government to come and act on its behalf to take these people to justice? Are they incapable of bringing them to justice in their own region? So, what is federalism?'

We all considered this.

'People say ethnic federalism doesn't take us anywhere. But I simply say that the ethnic federalism that came about in 1991 because of the situation we were in is a necessary evil that we cannot avoid. Because our identity, our language, our culture had been denied for many years, it was only through this way that we could restore and promote them. You know, if you scratch the surface of any party you will find out that the issue of ethnicity is underneath, but by the name it implies something else, just like we have the Federal Democratic Republic of Ethiopia. Does it mean it is federal? Does it mean it is democratic?

'There is nothing in a name. Therefore, for me every party in this country is an ethnic-based party. I am not saying it's a bad thing. It *becomes* bad when one ethnic group becomes a foe to another. Politically, it becomes bad when it is used as a tool of repression against others, when it is imposed. When somebody forces his own agenda on another, then the problems come. If you say to me, "Don't speak your language, speak only mine", then here comes a problem.

We have to appreciate our diversity. We want other people to sing in their own way, speak in their own language, celebrate their own culture, and wear different kinds of clothing. I think the idea of trying to bring everything into one is not a sensible idea.'

Kebede and I talked about this like other young Oromos trying to make sense of our times and the two predominant discourses. The first was the discourse for secessionism; the second supported a greater autonomy within the federal government—a better way of federalism that gives the Oromo a greater say in their affairs.

'Where does Bekele Gerba stand?' I asked. 'What does he see as a better way forward for the Oromo people?'

'Well, his stand is very firm,' Kebede answered. 'He always says that first the rights of the Oromo should be respected. The Oromos are located in the middle of this country. They have formed this country, they are part of this country, they will remain in this country. You cannot think about Ethiopia without the presence of the Oromos. They have sustained it and they are in the center of this massive land. What is very important is that their rights are respected. There should be no compromise. I can say, from what I have seen and heard, that he is not after secession.'

'I agree with this, I think.' I was cautious, though… unsure.

'But the problem is when the situation continues like it is now,' argued Kebede, 'when the exploitation, the eviction, the attempt to assimilate, to destroy our language, to destroy our culture, to destroy our identity goes on.'

Bekele Gerba was more philosophical. He believed that things could be put on the right track, and the wrongs could be righted. I am not sure, though, given our cultural practices of the past, the times of warriors and battles, that we can think of changing a government by any other way than armed struggle. I was ready to fight if necessary.

'I think that time has passed now,' asserted Bekele.

He did not envisage an independent Oromia or an independent land. He maintained this despite the dark days of 2014 and 2015 which he followed from his prison cell. Upon appeal to the Supreme Court, his sentencing was reduced to three years and seven months with a right to parole. The OFDM and the Oromo Peoples' Congress merged in 2012 to become the Oromo Federalist Congress, Oromia's largest registered political party. Bekele was appointed as First Deputy Chairman of that merged party while he was still serving his sentence. Although he was paroled and was eligible to be free in 2014, Bekele was released in the first week of April, 2015, only after he finished his sentencing.

'It is possible to change regimes and to confront governments by peaceful means of struggle. ' Bekele urged. 'We don't want to go to armed struggle; we don't want to show on television Ethiopians killing Ethiopians for power.'

3

In April and May of 2014, protests broke out across Oromia against a proposed 'Integrated Master Plan' to expand the capital, Addis Ababa (Finfinne), into Oromia regional territory. The design meant increasing the city to twenty times its present size by taking over prime agricultural land from Oromo farmers. The protests were led by students and many others participated. Security services, federal police, and the military Special Forces responded by firing live ammunition on peaceful protesters in many locations or beating them and innocent bystanders. There were many deaths, injuries, and arrests.

If it went ahead, the master plan would have displaced about two million households without compensation and nowhere to go. The consequence of such an evil action by the TPLF would have been disastrous. Taking our ancestral farmland would affect the lives of many Oromo and the design would divide the Oromia Regional State into two separate zones.

After his release from jail, Bekele Gerba spoke out against the land grabbing. 'What's more, my people are being pushed off their land by international investors. The greatest land grabbers are now the Indians and Chinese, but there are Saudi Arabians as well. Many families are being evicted and losing their livelihoods. Those who do get jobs are paid a dollar a day. This is a form of slavery!'

The truth was, as all Oromos knew, real state power remained with the elite of the TPLF, the main players in the four-party ruling EPRDF coalition. Decisions were made by the TPLF within the EPRDF, and regional state governments' role was to implement them. OPDO officials permitted extensive land grabs across Oromia and gross human rights violations committed against Oromo. The Oromia state parliament (*Caffee Oromia*), along with the state's executive branch, was constitutionally empowered to curb the implementation of this ill-purposed 'integration project.'

I am a runner, not a politician, but this is part of the story you are hearing and will tell others. The victims of Addis Ababa's land grab were families evicted from their only source of livelihood. Displacing Oromo farmers from their land without any consent or proper compensation violated their fundamental rights. Ethiopia has a duty to respect these, but all land was really controlled by the state. This made it easier for the government to displace farmers from their land, with a total disregard to other constitutional provisions, which protected peasants against eviction by the state.

As I trained in places near Finfinne, I mourned for my people. We refer to Finfinne as *Handhuura Oromiyaa*, meaning the Center of Oromia, the umbilical cord of our people—once a land that exclusively belonged to us, but its misuse was an ugly reminder of past injustices committed against us. There is very little Oromo identity left in the city—no official street names, landmarks, statues, etc. There are a few *Afaan Oromoo* schools and banks. Besides our land rights, we wanted *Afaan Oromoo* recognized as a federal language. Amharic was still Ethiopia's only official working language.

Some Oromos who remained in the city adopted a new identity, language, and religion, fully assimilating to a different social structure. Those who kept their identity as Oromos faced marginalization and discrimination.

I have listened to the arguments of those brave enough to protest against the new plan. 'It is part of this persistent need of oppression by Ethiopian authorities to keep the Oromo people in the shadows!' they say. 'They are violating our rights to self-determination.'

One speaker, a law student whose name I did not know, insisted that the current constitution guarantees the right of nations, nationalities, and peoples to determine their destiny, including the right to secede from the federation through a referendum.

'Remember this too!' he shouted above the milling crowd. 'The Oromo people's fundamental right to self-determination and the right to freely pursue their economic, social, and cultural development are protected under the common Article 1 of the International Covenant on Economic, Social and Cultural Rights. Expanding the territory of Finfinne without the participation of the Oromo people in the decision-making process is a violation of these internationally recognized rights to self-determination.'

He was later arrested, that young man, and I will tell you soon what happened to him. Kebede knew him and kept me informed of what was happening and I feared for him and others known to me who participated in the protests. I argued with myself about my decision to stay away from the marches and gatherings.

'The focus of my career is going abroad.' I remember saying this to Aduna, my brother, as I explained to him the risks of protest. 'I compete in the races in foreign countries and lead my life with what I get from there. If I get involved in the protests I will be arrested and blocked from going abroad for competitions. Preventing my exit to other countries would be enough to destroy my career.'

Every time I went to the Bole airport, a place always under military surveillance, I feared that 'They' would take away my passport. It would not take much to be detained on suspicion alone, because I was trying to help the protesters bn other ways, especially when members of my family were arrested. I gave money to support them and the officials could be watching me, knowing I was the one with the means to help.

'He has money. He's that rich athlete! He is helping others to protest! Arrest him!'

I dreaded hearing those words, but when the *ayyaantuu* in my village asked me for a donation to help those of our religion in trouble, I gave 5,000 *birr.* Then the party officials said I was helping terrorists. They spied on me and followed me when I went to Jaldu. I feared they would hit me and cause an injury.

'You must not come here when there are protests,' my mother pleaded. 'Leave now, Feyisa, before daylight.'

I did not go home as often as I once did when the security threats intensified.

Protests against the Master Plan spread beyond the city. In November of 2015, one occurred in Ginchi, that small town eighty kilometers southwest of Finfinne, where I turn off the main road to go to my village. Ginchi is the last town anyone could think of as a place of violence—it's a sleepy town surrounded by farmlands and a forest reserve in and around the small hills on the outskirts of town. Most of its residents are farmers and small-time traders who run the center of the town.

I like driving through it, seeing the youngsters holding up chickens or bundles of wood for sale. They wave and call out my name. Sometimes I stop and give them gum or lollies. You see all sorts of things in the villages. There was a time when I was amused at the sight of coffins for sale, some covered in plush fabrics, propped up amid the dust and dirt of the main street. Now the color of the red brocade is menacing, a reminder that the makers of coffins do a swift trade in Oromia. Then I see the animals, always the animals too, some poor old broken-down horses and pretty ponies with decorative bridles. The kids beside the road to Jaldu, with their goats and sheep, remind me of the boy I once was.

On a sunny Sunday, a group of young (and some old) residents of the town confronted a government inspection team of not more than half a dozen, according to the story I heard from a young grocery store owner. Residents suspected the officials were there to push through deals to take a nearby field used by local youngsters as a Sunday football pitch and to clear a forest reserve for an upcoming investment project. Officials from the Oromia regional state (to which Ginchi belongs) and the central government denied this, but it was too late to stop scenes of defiance and student-led protest that started from Ginchi and spread throughout the country.

The plans of the authorities in Ginchi triggered protests in at least 400 different locations across all the seventeen zones in Oromia. The brutal crackdown against Oromo protesters was led by the Agazi Special Forces and Liyu Police (special police). They were deployed in my Jaldu district, with heavily armed vehicles and security forces engaged in killing, dragging people from the streets, and taking them to detention centers. I thought of *Lola Mullataa Fayyisoo* (Mullata Fayiso's War), which was fought near here all those years ago, but the local people in this fight did not have guns or military leaders.

Protests in Ambo reached international news agencies. Ambo, the place where I was married, is a university city about thirty kilometers further west from Ginchi. The protest at Ambo University, a week after Ginchi, was lethal. Kebede and I both knew students there and a couple of those who escaped told us what happened.

'We were having dinner at the campus cafeteria when the power went off, not an unusual incident, but after what had happened at Ginchi and other places we were on edge. We wondered if the power cut was some kind of punishment against us for talking about the protests and how we would respond. Once darkness fell, we began throwing our cutlery and chanting "Say No to the Master Plan", a slogan adopted by social media activists.

'A few minutes later, the cafeteria was surrounded by campus police, but they agreed that we could air our grievances peacefully the next morning. That "hold it until morning" promise was not to come. The next morning, the compound was heavily surrounded by not only regional police but also federal police forces.

'On that Monday morning at 8:30 we moved out from our dormitories to start our peaceful demonstration, but police officers approached us and told us to stop. We continued shouting our slogans. More police arrived and started kicking some of us violently. We ran to our dormitories with them in pursuit.'

Most of the protesters were captured or shot; even those who didn't participate in the rally were forced to leave the campus. One of our friends, who wasn't planning to participate in the protest rally, was taken from his dormitory during the police chase. 'All I wanted was to sleep in my bed, but they broke into our dorm and took me and started beating me. I tried to tell them I wasn't a part of the protest rally, but no one was listening. Instead, one of them started hitting me on my face with the butt of his gun. Next thing I know I am at a hospital missing four of my front teeth. It was terrible there. The doctors and nurses were soaked in blood and tears and despair at the condition of their patients. We were many.'

Women went looking for their sons and daughters, calling their names, but most were not permitted to go into the hospital rooms. One mother remained standing outside, refusing to leave because she had been told that her son was there. Federal officers barred the way. A doctor, who knew this woman, marched up to her.

'What are you doing out here, nurse? You should be in there!' He grabbed her arm and took her inside.

'Which one is your son?' he asked softly.

She walked from stretcher to stretcher, her hand across her mouth in horror, unable to recognize him.

'I saw him only yesterday,' she whispered. 'He is tall...good looking....'

She identified him by his clothes. His face was no longer the one she knew. He was the student who had dared to stand up and tell his listeners about international law. He was gone.

'I want to take him home,' she told the doctor.

'You won't be permitted to do that yet. The officers will tell you he is a criminal. This body is a criminal. You will have to get clearance from the Justice Minister. You will be asked to pay money for his body to be released.'

Extortion to you, but we knew that similar claims were made during the Derg years. Regional governors were known as 'The Butcher of Tigray' or 'The Butcher of Gondar'. Revolutionary Guards killed tens of thousands suspected of disloyalty. Then, to claim a body, the family had to reimburse the government for the bullets used in the execution. More holes meant more revenue, so death squads used at least two bullets on each victim.

We've heard this story and many others in our own time.

Blood everywhere, from the bedclothes of a dormitory where students once slept in safety to the body bags which relatives were warned against opening. Funerals were attended by thousands—these occasions were still 'untouchable' by the security forces. They were present though, uninvited, at the services and the burial places.

I have taken part in traditional Oromo funerals of notable citizens, where men on horseback lead the coffins to the grave sites and ride around them, singing and chanting the praises of the deceased, telling the story of his life and deeds. They accompanied the body and spirit to the graveside, where the horses and spirit are released together to run free.

I have cried for the kids—I could not believe the number I saw there in Ambo and Ginchi alone. Not just university students, but many with no jobs, no homes, no help. No hope. They were witnesses to brutality on the streets every day.

I cringed when prisoners describe the methods of torture; mostly kicking and beating, particularly with fists, rubber batons, wooden or metal sticks, or gun butts. But then you heard of guards tying the prisoner in contorted stress positions often with beating on the soles of the feet, electric shocks, mock execution, or death threats involving a gun, beating with electric wire, burning, including with heated metal or molten plastic, chaining or tying hands or ankles together for extended periods (up to several months), rape, including gang rape, and extended solitary confinement.

'How would you bear it?' I asked Kebede as we heard the stories. 'One of my relatives was tortured for four months. They wrote down everything he said and read it back to him. They'd demand, "Did you do this?" Sometimes he's said things just to stop the pain and then later when it was read back, he denied it, and he would be tortured until he confessed again.'

'You could tolerate the torture for a couple of days perhaps.' Kebede had seen many victims of torture. 'Then you'd start confessing to the crime you did not commit to save your life. There is nothing you can do; a lot of people die in the prison due to torture. They are the ones who refuse to confess.'

When I am in a race, I am conscious of the sound of the pounding feet, around me and behind me. As I draw ahead, I listen for the feet and sometimes glance around to see how close the next runner is behind me. If I can't hear the footsteps, I am glad because I am safely in the lead. In Finfinne, before I left in 2016, I was also conscious of footsteps behind me, but on the street, not the racing track. Perhaps it was a policeman or a soldier. Keep going, increase the pace, don't look back, don't run, whatever you do. That is fear.

Bekele Gerba was released in advance of US President Obama's July 2015 visit to Ethiopia, presumably because holding a popular opposition leader in detention was not a good look for the President. On the other hand, at least one opposition party claimed its members were arrested before Obama's visit on suspicion they would make trouble. Obama went to Kenya, his father's homeland, before his big plane and limousines arrived in Finfinne.

There was much media hype about this first visit by a serving American president to Ethiopia, and no expense spared to smarten up places like the Sheraton Hotel, where he stayed. He was here for a couple of days in Ethiopia and the streets were buzzing with gossip about the million dollars or more that the government spent to accommodate the president and his entourage.

Obama was welcomed by Prime Minister Hailemariam Desalegn at the imperial palace, built in 1955 to mark Emperor Haile Selassie's silver jubilee, a grand place from what I've heard. I don't know if it's true, but it's said that the emperor even had a herd of stuffed animals, including cheetahs and lions.

Bekele was not impressed by the presidential visit and fearlessly told reporters that Obama's visit sent all the wrong messages. 'He shouldn't have shown any solidarity with this kind of government, which is repressive, very much authoritarian and very much disliked by its own people. Ethiopia's ruling party controls all of parliament. The Obama administration should pay more attention to the heavy-handed way its ally, Ethiopia, treats political opponents—and should help Ethiopians who are losing their ability to earn a living.'

Bekele was in the US when he said this, welcomed by the diaspora in Washington as a hero, just after the Obama visit to Ethiopia. Oromo supporters in the West had rallied in support, urging for his release from prison in their protest marches and banners. When he was in the US capital, the place of Western power, he agreed to a week of diplomatic work, talking to politicians, human rights groups and Oromo youth. His case was featured in the State Department's annual human rights reports.

'We begged him to stay here,' my friend Tolcha Wagi told me when I was in Washington myself, another dissident, just over a year after Bekele. 'He would have been a good candidate for the "Scholars at Risk" programme, but he went back.'

On the evening of December 23, 2015, Bekele Gerba was back home in Ethiopia, reading at his desk, with his wife and children nearby. Then came the knock at the door. Security men entered.

'We have come to take you in for questioning.'

'What have I done? I have served my prison term. Do you have permission to come into my house?'

They started searching the house as Bekele protested and his family watched helplessly.

Armed federal security forces had surrounded his home and they did not leave until their prisoner was forced into a vehicle and driven away, presumably to Maekelawi, where detainees' basic rights such as access to lawyers, family visits, and their rights not to be tortured, should all be protected by the Constitution. But at Maekelawi they were violated every day.

His wife and children were not allowed to see him, and they feared the worst. The day he was scheduled to appear in court, he disappeared. Later, he was taken to a hospital, where word got out that he had been beaten to unconsciousness during an interrogation at a military camp.

We were all anxious for Bekele, a quiet but forceful voice respected in our generation. In April of 2016, Bekele and twenty-one other leaders were charged under the Anti-Terrorism Proclamation. Bekele was accused of having links with the OLF. The Oromo political prisoners were publicly humiliated, in shameful ways.

'Before our court session last time,' Bekele said in a statement which we read on social media, 'we were forced to put off our formal black suits. We refused to do so because it is our constitutional right to put on any kind of clothes. We wore black to express our grievances and sorrow for more than 50,000 Oromo nationals languishing behind bars and also for the 200 or 300 peaceful protesters recently killed by the regime. Our actions were peaceful and in no way meant to affect the normal court proceedings.

'We were not only denied our rights; we were also verbally abused and insulted. Yesterday afternoon, the guards ordered all of us on today's court appointment list to get out of our cells with all of our clothing. From our collections, they selected and took away all the black ones and dumped the rest. We insisted they stop doing that.

'Other prisoners scavenged over our dumped-out clothes. They then brought some remaining ones and left them in our cells. They didn't stop there. They took us to dark rooms and locked us in there. They physically abused some of my comrades. They are here now, and they can witness what happened.

'We haven't eaten anything since yesterday. We were handcuffed until this morning. They abused us purely based on their racist ideals. Many Oromo prisoners were singled out for tortures and other physical and psychological abuses.

'Institutional racism is the hallmark of the prison house which we are in. They vowed to kill me, saying that all the mess they are in now came because of me. We therefore request this court to relocate us from this prison house, whose *modus operandi* is institutionalized racism. If we get back to that Qilinto prison today, we can't even be sure that we make it back to the next session of this court. Our lives are in real danger. We have been denied family visits. Even today, in this court compound, other people were prohibited from seeing us. We are not being considered as citizens. Why does the government want to run our cases out of public sight?'

Bekele and others were forced to attend court that day in miserably poor clothing, little more than undergarments. At another court appearance he wore an orange monkey suit and he was handcuffed. Qilinto prison is a terrible place. Kebede and I braved it as visitors and there were tears in our eyes when we talked about it. We never lost faith in Bekele, a brave man respected by other Ethiopians, not just Oromos. 'From prison he organized resistance to those who cause suffering and a time of mourning to recognize the suffering of families of those killed,' Kebede told me. 'Many people shaved their heads and grieved for those killed.'

No Oromo family was spared.

Bekele has a daughter and three sons. 'Like anybody else, like a human being, when you miss your family of course you feel sad,' Bekele said when he was asked about them. 'But my family is no different from other peoples' family. For example, there is a family that I know, the husband was in prison and when he was released the wife was taken to prison. Their children are growing up without a father at one time and a mother at another; my children are no better than these.

'And if only my family, if only a group of people enjoys normal life and the great majority are not doing the same, I think your happiness, or your joy cannot be complete. Of course, when I first went there, I thought my family would be affected badly, but they are very courageous, and very supportive psychologically. They were strong and, thanks to many Oromos, my children did not quit school and my family has not suffered as such economically.'

Would they be able to stay strong as the months turned into years for their imprisoned husband and father? Blessed with a son and a daughter, I thought about the cost of public protesting. I looked at Iftu, playing with our children, and I asked myself again, can I risk the good things we have here?

Then I compared my happy life shared with my family and friends to the youth groaning in jail or dead on the streets and I knew I must do something.

President Obama described Ethiopia as a country that was developing very well, but we knew better. We were the witnesses. I looked for an opportunity to negate the propaganda, because I knew that the claims made by him and other world leaders were wrong. I wanted to show the truth about my people to the world.

4

In Finfinne, the jacaranda trees bloom for months in the dry season, great masses of mauve flowers bright against the blue skies. They lift the spirits, these trees, defying the squalor and the poverty all around them. When Iftu and I started our married life, the jacaranda outside our house was in full blossom, but once the flowers finally left the tree, a few clusters reappeared in the spring, as if refusing to give way to the long rainy season to come. The big bunches are replaced by the occasional spray of vibrant color, which made me think about what life was like for most Oromo people. The days when our culture flourished seemed to be over, yet we had short seasons of celebration. We needed these times in our lives.

We were renting a house in Faransay, and Iftu devoted her time to making it a home. My clothes were perfectly folded and my meals carefully prepared. Even my running shoes were cleaned by Iftu. You will see many shoe cleaners on the streets of Finfinne and every other town and village of Ethiopia, kept busy in the rainy season, when the mud spoils many a pair of shoes, and at the height of the dry season, when shoes are thickly coated with dust. But Iftu liked to clean them herself back then and to fetch the water from the tank in the compound. I remembered my mother, the water carrier in our village, and the taste of the sweet spring water.

In our new life, I would run and rest and eat, run and rest and eat; Iftu would cook and clean; cook and clean. Many a time after a post-training sleep, I would get up and find her sitting, just waiting for me to wake so she could serve my meal. She liked her daily outings to the market, choosing fruit, vegetables, and spices and buying *teff* flour for the *buddeena* (*injera*) she made fresh every day. At night we'd sit and talk about many things. Iftu fretted about one of her cousins who went to school with her but could not find work after graduating from university. This was often the case for Oromo women competing for the better jobs.

'She will probably leave to get a job overseas,' Iftu told me. 'Girls need to marry a rich man to live comfortably here! It is hard to find such a man! Aren't I lucky?'

'We depend on my running,' I reminded her. 'Perhaps we won't always have such good money coming in. What if I am injured? Sometimes I will have to go away for a race and you will be left here. How will you manage then?'

Iftu had never worked outside the home. She left school and married me. She did find it hard, the first time I went away, to the Xiamen International Marathon in China.

'I did not know what to do with myself!' She was tearful when I returned. 'I go out to the markets, but I don't need much when there is no meal to prepare for you! My family is so far away!'

'We will get a bigger house,' I promised her. 'Then our family and friends can stay and keep you company.'

After a few more months, I bought a house in Bethel, in the center of town and reasonably close to the airport. Our new home was in a compound with high walls and a guard at the gate. I did not really like being so enclosed, but I wanted security for Iftu, who loved this home with its two big bedrooms, two bathrooms, and large kitchen/living area. We had parking space for two cars—my V8 and a Toyota Yaris for Iftu. She would be able to visit family and friends while I was away.

It may seem to you that I was getting very comfortable in a position of luxury, travelling overseas, flying first class, staying in nice hotels, and enjoying the good life wherever I went. I know it is true that when I first heard about Haile Gebresilassie driving a big car, I wanted to be rich and famous like him and I was becoming comparatively rich, if not famous. I trained hard and I lived well. Haile Gebresilassie is now a wealthy businessman. I made different choices.

Soon our new home was filled with people, sometimes our relatives, sometimes a friend or two. I always wanted a big family home where our family and friends could gather, like they did at my grandfather's when I was a child. I wanted my children to grow up surrounded by those who loved them. I wanted them to have someone like Geti, my grandfather's second wife, in their lives.

Our first child was born about one year after we were married. Our daughter is named Soko, which means 'gold', and I hoped that one day I would win an Olympic gold medal for this tiny baby. When she was older and showing off my medals and trophies to visitors, she said proudly, 'My Dad always likes to win!' I know of others who have called their daughters Kello, the name of the yellow flower that the Oromo love, and this is a good name too. Soko is our golden girl, very dear to me.

In our culture, only women are present at the birth—it is *safuu* (shameful or taboo) for a man to see his wife's private parts. Our family was always present at such special occasions and my mother stayed at our home for several weeks. If she didn't have anything to do back home in the village, she stayed longer. Iftu's family just visited; her grandmother was getting old and did not come to our house, but she was thrilled when we took baby Soko to meet her. We had two house servants as well, so Iftu could rest in the weeks after the birth.

We observed our traditional rituals after Soko was born. Iftu was fed *Buluka* or *moka* soup, made from barley, and *marqaa* porridge, made from *teff*, to make her strong and able to provide breast milk in abundance. On the fifth day, there is a process called *naqna dhiqaa*, which means the washing of mother and baby. Then the father may see the mother. Iftu looked lovely, dressed in a pretty gown to greet me and show me our child, freshly bathed and dressed, her little head peeping above the shawl.

The women there that day were celebrating, in what is called *Hillaancoo*, a song-dance (*Hillaancoo* means 'Something beautiful'):

Yaa hiillaancco, baga hiikamtee

Baga hoofkaltee, baga nuu galtee….

(O *Hillaancoo*, good that you are untied

Good that you are delivered, good that you have come home for us….)

Mother and child must stay in the house till the ninth day, the day of *ulmaa baha* (coming out of seclusion). Then they may go outside to enjoy the fresh air and sunshine.

I want to see such traditions continue, but in some places they are no longer practiced. For instance, men are not permitted to eat the porridge given to the women, who are welcomed with food prepared in anticipation of their visit. The men are given food made exclusively for them, but five days must pass after the baby is born before they eat *gesheroo*, a porridge made from the unrefined grain, *kinche*. I was shocked, after moving to Finfinne, when my friends invited me to their homes after their wives gave birth and served me *marqaa* porridge.

'How come you are feeding me women's *marqaa*?' I protested. 'I don't feel comfortable when you do this. According to Shoa's tradition, men do not eat *marqaa* prepared for the celebration of birth.'

Our traditions are not kept as faithfully in Finfinne as they are in the country.

Our culture celebrates the day of birth as very precious. It is like a wedding, when a lot of food is prepared and we invite our family and our neighbors to come and share our joy in a very special way. We also celebrate New Year (*Qaammee*) and *Masqala* (the equivalent of the Amhara *Meskel*) in August; and Christmas; *Qillee*, in January. Our very special festival is *Irreechaa*, which I have already described to you.

'I have never celebrated my birthday,' Iftu said after we were invited to a birthday party in America. 'I like the idea for our children, Feyisa.'

So we do this now—we celebrate Soko's birthday and that of her brother, Sora, born a couple of years later, in the Western way. In Oromia the name of Sora is interpreted as someone who looks after you when you are old! I think fondly of my plump son, like the 'Bogia' I once was, and try to imagine Iftu and I as old people, cared for in his house. I hope that home will be in Oromia, after all these troubles are over. We want our children to grow up knowing their heritage.

'As much as I can,' I vowed to Iftu as we tried to settle in a foreign land, 'I will help them not forget their language and culture.'

'If we want to teach them *Afaan Oromoo,* it will be difficult,' she replied quietly, 'as they will spend most of their time in a school where only English is used. We too must speak the language of this country.'

I struggled with speaking English, although I could usually understand it when written or spoken to me. I will always be able to speak my own language. 'I must do what I can for them, teach the traditions and celebrate our Oromo holidays.'

'If they know their language,' Iftu said wistfully, 'they will know their traditions too. I hope we can return soon to the places where they will have *Oromumma,* like us. We are the children of the *Qubee* generation and our own language is in our hearts as well as in our mouths.'

The words of the worker at our farm *daadoo* came back to me. 'You cannot separate the history of an ancient race from its spoken language.' You cannot separate a child from his birth language either. Or so I believe.

One of the Oromo cultural practices that I hope to teach Soko is our *gada* system, a political, military, and ritual institution. The Amhara/Tigre elite dismissed *gada* as contradictory to their autocratic, monarchic values; they rejected our law and government and declared the Oromo as stateless. The *gada* system operated effectively, until it was suppressed by King Menelik and subsequent rulers, and I have heard it said that some Oromo scholars compare *gada* with Plato's *Republic,* in which leaders were progressively trained until they reached maturity and assumed public responsibilities.

I'll explain *gada* to you as simply as I can, because it is complicated. It consists of *luba* (classes) that succeed each other every eight years in taking on military, economic, political, and ritual responsibilities. Each class remains in power during a specific term (*gada*), which begins and ends with a formal power transfer ceremony. The Oromo men are divided into five *missensa* (classes or parties), each with specific roles and functions to perform in five stages of eight years each.

Roles and responsibilities begin when you are young; that is, social or generational age and not biological age (which is one to eight years old; anyone born during that period is part of that *missensa*). The terms differ from region to region, but all boys are initiated as *itimako* or *ilman gamme* in the first stage, which begins the socialization process. The second grade, *daballe*, continues the socialization process as well as some military training; the third stage, *folle* or *cusa*, involves military service, under the direction of the *abba dula* (the father of war) and the *abba gada* (the father of *gada*).

In *qondala* or *raba*, the fourth stage, participants prepare to take over power from the exiting *luba* or *gada* leaders. They serve as apprentices to the ruling council, which includes the *abba seraa* (the father of law and justice). In our language there are two terms that express the concept of law: *ada*, or customs, practices, traditions; and *seraa* or *heraa*, law in the formal sense. *Qondala* or *raba* leaders attend council meetings but do not have any decision-making responsibility until the formal transfer of power at the end of the eighth year.

Then the leaders of the previous *missense* retire into an advisory role while the new leaders take on defense and governance in the fifth and final stage, *lubaa*. The system opposes despotic and authoritarian rule and makes provision for the removal of an unfit or corrupt official even if his term of office has not expired. An extensive election campaign is held to elect council officials: the *abba gada*, the *abba dula*, the *abba seraa*, and several others. They serve for one eight-year period only.

The election and transfer of power take place at the beginning of the Oromo New Year, in the *Jarra* ceremony, an event that ends the *gada* of the previous eight years and starts the next one. It is the beginning of a new period, the building of a new future, compared by some to the Greek Olympiad. The transfer-of-power ceremony is the time when the achievements and the failures of the past eight years are discussed, and expectations for the next eight years are outlined. After the ceremony, the council, the *Cafee*, makes laws that last the next eight years.

My desire to become a soldier may well have its origins in the *gada* emphasis on military training. We are trained in the art of warfare from the *daballe* stage, with instruction on precision in throwing spears, skill in horse riding, and self-defense. Centuries ago, when triumphant warfare meant survival for the Oromo, the *folle* and the *qondala* were organized in squadrons and led into campaigns by their the *abba dulas*. This is where the Oromo respect for heroes comes from, as our warriors proved themselves in battle. In modern times, the youth are still expected to learn the skills of horse riding and throwing spears.

According to *Tulema Gada* (the *gada* as practiced in Tulema), I entered the first grade *itimako*, after my father came out of the process seven or eight years ago. Now, if I were at home, I would be in *daballe*. The ages vary from *gosa* to *gosa*. I am older taking each grade than boys in the *Borana Gada*, for example, where the first stage is for younger boys. According to the Borana system, I would now be in *folle* grade, the third grade. The military training would suit me well, as I have yearned to fight the EPRDF government.

Most of the training related to military skills is now expressed in sports and competitions carried out away from the public or official eye of the government or explained as ritual or ceremonial rather than functional. This is why sports are so important to Oromos. Our cultural adulation has transferred from warrior to sports hero. Our champion runner, for example, is our warrior, our brave one, our protector.

The *gada* system is often discussed among young Oromo. It served our country well and we wish that the accountability of leaders and the right to recall, *bukisu*, those who fail in their responsibilities, applied to the current Ethiopian government.

I read as much as I can about our culture, while Iftu teases me about the books I have. 'Our house is like a library!' she said, dusting them and arranging them neatly on the shelves. I talked to her about the *gada* way of doing things.

'Most of our people respect and fear *Gada* very much,' I told her. 'There can be no doubt about the Oromo yearning for democracy and freedom as we knew it in the old days.'

'In a free Oromia,' she asked, 'do you think we will live under the *gada* system?'

'Democratic values have worked well before and can be restored and practiced again. Our liberation must draw on the past to be successful in the future. Think of some of the things we no longer have, like freedom of speech, the right to criticize government people or policies, and the right to debate public issues. In a free Oromia, respect for basic human rights will be restored.'

Just how to remove dictatorial power and replace it with democratic rule exercised the minds of Oromo everywhere in the world. Many of us believe that our political culture and values can at least serve as the foundations for a new democratic society, but until we were able to create it, we were engaged in a terrible struggle against a repressive government.

5

Iftu worried about my safety, especially when I started visiting prisoners in jail and giving them food and clothing. 'Feyisa, we have a family now. I want you to help your friends and family with money, but if you go to the prisons you will be watched, and a charge of some sort will be brought against you. Think how this will affect Soko and Sora.'

'I must do more, Iftu. How can we live the way we do while Oromo's sons and daughters suffer in jail?'

I did not admit to her that I dreaded being injured or killed in a staged car accident; or that someone might ambush me when I trained in the forests around Finfinne. When the doorbell rang at home, I told Iftu not to answer it. I went to the second floor and peered outside before I allowed anyone to enter.

'I am really fearful,' I admitted to Kebede when Iftu could not overhear. 'Being an Oromo makes us suspect.'

'We must not let them hold us hostage to our fears,' he said. 'Just keep on doing what you are doing and refuse to give in to your dread.'

I have always helped others with the money I earn from running. I don't even know the total amount of prize money I have won so far. I can't tell you where the money went.

'The money is as fast as you!' my mother scolded when she heard of another person asking me for a loan. 'It quickly comes and leaves. As an athlete, you should invest the money you get, once you have bought the special food you eat and paid your household expenses.'

'I have such a lot, Hadhaa,' I argued. 'I have to give to others.'

I didn't add that I wanted to do for others what she and my father had not done for me when I was a poor boy at school struggling to have books and clothes and shoes to run. But I now had a good relationship with Hadhaa, especially since our children were born. She was proud of me and boasted of my achievements to anyone who would listen.

I was helping some of her relatives as well. One day, after she had berated me yet again, I sat down and thought about what I had given away and I estimated that it must have been at least three million *birr*. That's about 200,000 US dollars. I remembered giving money to a boy with whom I once minded the animals in Jaldu, to help him through university. After that he borrowed 70,000 *birr* from me to farm his land and he promised to pay me back after a year. I didn't sign a contract as he was my childhood friend, but he never repaid the money.

There were many others like him who borrowed my money and I never saw it or them again. They had the attitude, 'Feyisa is rich. He won't miss this money.' There were young runners in my village I really wanted to help with providing the sports gear I never had when I first started. A pair of good athletic shorts was about 1,500 *birr* (50 USD) and I gave many to runners. I wanted those kids to have a chance.

Elite athletes in Ethiopia should give what they can to help needy people, but some only give through government mechanisms, anticipating something in return, even free land. I would prefer to help farmers buy seed and fertilizer rather than see their land taken from them. I don't think Hadhaa knew about all of the people I helped, but Iftu did. She worried less about the money than about my visits to the prisons.

Her attitude changed because of her brother, Tokuma. He was studying at the Mada Walabu University in Bale, about 400 kilometers south of Finfinne. He telephoned his sister one evening in January of 2016, when student protests continued at many universities in Oromia, including Mada Walabu.

'There has been a protest on campus,' he told Iftu, fear in his voice. 'Many students have been arrested.'

'Come here!' Iftu urged him. 'Bring your friends and stay until things quieten down. You'll be safe with us.'

'We'll wait another day. We don't think we should just run away.'

Iftu worried and fretted until a couple of days later when Tokuma phoned again. It was a Saturday afternoon, about four, when I was just leaving for a training session.

'Iftu, I am really scared.' Tokuma had not seen such violence as he described to us later. 'We are coming to Finfinne.'

The boys did not arrive that night and Iftu could not sleep, sure that they had been arrested. But they stayed the night at Bishoftu, at the home of one of the boys' relatives, before driving on to Finfinne.

'You must stay here now,' I warned them. 'No Oromo student is safe. We are hearing terrible things.'

Iftu fussed over them, making big meals, washing their clothes, exchanging news of family and friends. The boys loved Soko and Sora, playing with them and enjoying our home. They stayed for one week.

Then another friend at the university called. 'You can come back,' he assured them. 'Classes have recommenced.'

Iftu and I both tried to convince Tokuma and his friends to stay. What did it matter to miss a few weeks, when life on the campus was so risky? They did not listen. Perhaps I would have been the same, defiant and bold, as I was when I wanted to go and put out the Bale fires. Only two or three days passed before Tokuma telephoned again.

'The protest has started again! The police are chasing us! We have a place to hide but it may not be enough.'

'Stay where you are, Tokuma!' Iftu pleaded. 'Don't go back to the university.'

We knew that the police were particularly targeting students from the western regions of Oromia. They would know where the students came from. Tokuma and his friends, against all our advice, returned to the university and were immediately arrested.

'Tokuma is in Bale Goba jail!' Iftu met me with these frantic words and many tears when I returned from training. I had driven to Ginchi and then run south through Tulu Bolo to Waliso. This was a long run, with a couple of friends driving my car beside me and offering water. I was preparing for an important race, the Tokyo Marathon, which I hoped to win in preparation for the Olympic Games.

'My father has gone there to visit him,' Iftu went on, calmer now that I was home. 'Tokuma is to appear at the Oromia Regional State Court at Bale Goba. My father will stay there to hear the outcome.'

The court acquitted him, claiming there was no evidence against him, but our relief was short-lived. The federal police re-arrested eleven students, including him, accusing the state court of releasing them because they were Oromo. Tokuma was taken to that dreadful place, Maekelawi prison in Finfinne.

He was led to a dark room and stayed there for a couple of weeks. I had been told by others in Maekelawi that there were many people from different countries detained in different rooms. Arabs, Somalis, Nigerians, and so on were, among other crimes, caught while trying to traffic drugs through the airport. There were also white people.

One room was called *Chellema bet*, meaning dark house, or Siberia, because it was also very cold. Tokuma's hands and feet were shackled and he could not stretch his legs out in such a small cell. There was no mattress to lie on, no covering, only the clothes he was wearing. Biting insects bothered him constantly and he was always hungry, fed dry bread and tea occasionally. He was not permitted the use of a toilet except when on the way to the interrogation room. He was probably not eating enough to defecate.

He was beaten throughout the days in this cell. Sometimes a guard would go to his cell just to beat him, even though the small size of the cell made it difficult for the tormentor. Because of this, the beatings usually took place in the interrogation room. When he was taken from the cell to the investigation room, he was often blindfolded and dragged. The prison officials wanted him to confess to crimes he had not committed.

Tokuma was transferred to a circle-shaped room in which a very narrow sunlight beam enters through the ceiling. Detainees said this room was better than the dark one, but very overcrowded. There were children as young as fourteen, as well as political activists and other well-known figures. Prisoners were allowed a maximum of ten minutes of sunlight per week.

Next to the cell was a filthy toilet that they could use once a day; sometimes early in the morning, sometimes in the afternoon. If they had to go to the toilet at other times, the only option was a stinking bucket in the cell. Tokuma, accustomed to cleanliness and a nice appearance, could not wash himself or his clothes. The boy who was used to a good bed and soft covers at night lay on the cold concrete floor. Worst of all, he could hear screams and threats from the interrogation room throughout the night. He was in constant fear that the police would open the door and he would be the next one dragged to the interrogation room.

Tokuma and his friends suffered very badly in Maekelawi. Some prisoners, when asked what was the worst part, said, 'They put us with criminals, with the real criminals—murderers, thieves, mental people—it was very hard.' This happened to Bekele Gerba and many others.

Finally, prisoners made it to the section of the prison mockingly called the Sheraton, a place where they could at least move around. Natural sunlight came into the cells, but there was no electric light. The lack of water, insufficient food, filthy conditions, and poor hygiene added to the misery for a boy bruised inside and outside.

'Why won't they let us see him?' Iftu asked over and over again. 'We don't know if he is dead or alive.'

This was the usual pattern, denying prisoners the comfort of visitors and refusing to give any information to anxious families. We took food every day, registering the packages under the scornful eyes of guards who abused us if we asked about our brother. 'He is under investigation.' That was one way to describe torture and deprivation.

We were suffering now like many others. Kebede was sympathetic and angry on my behalf, but he knew the way things worked.

'Sometimes if they detain your family member, you need a fortune to even find that detainee,' he said bitterly. 'You may not know if Tokuma is alive or dead for at least two months. Sometimes all you know is that your father or brother or friend was arrested but not where he was taken. You go and ask the prisons and tell them the name of the person you are looking for and they tell you he is not there.

'After taking time and torturing that person, they still don't want to show you that person until he has somehow recovered. They detain people in a dark room where there is no single light beam. So, you suffer to see a detained person. You have to move around detention centers and prisons for months, paying bribes. When you see that detained person at last, you even think they did you a favor just for showing you that person.'

We knew these things happened, but it was worse when someone close to you was suffering. We were in great fear for Tokuma.

'One student was killed at his university,' Iftu's father told us, 'but no one knows who killed him. The victim was from the Amhara ethnic group. It is something at least that Oromo and Amhara were in solidarity during the protest, so the government is suspected of committing the crime to create tension and conflict between Oromo and Amhara students.'

Apparently, a bomb was thrown into the students' dormitories and one building was burnt down. Students do not have access to such an explosive weapon. There was one student whose clothes and school materials were burned in the fire, but police charged him for detonating that bomb.

'It doesn't make sense,' Iftu said, folding and refolding Sora's little trousers. 'If he burned the building why didn't he take his belongings before throwing the bomb?'

'This is the crime they are investigating,' her father said. 'Tokuma and his friends are suspected.'

A month went by before we could see Tokuma. He refused to meet our eyes, for fear he would weep, perhaps, and evaded our questions about the treatment he received. We heard about it all later. I think he feared there would be more torture if he spoke with the guards listening nearby, although it is doubtful they could understand *Afaan Oromoo*. One of the hardest things I have had to do in my life was to walk away with Iftu, leaving Tokuma behind, sitting there with head bowed and tears falling. He was just a boy. There was another time ahead, even harder, when I walked away and forced myself not to look back.

Tokuma was transferred to Qilinto (also known as Qillinxoo or Kilinto) prison. He and his friends were attending hearings at the Federal High Court at Lideta in Finfinne. Iftu made sure she was there on each scheduled date.

'All they do is adjourn the case to a future date!' Iftu came home tired and depressed after yet another court appointment. 'The court didn't say or do anything.'

The day came, though, when she was present as prosecutor's witnesses gave evidence, but the testimony of the witnesses and the charges presented against the accused were very different.

'The judges asked the witnesses to say against whom they were going to testify,' Iftu described it all for me. 'The witnesses mentioned the names of the accused persons and told the court they were there to testify against them. When the court asked the witnesses whether they knew the accused persons, the witnesses replied they only saw the accused persons on the date of the crime. The court asked the witnesses if they could recognize the accused persons, to which the witnesses responded that they can recognize the accused persons.

'Then, when the court ordered the witnesses to point to a specific accused, the witnesses pointed to the wrong accused person! One of the witnesses was asked to point to Tokuma, but he showed the court another accused person. These were the witnesses that were presented against Tokuma and his friends! What chance do they have against unreliable testimony accepted by the court?'

Tokuma and his friends were charged as terrorists. Other charges would follow, after another horrendous event which involved Bekele and Tokuma and Kebede. I will tell you about that before my story is finished.

Iftu and I became regular visitors at Qilinto. At first, she was afraid, but her kind and gentle nature could not ignore the suffering and the pain of the prisoners. She sometimes went alone, when I was training or resting or away running in another place. Soon she was visiting the prison three or four times a week.

'When I visit Tokuma,' she told me softly, apologetically, 'there are other prisoners whose families cannot visit, who are poor or too far away. I am taking food for them too. I give them some of your sports clothes and I also went to Mercato to buy more clothes.'

I took her hand and reassured her. 'I am glad you are doing this, Iftu. Now you understand how I feel. Tomorrow we will go together, with clothes and bed sheets and as much food as we can carry.'

'I don't even know them personally,' Iftu was making a list of what she needed to buy. She and her house workers would be busy all day cooking for the prisoners. 'I just see they are poor and in prison. When I visit they tell me their problems. They talk to my brother too and they help each other.'

We knew too much about prisons and prisoners. There were times when they arrested the suspect's family if they could not find the suspect. They did not identify those arrested, but they were often vulnerable old women and men, just to get to the suspect. The suspect then gave himself up so those in jail because of him were released. You wouldn't allow your father or mother to be tortured because of you, so you surrendered.

'I will go if they arrest my mother because of me,' I told Iftu.

'I don't know how I can manage if you are put in jail.' Iftu was thin and tired, from worry about Tokuma, pity for his companions in prison, and anxiety about me. 'I fear every day that it will happen. I hate to think of you in those places where they will hurt you. The compounds are packed and the prisoners look like animals herded together.'

I was afraid too, but I would not stop. I can tell you story after story, prisoner by prisoner. Here is just one, about a runner, Demssew Tsega Abebe, who placed third in the Houston Marathon, 2012, when I ran first in the half-marathon. I know Demssew well. We have run together. I often met him training around Sululta, twenty kilometers north of Finfinne, and preparing like me to qualify for the Olympic Games in Rio de Janeiro. We sometimes talked about our situation after training.

'My father's land was taken by cadres of government supporters,' he told me. 'Our family and all the farmers were dispossessed. My family has nine children including me and most families are about the same. We had twelve acres of land. We were left with only four acres. How are we to feed the family? The animals?'

We sat down to pull on tracksuits and I nodded, waiting for him to tell me more.

'The government tent doesn't care, but I do not forget. I ran away with my family and our precious land was given to TPLF cadres. My father is an Oromo elder, Feyisa. He is the one at festivals who says, "God bless our people, God bless our animals, God bless our children." How can they be blessed in these times?'

I shook my head. This was a question I often asked myself.

'In 2005 we had the election in Ethiopia, and you know, Feyisa, that our people were ready to elect another government. This government had taken our land. We wanted it back. My father demonstrated with many others. When the police came, I saw one of them hit him with the butt of the gun. They hit me too, and my brother—we were just kids. I was about fifteen.' Demssew's hands were shaking as he described the scene. 'My mother was pregnant and went to the hospital in shock. My Father was in prison for one month, beaten and tortured.'

'What happened to you and the other kids?'

'We are worried about our land. We sold our animals, but no money left. We did not have enough to eat—all of us hungry, going to school, ten kilometers away without food or the proper uniform. After Grade 8 I dropped out of school.'

I understood this situation well. 'Go on,' I said.

'Then I decided to start running. After I dropped out of school I started running—I think: *I can help my mother*. I am happy when I am running. I run with friends, I teach myself. I only had soccer shoes, not good for running. "Oh my God," the others say, "these are not for running! Not right for the road!"

You can see how I related easily to Demssew.

'After I won a competition, I joined St. George's Sports Club in Finfinne. It is hard to improve though, without proper food and right conditions.'

He had a good record, built slowly like mine. I invited Demssew to my home to meet Iftu and share one of her meals. 'I see your good life, Feyisa,' he said as he left. 'I envy you. If I keep going, I hope to be like you one day.'

This was not going to happen. The government authorities asked every athlete to join the EPRDF. I refused every time, although I dreaded the reprisals to my career. I was lucky. They asked Demssew at least ten times. Each time he refused, and they waited for the chance to punish him.

'I know they watch my family,' he said. 'We have protested against them and they never forget. They cannot force me to join, but they can make it hard for me to run. I had a marathon to compete in Dubai, but because one of the organizers was a TPLF man, he said, "If you are not a member, you cannot participate." I am sad. I had done much training. I cry. My wife says "Don't worry. Perhaps you have to wait for another competition. Don't worry."'

I thought of Iftu, who had not faced this challenge yet. Her time would come.

'My wife was making hope for me,' Demssew went on. 'In June of 2013, I had an invitation from the organizers of a race in China to participate. Again I was excluded. Then I think: *I must demonstrate. I will do something to show the world what is happening here.*'

This sounded just like me, but Demssew chose a local protest, hardly likely to make the censored news in Ethiopia, let alone other places. It also had an inevitable outcome. I did not see Demssew after this time, but we met again some months after I made my own protest and he told me what happened. In December of 2015, he was on his way back from training when he saw a demonstration in Sululta. Oromo there were protesting the government land grab.

'You know, Feyisa, that many of us are angry because the government has stolen our land. For a long time the ruling regime has been seizing the land of farmers like my father. They sell the land to foreign companies or give it away to loyal cadres. Why should my father become a day laborer, barely earning enough for my family to live on?'

This much I knew. I wanted to hear about his arrest.

'Five of us athletes are together that day when we join the protest. I didn't think I would be arrested, which is stupid, but I am and one other from our group. The others hide—disappear in the crowd. The security agents know me from the television—they are targeting me. They take me to prison. They demand, "Why are you participating in an illegal demonstration? You are a supporter of the Oromo."

'They torture me. I don't say anything. They beat both feet with a plastic baton to cripple me so I cannot run again. They put the pistol in my mouth. They want to punish me for demonstrating and to prevent me running again. I am worried—I have a kid by that time.'

'What were the conditions like?'

'For three days I was just wearing my sports uniform—a jacket and training pants. I am too cold, and my feet hurt. No food or water at first. Then in the morning and evening, we get bread and tea. No toilet, only a container in the room.

'There are three torturers. They blindfold me and insist that I confess. My friend is not as famous, so he is not beaten as badly, and his feet are not damaged. My wife comes to visit me, but they don't allow her to give clothes and food.'

The same for his family as for Tokuma's.

'I was released after three days, limping badly. I was afraid to go to the government hospital because they might arrest me again. I had my visa for the Houston races in January of 2016, Feyisa. But I could not run.'

I have performed well in Houston, where I held the record for the half-marathon event: 59:22 in 2012. I was not running there in 2016 because I was concentrating on the Tokyo race. Barely able to walk, Demessew boarded the plane to Houston with his team. But instead of running the marathon, he stayed in the country and applied for asylum.

I heard the end of his story when I arrived in the US. He is a brave man who suffered much more than I did. He is the face of Ethiopian athletes punished for protesting their rights. I am glad that an Ethiopian athlete, Lelisa Desisa, came first in the Houston half-marathon that year, and two others were placed first and second in the marathon. Demssew should have been one of them.

The message to the outside world remained the same. Ethiopia was the home of elite runners. No mention ever made of the fact that it was also the prison of peaceful protesters.

The long arm of injustice reached as far as Kenya, the land of some of my athlete heroes. Government investigators went there and arrested Oromos who are now Kenyan nationals and deported them. First stop, Maekelawi. I knew because I talked to a young man called Halkano, brought from Kenya and imprisoned in Maekelawi. I gave him food and clothes.

In relation to this, a decision by the Supreme Court of Kenya on an election result made me proud to be African. Ruling that President Uhuru Kenyatta's victory in the 2017 vote was marred by irregularities and illegalities, the court ordered a fresh vote to be held within sixty days, the first time judges ever overturned a president's victory in an African election. Six judges on the bench upheld a petition by Kenyatta's challenger, Raila Odinga, who claimed that systematic fraud had denied him victory. Outside the building, as well as in slums across the capital, Nairobi, and in Odinga's strongholds in western Kenya, the crowds shouted in disbelieving joy.

Many of the same people had been running for their lives, as police used live ammunition to crush protests triggered by the electoral commission's official declaration of Kenyatta's victory. People were killed, including a six-month-old baby beaten into a coma from which she never recovered, and a teenager hauled out from under his bed and beaten to death in front of his parents. This sounded too much like Ethiopia.

I read the reports online, silently cheering the victories of the poor people. One man said, 'We expected the worst and have been given the best. We have been vindicated and justified. The oppression of Kenya's people has been ended by the stroke of a pen.'

The supreme court made legal and political history in Africa by making a ruling once unthinkable—one that could make other courts on the continent willing to follow. I didn't care whether the decision was right or wrong. What made me happy was knowing that courts can have such positive authority in Africa. The court controlled the power of a president. I hoped this could be a lesson for Ethiopia, but I doubted the government would learn from it.

I felt as happy as if I were a Kenyan myself! This may not mean anything in Western countries, but when this happened in Africa, it made me glad.

Inevitably, Uhuru Kenyatta was re-elected after securing more than 98% of the vote in a contentious rerun election boycotted by Raila Odinga. He urged his supporters to boycott the election too, and activists tried to stop the vote. The usual violence was inflicted on the protesters in Kenya. That country has its own tensions in about forty ethnic groups, whose bonds, I expect, are often stronger than national identity.

Kenya, like Ethiopia, could disintegrate as a nation. However, I tell you that I did not want our country to disintegrate. There are a lot of ethnic groups that have been facing the same problems as the Oromo. These people live in Oromia and in other regions of the country, in Amhara, and even in Tigray.

As I see it, the struggle should include others wanting their freedom, the same as we did. When we get our freedom, we should not forsake other oppressed people. By the time we get our right to self-determination, we should stand for the rights of others. I think that my landlocked country is comparatively small—it only takes a short time for an airplane to leave it. A lot of people would suffer if it is split into different independent countries. Oromia won't face economic hardship if it secedes; Oromia has enough natural resources on which the Ethiopian state depends. But I did not believe this was the way of the future.

What did I wish for my country? I wished it could be a place where human beings and their rights were respected. I wanted good governance and an end to violence and repression. I was a witness to atrocity and grief, a spokesman for a country that had never known real peace.

Sometimes I dreamed at night of the tortures inflicted on innocent people. These torments were too cruel to use on the most hardened criminal. There is a place near the hospital, Tor Hailoch, in Finfinne. If a detainee went through other tortures, he could then be put in a hole there full of big biting ants. He would confess to the crime he didn't commit after being bitten by the ants. I have heard too of detainees hung by their hands so that they couldn't sit, then containers holding two litres of water were attached to their testicles, left overnight.

Let me tell you what happened to a young man who is a family member. He told me that the administrator of that district tortured him by beating him repeatedly. At last, the administrator was tired of beating him and ordered a security guard to continue beating this young man. The security guard beat him the whole night as he was ordered to. You will read of these horrors and worse in reports by Amnesty International and Human Rights Watch, for example. They were not just the bad dreams of an angry Oromo man who wondered how much more his people could take.

Have you ever seen the impact when a bird gets in the way of a fast-moving vehicle? I saw this happen when I was out running beside the road. I heard the thump and turned to see the feathers flying in all directions, some floating to the ground around the limp body. The driver went on his way, heedless of the bird, just another pigeon of no value. At first, because I was nervous, even in a democratic country, I imagined that it could be me, killed like that as I ran alone early in the morning. First the thud, then my body on the roadside. Perhaps I would not die but be left permanently crippled in a road smash, like Abebe Bikila.

I thought of the similarity to Ethiopia, where the might of powerful government forces hit the protesters with huge impact, taking the life of their own country, scattering their people as heedlessly as feathers. How often have I longed, when peace seemed unattainable, to gather my people together to flee in a great exodus from the evil that took Oromo children from their poor homes and their parents from impoverished villages. It was easy for me to leave, but not them. Maybe, Kebede suggested, they would not want to go even if they had the means. 'I wouldn't go. We need all our people to return from exile and live in a peaceful country.'

Not long before I left the country of my birth, perhaps forever, Iftu came home from a visit to Tokuma, very distressed.

'They prohibited us for giving food to Tokuma and the others! Why? What will happen now?'

What happened was predictable. The prisoners were given low quality minimal meals prepared in the prison. Many of them got sick, some died. Their morale, given a little boost with good food brought by women such as Iftu, suffered and the bad diet made their lives so much harder to bear.

6

Depriving human beings of proper food and clean water is a terrible torture. I have known hunger, but not for many years now. Elite athletes are very healthy because of the constant exercise and careful diet. I try hard to lose some weight whenever I approach a competition, eating simple food like rice and vegetables. In Ethiopia, two weeks ahead of the race, I ate less. I stopped eating before my stomach was full and my weight decreased when I did that. I thought the same system should work in the place of exile and I decreased my intake of food for a while. I almost fell when running, my energy exhausted. I wonder if the quality of food in Ethiopia is superior to that of America, as the Ethiopian food is all organic. I had to adjust my diet along with everything else.

I sometimes looked at the medals I have won to remind myself of who I am and what I stand for. I was no longer in the place where I truly belonged.

I recall so many places and races now, that they blur in the memory, but I remember a couple in particular. I did not win a medal at the London Marathon in 2013, but runners remember it because it was held six days after the bombings at the Boston Marathon, won by Lelisa Desisa. The London race began with thirty seconds of silence to honor the victims of the Boston bombing and many runners wore black ribbons.

The April weather in London was ideal for running and colorful crowds packed the streets, undeterred by what had happened in Boston. Every major race has some controversy or other and this time it involved Mo Farah, who started the race, but withdrew, as he had planned. Mo was accused by some of making more money by signing a lucrative contract to run just the first half of the race before making his debut over the full marathon distance in London the next year.

Mo said that his decision to accept the London Marathon's unusual 1½-race deal had nothing to do with cash but was an opportunity to learn about the race without damaging his track preparations for the World Championships in Moscow. 'My aim is to come out here and learn about the race and get used to the course so that next year I'm ready to go. When you become Olympic champion and everything else, when you go into a race, yes there are rewards. But for someone to say, "He's only doing it for those rewards", that's wrong. It wasn't a case of "Yes, I'm getting so much so I'm going to do it." If I did that, it would be wrong, and that's one of the things that hurts.'

It hurts when you have to withdraw from a race too, as I did at those World Championships in Moscow. I was struggling till about the 10-km mark, about fifteen seconds off the lead. Then I managed to catch up to the lead group for a while, but I was in pain and had to stop. It also hurts to read the reports that say, 'Lilesa failed to finish'; listed in the stats as DNF—Did Not Finish. It takes no account of all the work you did to be there for the race. Mo did well in Moscow, as expected, winning gold in the 5,000- and 10,000-meter races.

When you win, the media pounce, wanting to be the first in their own race to get your story. I remember best my win in the Tokyo Marathon in February of 2016, the first marathon win I'd had since the Xiamen Marathon in 2010. I had my twenty-sixth birthday at the start of the month and I had run in seventeen marathons. Now I was running in Tokyo, the scene for Abebe Bikila's second Olympic triumph.

As I have already told you, I recognize the signs in my mind and body that tell me if I will perform well that day. The clear skies in Tokyo matched my mood and I ran easily from the start. In distance races, as short as the 800 meters and as long as the marathon, we are joined by rabbits, runners tasked with leading the race to a certain point (usually about halfway), doing the hard work while the other runners save their energy, then exiting and watching the finish from the sidelines.

Some of the major marathons ban them, but others use rabbits, sometimes as many as a half-dozen. In races longer than the 800 meters, there are frequently two rabbits pulling the field along. There is grumbling about it, but not much from competitors, because we believe the rabbits that run an even pace help everyone. None of us gets upset at the Kenyan pacemakers, who are doing the same thing. We had three rabbits in the Tokyo race and they dropped out at the 30-km mark.

The main opposition for me came from the Kenyan, Dickson Chumba, but in the end it was another Kenyan, Bernard Kipyego, who came in second behind me. I finished in 2:06:56. I began flexing my arms in celebration a kilometer from the finish line!

'It was a tough course,' I told the waiting reporters, 'but I am happy to win. Since my training went well, I knew I could come up with good results. Chumba was running fast from 30 to 35 km, and I knew I had to stay with him. After 40 km, he was not able to keep up the pace and I went to the lead.' I paused and grinned. 'I feel like I have just bought a ticket to Rio!'

That decision remained with the Ethiopian Athletics Federation, but I knew I had to have a good chance. I've broken 2:08:30 nine times, including Tokyo, and broken 2:7 four times, counting Tokyo. My personal best is 2:04:52. Ethiopian runners dominated the Dubai Marathon in January, as they always did—Haile Gebresillassie had the record of winning Dubai three times—but the Dubai competition was not supposed to count in the selection process for the Olympic team. I have run Dubai, coming fourth in 2014. Other top Ethiopian runners were set to compete in Boston and London too, before the final Olympics selection and, sure enough, they were placegetters, including Kenenisa Bekele coming third in London. His times were significant, as you will soon see.

The IAAF (of which the EAF is a member) has a way of determining which runner and which team scores best over the major marathons. Each race is scored separately, and team results are decided by the aggregate of places recorded by the scoring athletes of each team. Points are awarded in increasing order: 1 for the winner, 2 for second, 3 for third, etc. The team with the lowest aggregate of points will be judged the winner.

If a team fails to finish with a complete scoring team, the runners finishing in senior races shall be counted as individuals in the race result and be eligible for the individual prize money. In all races, IAAF member federations may enter a maximum of eight athletes, but no more than six shall be allowed to start in each race, with four to score.

I finished in 2nd place on aggregate result of major marathons in 2015–2016, but I didn't win any prize. Only the person whose aggregate result is first gets the prize. There are six major marathons in a year and they all are on the same level: Chicago, Boston, New York, London, Berlin, and Tokyo. You get 25 points if you win Tokyo. If you win another of these marathons your points would become 50 in total. If there was no other athlete that got 50 points in running these major marathons in that year, you win USD 500,000.

You don't need to compete in all of the marathons. The 2nd place gets 15 points while 3rd place gets 10 points. I didn't know that there was such a rule. I came to know of its existence when they told me that my aggregate result was 2nd after the race in Tokyo. Eliud Kipchoge was the winner on aggregate points. I was surprised when they called my name and said I was 2nd place on aggregate points.

Iftu is amazed at how much I earn. We are both such innocents when it comes to finance and we need to be more business minded because I won't always win such big money. I have often told her the story about Haile Gebresillassie driving a big car in Finfinne. Now I was driving a big car too.

'Do you know, Iftu,' I reflected when we were relaxing at home, the children in bed and the house free of visitors for once, 'cars must have always been a status symbol for athletes. Abebe Bikila was given a white Volkswagen Beetle by Haile Selassie. I was about twelve when I saw Tesfaye Jifar on television after he won the New York Marathon. He came from a family of ten children in Lencha, near Ambo. The ox on the farm gored him when he was fourteen in the right eye, permanently blinding it. Imagine an athlete, needing good peripheral vision, with such a disability.'

'What has that got to do with cars?' Iftu yawned. She'd had a long day with Soko and Sora.

'When his wife Etenesh drove Tesfaye to the airport, she asked him what he would do for her if he won. He said, "I'll give you a brand-new car."'

'Did he keep his promise?'

'Yes he did. She got a gold Pontiac.'

I didn't add that Tesfaye tore his Achilles tendon in 2005 and that was the end of his career as an elite runner. The last time I heard he was driving a Lincoln taxi in Boston, trying to arrange for his family to join him.

'I'm happy with my Yaris,' Iftu said sleepily. Little did she know that one day she would be in the same predicament as Etanish, separated from her husband. I hadn't even thought that far ahead.

Iftu, drowsing beside me, wouldn't be watching Diamond League on television that night! The IAAF Diamond League is an annual series of elite track and field athletic competitions held at different places around the globe. Iftu doesn't want to miss it, but I don't usually watch. I prefer soccer. Iftu fell asleep, but I know when I am away and about to run a race she won't sleep. She is too nervous for me. I have told you already that I don't get nervous, which is surprising when you consider the prestige and purse at stake.

My family and friends marvel at the money to be made by athletes. For example, in the Dubai Marathon they pay USD 200,000 for 1st place, 80,000 for 2nd place, and 40,000 for 3rd place. There is a huge gap between the prizes, but I think they do this to encourage competition. If you run a new world record, you win USD 250,000 and the first five men under 2:04 win 50,000.

Your sponsor also pays you. I won eleven million Japanese yen (around USD 120,000) when I won the Tokyo Marathon. I was paid USD 70,000 for accepting the invitation to participate. In addition, Nike awarded me USD 50,000 because I won the race and added 50,000 on my contract for the next year. So, when you add all that up, Nike gave USD 100,000. All together I got 120,000 + 70,000 +100,000 = USD 290,000 on the Tokyo Marathon alone.

I wear Nike products in training and competition; the latest designs they make each year. I am not allowed to wear other brands, as they pay me to wear their product and market it. Sportswear companies make a lot of money from athletes but so do we. It amazes me to think that this barefoot boy is given thirty pairs of shoes in a year. I have heard about barefoot style shoes— one of them is called Bikila! Experts suggest that we should run barefoot, as we once did, especially if we hope to run sub-two-hour. This is unlikely to happen because almost all of us have shoe sponsorships to honor.

You may think it is immoral for athletes to earn so much. How can it be justified? I don't know the answer, but sports and sports men and women have always had a large following. People all over the world love the glamour of elite athletes and are fascinated by their sleek bodies, focused minds, and dedicated lives. They admire us and follow us as stars or celebrities. Some of the best athletes I know are among the heroes I most admire. I like to think we are role models if we act responsibly, give generously, and run honestly.

We have pressures too, such as obligations to our sponsors to perform well or risk having the sponsorship withdrawn. There is always the risk of injury....

Another concern is having a reputable agent. My first one was from the Adidas company, Gianni Demadonna, an Italian. I didn't have a disagreement with him; he did a lot of good work to develop me. My second agent was an American, Hussein Meki, from Philadelphia. I disagreed with him on some financial issues: I didn't like that he was unreasonably taking the money I labored to get. I am with my third agent now, Federico Rosa, another Italian, and I like him.

After I came home with the big purse from Tokyo, I decided to build a new house in Sululta, where I do most of my training. Houses as well as cars are the status symbols, the evidence of success. It is true that I was proud of my achievements. The new house was very big and Iftu said it took her all day clean it.

'You have house workers for that,' I remonstrated. Iftu has a kidney problem that goes back to the days when her grandmother wanted her to run like Derartu Tulu. 'You should rest more.'

When we moved to Sululta, Iftu and the children sometimes came in the evenings to watch me training. I liked having them there, the little ones running about under Iftu's watchful eyes. They were energetic and I was thankful for their small perfect bodies and inquisitive ways. When I left my country, I missed my favorite places as much as I missed my wider family— places I visited many times, occasionally with Iftu—The Bale Mountains, Wanchi Lake, Dandi Lake. I had a plan to build a house at Wanchi Lake and was looking to buy land. There is a place called Senete in Bale Goba, the highest place in Oromia, which I visited. I didn't visit Hararge, Wollega, and Borana, but I wish now that I had. If I ever returned to Ethiopia, I wanted to see all of it—go to the places I have only read or heard about.

One of my favorite places is Sodere, about 120 kilometers south of Finfinne, known for its hot springs. You would call it a spa town. I invited my friends to join me there every Sunday, as I didn't train on that day. After intensive training on Saturdays I felt exhausted and the hot springs on Sunday were good for recovery. I also took a masseur with me to ease the tension in my muscles and relieve the soreness in my legs and feet.

7

Building the big house in Sululta probably seemed like a futile extravagance to some people. By the time we moved in, I was anticipating Olympic selection. I had made up my mind that I would use the Olympic Games opportunity in some way, so what was I doing with this big house? If nothing else, I reasoned, it was an asset for Iftu and the children. If I was killed or imprisoned and the prize money was gone, she had something.

The year of 2016 was like a decisive point in a marathon, perhaps about three-quarters of the way, or thirty kilometers into the race. By then, you know who the main contenders are, what your mental and physical state is, and what it will take to win the race.

While we were agonising over Tokuma and I was planning my strategy for the Olympic Games, events were coming to a crisis point in Ethiopia. On January 12, 2016, the government announced the cancellation of the Master Plan for Finfinne. We will never know for sure the exact figures, but human rights groups say that at least 150 people died and another 5,000 were arrested by security forces during protests about the Plan.

Add to this—and I haven't touched on these at all in my story—Ethiopia was engaged in about ten domestic armed rebellions, in the regions of Oromia, Tigray, Amhara, and Gambella to the west. There was also long-standing rebel activity in the south-eastern state of Somali, also known as Ogaden. Besides the border dispute with Eritrea, which sparked a war in 1999–2000, the country shares unstable borders with Somalia and South Sudan.

'Do you think the plan has really been scrapped?' I asked Kebede when we met in one of the Kaldi's coffee shops that are popular in Finfinne.

Kebede shrugged. 'I'm sceptical. Will the cancellation really be implemented? Both prime ministers, Meles Zenawi in the past and Hailemariam Desalegn now, have never given in to "terrorists". They recognize that Oromo students and opposition activists present the most serious threat to their government.'

We sipped our coffee in silence.

'I'd like to think,' Kebede went on, 'that the OPDO is finally recognising the error of its ways.'

In a move that took us all by surprise, the OPDO said that, after a three-day meeting, it had resolved to 'fully terminate' the plan. Such rejection of official plans by government members was unprecedented in Ethiopia. Could it also be seen as acknowledging the legitimacy of the protests?

In the face of the large Oromo constituency, the OPDO must have realized that supporting the master plan undermined its grassroots support and influence within the EPRDF. I think I may have already told you that the EPRDF is made up of four ethnic-based political organizations: the TPLF, the Amhara National Democratic Movement (ANDM), the OPDO, and the Southern Ethiopian People's Democratic Movement (SEPDM).

In a televised statement, the Oromia branch of the EPRDF announced the plan had been 'scrapped' after discussions with local residents. The government said it had 'huge respect' for the Oromo people who opposed the Master Plan. But the statement was evasive about the reasons for the opposition, saying it was based on a simple misunderstanding created by a 'lack of transparency'. The announcement was met with derision by activists in Ethiopia and in the diaspora, claiming that the concession was a small victory for protesters but would not be the end of the dispute.

'These concessions are not gifts from the ruling party.' This was Kebede's view. 'It's a hard-fought victory that cost us many Oromo sons and daughters. There will be more. This is a time to mourn, not rejoice.'

The Oromo people were not ready to accept the announcement as a lasting solution to their cries for freedom from eviction, relief from systematic exclusion, and the end of mass incarceration. We had to force the implementation of radical changes. Protests in some Oromia towns continued, including Ambo. Peaceful demonstrations and sit-ins were taking place in schools across the Oromia region.

Tokuma and his friends were still in jail. As the months of 2016 dragged on, they became more despondent. Bekele Gerba was still in jail too, asserting that he was stronger than he was before he went to prison. 'I consider myself more prepared and stronger than before,' he said in a message to his supporters. 'And I can never be out of politics; I don't want to be out of politics.'

We needed his powerful statements to give us hope and courage. As I was counting the cost of what I planned to do, formulating my own life strategy, his words helped me. 'I have dedicated my life to fight injustice, inequality, racism and oppression with passion. To fight for the human rights, dignity and equality of my people by peaceful means and pay any price for this struggle is an honor for me. If I have to ever apologize in this life I dedicated for the struggle it is only for two things. One, if I chose not to speak against the sufferings and anguish of Oromo people enough; and two, if my motive in hiding this suffering was for a lesser purpose than the brotherhood of all people, I will ask the Oromo people to forgive me.'

A poem he wrote in prison appeared on Facebook: 'We Will Never Stop Our Journey!'

Daandiin keenya qoreen guutee	Myriad thorns on our paths
Dugdi keenya ulee quuftee	Countless sticks (beats) on our back
Abdiin osoo hin dhalatin	Before a hope exists
Ifa hin argin	Before we see the light
Nurkaa duute	Our hope obscured
----	----
Nideemna hindhaabbannu	We keep moving we never stop
Miilli nubututes nuti abdii hinkutatnu	Though our feet are worn, we won't despair
Biyya hawwii keenyaa Hin hankaaknu ni geenya	We won't fail we will arrive our land of hope
Karaa dheeraa sana	That long journey
Dheebotaa beela'a	In that hunger and thirst
Imimmaan lolaasaa	With tears washing our face
Dhiiga dhangalaasaa	In that bloodshed
----	----
Dukkana kaleessa qabsoodhaan ibsinee	Illuminating our yesterday's darkness with struggle
Ifa boruu arguuf harrarra dhaabannee	We will see tomorrow's light from today
Kunoo ilaalaa jirra biiftuu ba'uuf jirtu	Here we sight a glimmer of light
Urjiin bilisummaa yommuu calaqqiftu	When the stars of freedom shine.

V

I

The best time of the day at the new house in Sululta was in the evening, after I finished training and we had eaten our meal. When the Olympic Games were drawing close, I wanted to tell stories to Soko and Sora, *Oduu Durii* in our language. Iftu sat beside me, with Sora on her lap and Soko nestled between us. My mother, their grandmother, was sometimes there too and she listened, her eyes faraway at home in Tulu Bultuma village, in the *aanaa*, or district of Jaldu, West Shoa Zone, Ethiopia. Sometimes she corrected me or added a detail I had forgotten.

As the day of my departure approached, I talked about Olympic heroes. I never returned to formal study, but I found out a lot on the Internet. 'Tell us the story of Pheidippides!' Soko begged each time. I know the legend well now, with all its variations.

'Pheidippides is a day runner,' I always began with this, as the idea of a day runner appealed to me. 'Others call him a courier or herald.' These words were also taking on new meaning. 'He is sent to Sparta to ask for help when the enemy, the Persians, land at a place called Marathon in Greece. He runs about 240 kilometers in two days! But the Spartans will not be able to come immediately to help. Pheidippides has to run all the way back to the army in Marathon and tell them the bad news.'

'Tell us how he dies!' This was the bit that Soko liked best and she was impatient, bouncing up and down. Sora thoughtfully sucked his thumb. I was not to be hurried—the would-be soldier in me wanted the military part told.

'The Greeks decide to send about 10,000 soldiers out to meet the Persians, whose force is about three times larger. No one knows the whole truth about the famous Battle; although the Persians greatly outnumber them, the Greeks somehow crush the Persians.'

I paused and grinned at Soko. 'Go on, Baba, go on!'

'Pheidippides runs in full armour, hot from the battle, all the way to Athens, about forty kilometers, to announce the victory. All he can say is, "Hail! We are victorious!" and straightaway dies.'

'Hail! We are victorious!' Soko repeated, clapping her hands. 'Tell it again, Baba!'

'Time for bed,' Iftu decided. 'Baba will tell us another story tomorrow night.'

Iftu liked to hear the story of Spiridon Louis, who won the first modern-day marathon at the 1896 Summer Olympics. Her hopes were high for my Olympic gold medal. The children were not as interested in Spiridon Louis, but I saw myself in his ordinary beginning. He was a water carrier, a detail that Hadhaa insisted upon as we relived Louis.

'He is born in the town of Marousi, which is now a suburb to the north of Athens, into a poor family,' I explained. 'Louis's father sells mineral water— like we get from Ambo—in Athens, a city then without a central water supply, and Louis helps him by transporting it.

'The Greeks are very enthusiastic about the first Olympic Games, but disappointed that no track-and-field event has yet been won by a Greek competitor. The victory of an American in the discus throw, a classical Greek event, hurts. Because of its special history, the public desperately wants the marathon to be won by one of their countrymen.'

The kids were yawning, Hadhaa went to the kitchen, but Iftu wanted the rest of the story told.

'They gather along the dusty road to watch the runners. The next bit may not be true. Louis makes a stop at a local inn to drink a glass of wine, although some say he just ate half an orange and drank a glass of cognac, another strong drink. After asking where the other runners are placed, he declares he will overtake them all before the end. And he does!'

'What do the spectators in the stadium say, Soko?' She always liked the end part of a story.

'"Hellene, Hellene!" And two Greek princes meet him and run with him on his final lap.'

'For a finishing time of 2:58:50.'

Iftu repeated the winner's words to me, smiling. '"That hour was something unimaginable and it still appears to me in my memory like a dream. Twigs and flowers were raining down on me. Everybody was calling out my name and throwing their hats in the air."'

Hadhaa returned for the bit she liked to hear. 'The king offers Louis any gift he cares to ask for and all Louis can think of is a donkey-drawn carriage to help him in his water-carrying business!'

We all laughed, even though we had heard the story a few times now. Spiridon Louis retreated to his hometown, never again competing in running. He lived a quiet life, working as a farmer. Perhaps this will be my final destiny one day. He also worked as a local police officer, then was arrested on charges of falsifying military documents and imprisoned. After more than a year in jail, he was found not guilty and acquitted. I wished such a verdict could be reached for Tokuma and Bekele Gerba and many others.

The story ended for me with Spiridon's appearance as guest of honor at the 1936 Summer Olympics, held in Berlin. After bearing the standard of the Greek team during the opening ceremonies, he was received by Adolf Hitler. Spiridon Louis offered Hitler an olive branch from Olympia, the birthplace of the Olympic Games, as a symbol of peace. Imagine that, a peace offering to a ruthless leader whose hatred of the Jews was something like our government's loathing for the Oromo. I applauded African American Jesse Owens, who shattered Nazi beliefs in Aryan superiority and a Master Race with his four gold medals in Berlin.

It was ironic perhaps that a Korean runner won the marathon, competing for the Empire of Japan team. Japan soon showed itself to be an aggressor, like the Italians in Ethiopia. A few years after the Olympic Games, Hitler's forces invaded Greece, but not before the Greeks defeated the Italians in battle as soundly as they did the Persians at Marathon. Spiridon died without witnessing the invasion of his country.

'Hatred, imprisonment, war,' I voiced my thoughts aloud to Iftu. 'Will it always be like this for Soko and Sora?'

'After what has happened to Tokuma,' she said, picking up their toys from the floor, 'I fear for them.'

She looked up at me with tears in her eyes. 'And you, Feyisa. You are so angry sometimes. I know that when you hear of yet another wrong you don't eat. People love and respect you, but I know how persistent you are and how angry you get. You must not do anything out of anger.'

'I must do more, Iftu. I cannot promise you that I will always remain silent.'

Iftu sat beside me and took my hand. '*Badiin biyyaa wajjinii badhaadha*,' she said softly. '"Sharing burdens with everyone is a blessing." We are doing that as best we can, going to the prisons and sharing our home and money.'

But it bothered me that the Western world for the most part did not know or did not care about what was happening in Ethiopia. What would it take to gain attention?

I thought of what it took to have Mamo Wolde, the Olympic marathon runner, released from prison. Soko and Sora heard his story too.

'You have heard my stories about Abebe Bikila,' I began. Soko nodded and jumped up and down impatiently. Sora stared at me solemnly before seeking refuge on his mother's lap. 'He is struggling with an injury when he goes to Mexico City for the Games in 1968. He has started to limp, because of hamstring problems.'

Soko rubbed the back of her thigh in sympathy. She knew about hamstrings.

'There must have been something more,' I continued, 'because Abebe Bikila tries to convince his coach that it is nothing and that his massages will help it to go away.'

I was on familiar ground here for I have had similar problems, insisting that only a certain masseur in Finfinne can always put it right. I am stubborn.

'Anyway, Abebe goes to Mexico City to run the marathon and so does Mamo Wolde. Some people say that the two athletes are good friends, but others disagree. One man says that when they train or race together, Abebe shouts, "Get back, Mamo!" Mamo is an experienced runner; he competes in the 1956 Olympic marathon before Abebe races in Rome. There are rumours too that Abebe, my hero, is drinking too much.'

'What happens in Mexico?' Soko as usual wanted to hear the end.

'Abebe has not even reached halfway when he turns and signals Mamo to join him at the front of the race. This is what he says:

"Lieutenant Wolde."

"Captain Bikila."

"I'm not finishing this race."

"Sorry, sir."

"But Lieutenant, you will win this race."

"Sir, yes sir."

"Don't let me down."

"No, sir."

'Mamo takes off and wins easily. Afterwards Abebe comes to attention and salutes; Mamo returns the salute.'

Soko and Sora both demonstrated the salute with me.

'Mamo Wolde wins the bronze medal at the Munich Olympics in 1972. Abebe Bikila is there in a wheelchair, paralyzed after a road accident in his Volkswagen. Mamo is promoted to captain in the Imperial Guard.'

'Emperor Haile Selassie promises Mamo a nice house, but he never gets it because the Emperor and his men are killed. The Derg take over and Mamo is given a lowly job in a *kebele*, a sort of neighborhood council, and, although his first wife dies, he marries a young fan, Aberash. Mamo and Aberash are Oromo and they have two children.'

I met Iftu's eyes, trying to read something in them.

'Mamo is a great storyteller and can be funny.'

'Like you, Baba!' said loyal Soko.

'He goes to Houston, where I have won races. A fan comes up to him and says, "I love you!" Mamo says, "Lady, love means sweat in Amharic. Don't say love. Don't put your love on me!"'

Soko giggled and planted a damp kiss on my arm.

'Back in Ethiopia the new government takes over and imprisons anyone suspected of killing people in the Red Terror, including Mamo. He is there for years before the West takes notice—he hasn't been charged with a crime. When the International Olympic Committee demands an explanation, it is told to wait for the verdict of the court.'

Iftu studied her hands. I knew she was thinking of Tokuma.

'Aberash believes her husband is innocent. "Here is what happened," she says. "It was 1978, at the height of the Terror. Mamo said one night he was ordered by a top *kebele* official to put on his uniform, with his pistol, and go to a nightclub. Mamo thought this was protocol, that he was to meet an important visitor. When he got there, he saw the official and some others had a boy with his hands tied. He was about fifteen. He might have been in some youth group, fighting against the Derg. The official took the boy out and shot him. Then they told Mamo to go to the body of the boy. At first he refused, but at that time to refuse an official was to be dead yourself, so finally he went. The boy was dead. The official told Mamo to shoot the body again, because there had to be two holes. The policy. Mamo said he went to ten feet away and shot and purposely missed. Lots of people saw him miss.

'In 1992, when the court took testimony, many witnesses said Mamo didn't kill anybody. Only one accused him. The official who shot the boy wants to blame Mamo to save himself. The prosecutors say they have to keep him in detention until they bring charges, but they never do. He just waits."

'Mamo is ill in the End of the World Prison and all he can think about is clearing his name, getting out, and using stone to rebuild the mud and sticks house his family lives in. He is a penniless, imprisoned hero. At last, with huge support from sporting ambassadors, runners, churches, schools, and many others, Mamo is released. Even Haile Gebresillassie raises money to help pay off his prison debts.'

I thought warmly of Haile then and I still appreciate his show of support for a man who was most likely innocent. But how could Haile say over the years that our country was at peace? He must have known friends and relatives in prison. No one was spared the association. I glanced at Iftu before I finished the story.

'Mamo and Aberash have made a pact. When she is visiting the prison one Sunday, he takes her hand through the fence and whispers that the only reason he is alive to receive such things as flags and invitations to marathons is her tireless struggle to visit him with food and support and the sight of his kids growing up safe and strong and loving. "So," he says, "I am going to make a vow. When I finally get out of here—and I am going to get out of here—and when I receive another invitation to go out of the country and be celebrated, I'm not going to go, not unless I can take you too, because you are the marathoner here. You are enduring as much as I am."

'Aberash is overwhelmed. She wets her fingers with her tears and touches her husband's hand with them in acceptance, because no Ethiopian man can show greater love than by taking his wife out into the wider world, proudly introducing her to other peoples and other cultures. She has often said that being able to visit the places where Mamo has run and meet the people he's run with is her greatest possible dream.'

This was a long story and Sora was asleep, Iftu's arms around him. Soko had her hands clasped around my neck, listening, but probably not understanding everything. Like the boy I was, listening to my grandfather, she loved the sound of the stories, the expressive way I told them, and the peace of the room when all was well with us. 'At last Mamo is released from prison and goes home to Aberash and his children. "Thank God, I am free at last," he says. "I hold no malice toward anyone. I've been found guilty, yet I consider myself innocent. I served more than nine years in prison and that's enough. I've nothing else to say."'

Mamo dies not long after his release, before he can keep his promise to Aberash. At his funeral, Ethiopian athletes, including Haile Gebresilassie, form a guard of honor, dressed in green, yellow, and red Olympic uniforms. Mamo is buried in St. Joseph's Cemetery in Finfinne, next to Abebe Bikila, who died soon after the Munich Olympics. Bronze statues of the two heroes were built at the graves, but Mamo's is not there any more.'

Iftu was silent, twisting one of Sora's curls around her finger. Soko was on my knee, touching my face and studying me.

'What happened to Aberash and the children?' Iftu asked softly.

'The children, Tabor and Addis Wolde, moved to Iowa, in the United States. Aberash joined them there.'

We put our children to bed and Iftu said she was tired too and went to bed. Something was bothering her. I returned to the lounge room, thinking about my flawed heroes. Abebe Bikila became arrogant and drunken before his last Olympic race. Mamo Wolde's story of innocence was disbelieved by some people and he seemed from my reading to be too much in bondage to Abebe Bikila. Haile Gebresillassie built a business empire, not standing up publicly for his Oromo brothers and sisters.

I questioned my own motives in the action I planned to take. Elite athletes are rewarded when they are successful and I enjoy the attention when I win a race—the microphones and cameras of the media, the trophy in my hand and the purse in my pocket, the return home tired and triumphant. This opportunity, if I got it, would receive attention of a different kind and have a predictable outcome. I would be a hero to many and an enemy of the state to others. I might be separated from Iftu and the children for years, like Mamo Wolde, Demssew Tsega Abebe, or Tesfaye Jifar. I might be killed.

I was sure to be misunderstood. Criticism and condemnation are painful, like blisters on the feet. For days your training is impeded because of the sores which resist all your attempts to soothe them. You use bandages to cover the spots and you get back up on your feet and run despite the hurt. Sometimes the blisters take weeks to heal properly and the scars remain.

I needed sleep. I was training early in the morning and a clear head was necessary. A double-minded man is unstable in all his ways. If I were to perform well at the Olympics, I had to be fully prepared, yet sleep sometimes eluded me when I brooded on the wrongs all around me that I could not put right.

<h2 style="text-align:center">2</h2>

Why was I thinking about Eliud Kipchoge? It must be the thought of running the race despite painful blisters. Eliud and I both competed in the Berlin Marathon in September of 2015. He ran much of the race with the insoles hanging loose from his shoes, a footwear malfunction that caused pain and distraction through the last part of the race. At the pace we were running, he could not risk stopping. He determined to finish the race.

Conditions were cool and sunny and the front runners were hopeful of breaking the world record of 2:02:57, set by Dennis Kimetto in Berlin the previous year. Kipchoge, the 2015 winner in London, was the one most likely to do it. The men's elite field in London was dubbed the 'clash of the champions' by race organizers: three Kenyans—Eliud, Wilson Kipsang, and Dennis Kimetto—were the main contenders. In Berlin, however, Eliud's hopes of a new record were dashed, all because of faulty shoes and blisters. He won, though, in 2:04:00.

Eliud is a gracious man, well-liked among the runners. He told us afterwards that the glue on the insole did not stick. 'It is a good shoe and I have tested that same shoe in training, but that is sport. I have to accept it. I think I would have run faster than that, but I don't know the time.'

I have read a lot about Eliud Kipchoge, following his career and that of other Kenyan runners who intrigue me. He started out running shorter distances and some people were surprised that he did not move to road running earlier. I have heard him insist that the lessons he learnt on the track were crucial to his success. 'It is an old-school mentality to run on the track first and then move to the road. Running is not only a physical exercise but also mental, so we had a good plan with my coach and manager to compete for ten years on track and then make the transition to the road. After making the transition it was very smooth.'

You'll notice that Eliud is able to use his track speed to run clear of the field well in advance of the finish line. Another Eliud, the Kenyan runner Eliud Kiptanui, ran second in Berlin and I came in third with a time of 2:06:57. Two other Kenyans followed me in fourth and fifth place.

The race in Berlin was important to us, as part of the lead-up to the Olympic Games. Kipchoge planned to take three weeks off to recover before targeting a spring marathon, but like me he was mostly looking ahead to the 2016 Olympic Marathon. Our minds were fixed on Rio de Janeiro. Eliud won the London Marathon in April of 2016—he would be in the Kenyan team at the Olympic Games, no doubt about that. I won Tokyo in February, when I was so buoyant that I reckoned I had just bought a ticket to Rio! The truth was that I had doubts about my selection.

You never knew what could happen with the Olympic Games committee of the EAF. Instead of trials, where the top-three finishers qualify for the Olympics, selection is weighted on past performances. Kenya has a similar selection process. The process had problems and, from all I could make out, the persons who made the selection were not experts. They issued the rules of selection a year ahead of the Olympics, including the rule that they would select an athlete who had run only two marathons in the year. This was based on the assumption that an athlete who ran more than two marathons would have exhausted his energy.

The second requirement was that an athlete should only be considered for selection if he ran the World Marathon Majors—Chicago, Berlin, Tokyo, New York, Boston, and London. They would not consider other marathons like Dubai. Performance in the Athletics World Championships in 2015 was another factor.

But they did not respect the requirements they issued themselves, because, when athletes ran the Dubai Marathon and registered fast times, they were eligible. They also selected an athlete who ran three or four marathons within a year, disregarding the rules. I ran only two major marathons, Tokyo and Berlin, to observe the rule, although I could have earned good money running in Dubai. Other athletes registered fast times in the Dubai Marathon, held in January, as the flat course is favorable for marathon runners. When they selected athletes who ran the Dubai Marathon, I challenged them with the rules they had issued.

'You are ignoring your own rules!' I argued. 'Dubai is not supposed to count. And how do you explain the selection of the runner who ran more than two marathons? We are all training and planning for selection, but you are not giving us a fair chance.'

Others protested too and the selectors reversed their decision and excluded those athletes who had not followed the rules. Then *they* were angry and said, 'You have already selected us! You cannot leave us out now!' The dispute was unsettling to our schedules and our expectations.

I think it was a wrong process because members of the selection committee were unqualified and incompetent. I am not accusing them of being corrupt. I had fulfilled the requirements and should have been selected as number one on the list, but at one stage I placed fifth, which meant I would have been an alternative or what you call a reserve only.

Tigist Tufa, the 2015 London Marathon champion, was supposed to be Number 1 on the women's ticket. She met all the criteria. She took her protest to the local media and her case was reviewed. She was allocated Number 3. If nobody complains, nothing is done.

The major upset was the exclusion of Kenenisa Bekele from the team. He had changed from shorter distance to marathon, like Eliud Kipchoge, and made his marathon debut in Paris in 2014. He had missed more than a year of marathon running because of injury, but returned to finish third at the London Marathon in April of 2016. He had also won the Great Manchester Run 10-km race the following month.

We have not had a good relationship. Aside from that, I did not think Kenenisa had the right qualifications for Rio de Janeiro. But because he is such a talented athlete, a three-time Olympic champion and a world champion over shorter distances, his exclusion came to represent our athletes' general discontent with the EAF. I followed the public protest, but I did not participate.

At a news conference, Alebachew Nigusse, president of the EAF, said that Bekele Kenenisa had a big place in our athletics history, but he failed to qualify. 'That's final and there will be no re-run of the marathon results. We couldn't really change the criteria again to bring him back just because he is Kenenisa. We are sorry but that's not possible.'

Then Haile Gebresillassie and about 100 other athletes protested against the EAF outside its headquarters at the National Stadium in Finfinne. The athletes disagreed with the qualifying rules, claimed they were told too late about them, and protested against what they saw as mismanagement by officials. They were not arrested.

Kenenisa complained about a lack of competence and accused officials of chasing personal interests. In his opinion the selection process was biased and the result unjust. He threatened to never run for Ethiopia again.

In another televised interview, I heard his bitterness. 'The Federation set criteria they knew very well would rule me out. I finished third in the

London Marathon (in April) when I was far from 100 percent fit. I'd done my preparation in full. Everyone knows that London is the toughest marathon, except the people from the Federation. There is a group there that knows nothing about athletics. According to their criteria, I'm only seventh in the selection list. That they did not consider what I have done for Ethiopian athletics is one thing, but the problem is that they have not considered that my performances have been no worse than those who have been selected.'

Haile Gebresillassie addressed the gathering of athletes claiming that the Federation was marred with incompetency. Then he said something that made me very cross. 'If I was on the selection committee my first choice would be Kenenisa. An athlete like Kenenisa, it doesn't matter if he wins or not. Morally his presence means a lot for the rest of the group. That's why I wish to see him in Rio.'

Journalists picked up the story, adding their own bias. Fikir Yilikal, a sports journalist with Radio Bisrat for a long time, said that he had never before seen an organized protest such as this one from Ethiopian athletes. He saw the relationship between the federation and the athletes as a problem, daring to say that the current leadership was not fit to lead. Yilikal said there were doubts about training programmes too. He gloomily predicted: 'I don't expect glamorous results in Rio as in past Olympics.'

Our preparation for the Games was also disrupted by concerns over Ethiopia's drug-testing systems. A few months before the big event, the IAAF governing body named Ethiopia as one of five countries in 'critical care', so the EAF announced that it would carry out doping tests on 200 of us. Six athletes were suspended on suspicion of doping and two were barred from competition for four years after testing positive for banned substances.

Competitors and organizers were sure to look at Kenya and Ethiopia with suspicion because our runners dominated the distance races. Both countries are listed as having Regional Anti-Doping Agencies, a programme of the World Anti-Doping Agency, designed to help in regions of the world where no quality anti-doping activities have been established. Athletes from countries with well-funded anti-doping programmes (like the United States and United Kingdom) are tested more frequently than athletes from countries without the funds. The World Marathon Majors attempted to change this by contributing funds to the IAAF for additional testing elsewhere, especially in Kenya and Ethiopia.

Most elite athletes want a clean sport culture. I've heard that Kenyan athletes also took protest action some months before the Games against their own home federation, Athletics Kenya, following allegations of corruption among officials. It's sad but true that African countries are often treated with mistrust, but it it's also true that not all officials are corrupt and nor are all the athletes.

Anyway, you may remember that I told you about Haile Gebresillassie becoming President of the EAF after the Games. One of his first declarations was about the EAF's decision to start imposing lifetime bans on drug cheats as a way of restoring credibility. Haile's 'zero tolerance' is stricter than that imposed by the International Olympic Committee (IOC). Under their rules, athletes who fail drug tests can face four-year bans, but after that they are allowed to represent their country in any international event, including the Olympic Games. Haile reckoned he was living proof that an athlete can succeed without drugs and that was true for most of us.

All the controversies seemed like a vote of no confidence for the chosen Olympians, undermining our chances and causing more trouble. There was also criticism about the absence of Lelisa Desisa, another Oromo runner born just a couple of months before me, who had won Boston a couple of times. Lelisa was a sentimental favorite to many Ethiopians who followed the sport. He was not hurt in the Boston Marathon bombing that shook us all in 2013, but he returned his winner's medal to the city, in honor of the victims of the bombings. I can recall hearing him say on television, 'I am the champion, and in a few hours my happiness is sadness. Sport should never be used as a battleground.' That should also apply to the selection process for elite athletes. Lelisa and I had a good friendship, but his regard for me faltered when I chose to protest.

Lelisa Desisa was listed as an 'alternate' along with Olympic gold medallist Adhane Tsegay. Bekele made a late attempt to get on the team in the 10,000-meter event, but he 'failed to finish' at the trials at Hengelo, in the Netherlands.

The EAF finally announced its men's marathon team for the Olympics: Tesfaye Abera, the 2016 Dubai and Hamburg Marathon winner; Lemi Berhanu, the 2016 Boston Marathon winner; and Feyisa Lelisa. None of us had participated in previous Olympics.

We moved to the Ararat Hotel some weeks before the Olympics to sleep and eat there, but we did not train together with the same coach. We all had our own coaches and trained separately at familiar places around Finfinne— in Bishoftu, Sululta, Kaliti, Entoto, Sendafa, and so on. I wanted to give this Olympic chance my all, so I told family and friends to honor my need for total focus without distraction.

'I do not want to have anything disturb my concentration,' I explained to Iftu. 'Even if my father should die, do not tell me about it until after the race.'

I had determined to make a public gesture, a protest sign, knowing it would only be effective if I won a medal.

The EAF held meetings to give advice and instructions, but I didn't attend, nor did I go to the farewell party arranged by the President of Ethiopia, Mulatu Teshome, at the National Palace. My heart was not in meeting him and his top men when many people were being killed and many more tortured. I was angry and I didn't want to see them, but most athletes were happy to go to the party. How could I feast with the people who killed my Oromo family? They spoke to us as if we were children and didn't have knowledge about anything. They falsely celebrated us by saying, 'You are the country's ambassadors. Maintain the culture of victorious athletes and hoist the national flag at the Olympics!'

Seventy-seven delegates were going to Brazil—forty-one athletes, twenty-seven officials, four distinguished guests, and five journalists. Apart from the coaches, most of whom were Oromo, the extras didn't contribute anything. They went there for the overseas trip and the entitlements. They were mostly Tigre and some Amhara who were loyal to the Tigres and not one Oromo among them. The dissident athlete kept his distance—training, eating, sleeping…training, eating, sleeping….

3

The wet season, *birra,* started as our training intensified. Long lines of bright umbrellas appeared in the streets, held by those waiting for ages in the rain for buses and taxis. A grey cloud descended over me, to match the skies, but now and then the sun shone, until the thunder heads built up once more. The cause of my concern was Sora, while the chatter and charm of Soko gave me the glad times.

Ever since he was a baby, Sora had not wanted to have much to do with me, always favoring Iftu. He was a chubby child with a grave expression, shrewd and watchful beyond his years. In the weeks before I left for the Olympic Games he would not eat if I did not feed him. Sometimes I came home from the Ararat Hotel or running on the roads near Sululta to find Sora stubbornly refusing the meal in front of him and Iftu anxious because she could not understand the change in his behavior.

'What is wrong with him? He only wants you now, all the time.'

'Perhaps he is just doing what boys do,' I suggested, although I couldn't imagine ever preferring my father over my mother or Geti.

Sora cried if I left the room or the house without him. My bedroom was on the second floor and he could not easily manage the stairs. He cried for me to come and get him. Often as I lay resting after training I would hear him call, 'Ababa!' over and over again, till Iftu distracted him, usually showing him my car to reassure him that I was at home, or taking him for a walk outside in the compound. In a way, I was glad to be at the hotel much of the time, because there I did not have the small figure trailing me, crying to be fed or picked up.

Sora's eyes were disconcerting when I fed him. He stared into my eyes, as if he could see beyond them into my thoughts. I wondered, could he see in my eyes what I planned to do? Could a child so young be taking responsibility already for his name, wanting to look after me?

Sora's beseeching ways unsettled me so much that I worried about my situation day and night. At one point, after he had implored me once more to feed him, I wanted to change my mind about the protest in Rio de Janeiro. As I ran along the muddy roads near our home, his face was before me and my vision blurred with rain and tears. 'I must not let this opportunity go,' I said aloud to the trees that I passed. 'Sora will be OK. I am probably imagining that he knows something and tries to hold me back. I am protesting for him and Soko as well as all Oromos so that one day they will live in a free Ethiopia.'

I was very emotional at that time. I was feeling more intensely the deaths and tortures of others. I wanted to take my wife and children to a safe place before I left, but I could not see how to do this. When Iftu gently questioned my silences and restless sleep, I hoped she was satisfied with my replies.

'All the arrests and the killing, Iftu. They get to me sometimes. Look at the blood in the puddles on the streets and the battered bodies lying still while the rain falls on them. You feel it too when we go the jails and see how pitiful the prisoners look.'

She nodded, putting one arm around my shoulders and resting her head against me. We sat like that for a long time, as I argued with myself about telling her my plan. Deceit was adding to the darkness in my soul, but she would try to stop me, and I might be easily persuaded while she was close and warm and caring. Most of all, I did not want her implicated in what I was about to do.

I had a plan to distract my thoughts and to distance myself a little from the family. I was going to Jaldu to arrange the planting of many trees on the land where I once cared for animals. Ten thousand trees are there now as a memorial for the trees and the Oromo youth cruelly cut down. I saw Sora's eyes in my mother's, though, when I asked if I could plant the trees on her land. I think she suspected my motives, seeing with a mother's eyes that there was something here she should know about. My father's long stare, as if for once he could see in the request something bigger than himself, also stayed with me as I left Jaldu.

All the rain-soaked homeland looked vulnerable and forlorn as I drove away, in mourning for its children. Oromo soil, *Biyyee Oromoo*, soil of my father's land. *Biyyoon biyyaa abbaa koo nagaa nagaa.* The soil of my fatherland, farewell.

From that day, when I left Jaldu for the last time, I knew there was an alien spot inside me—a lonely, cold, unhappy place—the place of grief deeper and more desolate than anywhere I went for my grandfather or Geti or the dead sheep or for Bilisse. I didn't want to go there, but my thoughts and feelings dragged me there day after day. *Kan booyee nu raasu garaa garaa…*What cries and trembles is the heart, the heart….

My need to remain steadfast was met by the events of Friday the 5th and Saturday the 6th of August, 2016, just days before I departed. Through social media we all heard about the Grand Rally for Freedom, Justice, Liberty, Dignity, and Democracy for All. Its Facebook page described the event as a national act of protest by the Oromo and non-Oromo citizens of Ethiopia to gather in unison to express deep-seated mass grievances, country-wide anguish and suffering, and widespread violation of rights perpetrated by the TPLF regime.

In every month so far in 2016, many thousands across Oromia had taken to the streets, demanding an end to forceful dispossession of their ancestral land and the land grab, the release of political prisoners, and the rule of law as opposed to the rule of the gun and prison. Ethiopian security forces responded to peaceful protesters as they always did, using excessive and disproportionate force, including live bullets as a standard crowd-control tool. But the state's extraordinary measures only encouraged more anger and inspired more street protests.

Both the protests and the brutality were unprecedented, even in EPRDF's long history of violence. I read that security forces killed more than 1,000 people in Oromia alone by the end of the year, hundreds were wounded, and record numbers of arrests and disappearances were reached. The maze of military training facilities and concentration-like prisoner holding camps, was difficult to negotiate. Many innocent people remained in jail on dubious terrorism charges. Youngsters like Tokuma were giving up hope of knowing freedom again.

The Grand Rally was an ambitious undertaking, staged in all the major cities and district towns of Oromia. It was intended to be a peaceful rally, but some saw it as a national day of rage to protest the Oromo people's continued marginalization and human rights abuses. I planned a peaceful protest myself, yet I knew there was anger underneath my outward calm.

During the Grand Oromia Rally, participants were to stay connected using mobile phones and social media platforms. I dared not march publicly. I had to stay focused. My time would come soon enough—a time to speak to the outside world.

I have not yet explained to you an underground activist network, known as *Qeerroo*, which organized the Oromo community for the Rally. *Qeerroo* in its widest meaning refers to 'strong active youth'. When the Tigrayan-led minority regime pushed the OLF out of government, the activist networks of *Qeerroo* gradually blossomed as a form of *Oromummaa* or Oromo nationalism.

'The *Qeerroo* are the voice of the people,' according to many. 'They are the vanguard of the Oromo revolution.'

Their platform was radical: *We, Oromo and all other oppressed peoples' students, declare to the world and the Ethiopian peoples that we are committed to be first in torching the revolution. Given the recent history of Oromo students' movement, we are cognisant of the price of freedom. We are determined to die in freedom rather than live in slavery. We are confident that soon the remaining Ethiopian peoples would follow us in upholding the torch of the revolution so that their oppression, suffering and slavery end here and now and give way, once and for all, for liberty, freedom and democracy to prevail.*

Their fighting words and notices of the rally drew the ire of Prime Minister Hailemariam Desalegn, who announced a ban on demonstrations which 'threaten national unity' and called on police to use all means at their disposal to prevent them. The means inevitably included lethal weapons and savage beatings.

The protesters, mostly students, were not deterred. They chanted anti-government slogans and waved dissident flags: *We want our freedom! Free our political prisoners! Stop killing Oromos! Don't kill innocent Oromo students!*

I followed the rally from my hotel room as many of them raised their arms and crossed their hands in a peaceful protest gesture of civil resistance—the gesture I would make my own. The clenched fists show coiled power, while the fists facing outward reveal that there are no weapons in hand. When you cross the wrists, you are showing voluntary restraint, though to some this indicates the bonds of slavery—shackles or chains. The arms raised indicate a defensive posture against assault. I moved away from the window and raised my own arms, in solidarity. One day soon the world would see the sign and I would explain its meaning.

The rally turned deadly and I could hardly bear to hear the shots and screams. Reports told of many killed and many more arrested. Before the only state-controlled Internet service provider shut down across the country for two days, word got out. The plight of the Oromo people received the biggest single-day coverage when international media outlets reported widely on the peaceful protests and government repression.

Electricity was turned off in many places and an unnatural silence and darkness covered the land. Yet, to those who followed the troubles of our country, there was a glimmer of hope. Perhaps the Oromo protest movement had started to change the political landscape of Ethiopia and shaken the regime's foundations. Different groups were revising their attitudes and standing with us. Protests had spread to the Amhara region and the Amharas and the Oromos were starting to come together, after long years of antagonism.

Some of the protesters at the Rally chanted, 'Wolkait Tegede!', the name of a fertile border land between Amhara and Tigray which was forcibly annexed from Amhara and rezoned as Tigray. It was a serious flashpoint between Amharas and Tigrayans. Beyond the geography, the issue was also about language and culture. Under the current arrangement, children in the Wolkait Tegede were forced to learn Tigrigna. The Amhara in Wolkait could not receive public service in Amharic, and so on. The Tigray region did not promote or develop the Wolkait people's culture. So it was about representation, culture, language, and accessing public services.

The demands of Amhara people to stay in their own region were as legitimate as Oromo demands to stay in their region. It was good to see that the two largest groups had started to support each other, recognising common grievances.

The United Nations High Commissioner for Human Rights, Zeid Ra'ad Al Hussein, reacted to the protests. 'I do urge the government to allow access for international observers into the Amhara and Oromiya regions,' he said, 'so that we can establish what has happened and that the security forces, if it is the case that they have been using excessive force, do not do so and promptly investigate of course these allegations. Any detainee who has been peacefully protesting should be released promptly.'

There was one detainee I wish had been released promptly, but I did not even know that he had been arrested. I had not seen my friend, Kebede Fayissa, for a few weeks. He had taken employment in a place outside Finfinne, called Melka Gefersa, on the road to Ambo. He was busy settling into his job and helping care for two children.

I was preoccupied with training and dividing my time between home and the Ararat Hotel. I was determined to separate myself from the usual distractions. It didn't occur to me that Kebede would have taken part in the protests—he had never done so before. How was I to know that he was arrested anyway, from the street where he worked?

I thought of him as I brushed my fingers over the tattoo on my right shoulder. I had chosen an *Odaa* tree, an Ethiopian sycamore, colored in red, black, and green ink, a brand name imprinted on me, a symbol of Oromo pride. Soko liked to stroke the tattoo and I hoped that its meaning rubbed off on her, the next generation of Oromo.

She and Iftu were excited when I brought my Olympic uniforms home to show them.

'Did you have a fitting?' Iftu asked, holding up the green track suit jacket with 'Ethiopia' emblazoned in yellow on the front.

'No need,' I said. 'They asked me my size, I told them "Medium," and this is what I got.'

'Try them on, Ababa!' shouted Soko. 'Let us see you all dressed up!'

'Let's all dress up!' Iftu was in a playful, proud mood. She put on the green and white top and dark green trousers, smart dress wear, giggling as she held the waistband of the trousers to stop them falling down.

I entered the spirit of their game, determined to be cheerful and not give away my thoughts. I pulled on the red racing shorts and green singlet. I chased Soko, who was running around with the green and white scarf tripping her up. I lifted her up and she squealed and kicked.

'I will win a gold medal in these clothes, Soko! Gold, for my golden girl!'

I wanted to win, to make my point in the best possible position. I touched the emblem of the Olympic rings on my singlet and vowed that I would not run in vain. I looked down to Sora, sitting among the clothes on the floor, staring at them glumly. I picked him up and hugged him, but he struggled free and ran from the room. One day he will understand, and all this will be part of the *Oduu Durii* he tells his children.

Often people asked me how I felt about wearing the Ethiopian uniform. Did I feel as if I were somehow betraying Oromia, the birthplace of many great athletes? '*No,*' I gave a firm reply. 'I was proud to wear the uniform. So long as I was in that country it belonged to me too. The uniform didn't do any wrong to us, it was the dictator government that killed our people. I didn't feel sad, but proud to wear the uniform for the race.'

The Games had begun with an opening ceremony on Friday, the 5th of August, the day that the Great Oromia Rally started. On television I watched the happy spectacle of athletes in their thousands marching into the stadium and compared it to the thousands marching in the streets of Oromo cities. The two gatherings were many miles apart with the world's spotlight beaming on one and small phones flashing on the other. But they both made many sacrifices, and both wanted victory for their country and themselves. I was not in the first group of athletes to leave Finfinne for the Games. I prepared to leave with the second group, on Wednesday August 17th, ready for the race on Sunday August 21st.

Iftu helped me pack my bag as she had done many times before. I could not take extra clothes because she would question me. I chose a few sports clothes I used for training. Soko ran to find the pair of shoes I wanted to wear as well as the ones for running.

'Is one pair enough?' asked Iftu. 'You may need another pair, don't you think?'

'One pair is enough.' Dear Iftu, so unsuspecting. I expected Nike would send me more clothes and shoes wherever I was. Wherever I was. I had not thought beyond the race. Perhaps I would be back here in jail, with no need of running gear.

We walked out of the house and got into the car. Iftu was taking me to the airport. She wouldn't be able to come into the terminal—a security rule prevented that. Our goodbye at the car was brief and awkward. I hugged them all. Sora was trying to run after me; he was screaming 'Ababa!' and Iftu was holding him back. Soko was waving and calling 'Good luck!' *Carraa gaarii siif haa ta'uu!*

The other athletes travelling with me were wearing the Ethiopian dress uniform, but I was not. I wore the Oromia flag (black, red, and white) as a scarf around my neck.

'Whose flag is that?' asked a journalist in Amharic. His tone was mocking. 'That's not the Ethiopian flag. Why are you wearing that?'

'It is the flag of Oromia!' I answered in *Afaan Oromoo*. I smiled, happy to pause for an interview. Who could stop me leaving the country now? 'If you want to talk to me you will need an interpreter. I speak the language of my country.'

The journalists looked at me curiously, but they found one. 'I can understand Amharic,' I told him, 'so I will know what the questions are and the answers you give. Make sure you interpret what I say in *Afaan Oromoo* to Amharic without changing the meaning.'

They were all flustered, I think. They begged me to put on the Ethiopian uniform, but I refused. They took another athlete's jacket and put it around my shoulders to conduct the interview and take photos.

'I have no hatred for this uniform,' I told them all. 'I will wear it on the day, but I am going to the Games as an Oromo runner, like many others before me. I love my country, but I want to show off our Oromo flag, to which I owe my first loyalty. You think this flag is that of a backward place, but you are wrong. I am proud of my heritage.'

I listened to the interpreter repeating what I had said and saw the journalists pause in taking notes. They decided to take another approach—thinking, I suppose, that I was not a very likely team player.

'Will you do teamwork with the other Ethiopian athletes in the marathon?' asked one. He sounded accusing.

'No, I won't want to do that.'

'Why not?'

'I want to use my personal tactics for the race. I will run on my own.'

I had no intention of implicating Lemi Berhanu and Tesfaye Abera in my bigger plan for the race. We would be seen running separately. They had already told the journalists that they were planning teamwork, so I was regarded as a reluctant starter. The journalists reported that I was refusing the uniform because I was going to the Games involuntarily! If only they knew. Well, they know now.

I walked away from them that day, dragging the bag of next to nothing for the life ahead. My luggage was light, but my heart was heavy. Do you remember the boy whose father made him run all the way to Gojo and back carrying a load of grain for the grinding machine? He longed to put his burden down and rest, but he could not, except briefly while he waited his turn. That same boy has carried the great weight of Oromo grief for years, with just some brief respite because of Iftu and the children. I cannot carry it any further than the men's marathon in Rio de Janeiro.

4

Others are bothered by long flights, but I had no trouble sleeping the hours away, even on this journey, when I might have stayed awake, brooding. I had visited Brazil before the Olympic Games, so I knew a little about what to expect in that country. I went to São Paulo at the end of 2015 to compete in the Saint Silvester Road Race. Its course is only 15 kilometers (9.3 miles) long, less than half the length of a marathon, but the race is made more difficult by the intense heat of the Brazilian summer and the obstacles such as steep and winding streets.

The race attracts thousands of runners from many countries, with Ethiopia and Kenya (as usual) competing for top places. The heat does not deter the spectators, as it is held on New Year's Eve and the city is in festival mood. The race starts on São Paulo's Avenida Paulista flanked by tall forbidding skyscrapers. I have never liked the feeling of being shut in by those big structures.

Stanley Biwott, the Kenyan, won in a time of 44:31. He'd won the New York City Marathon just a couple of months before the race in Brazil and he would be competing against me in the Olympic race. My time in São Paulo was 44:38 and I was in third place after Leul Gebresilase Aleme, another Ethiopian, destined to win the race in 2016.

I travelled to São Paulo just when the mosquito-borne Zika virus was a major health scare in Brazil. Then, early in 2016, a global health emergency was declared. The risk was unlikely to deter most athletes, but the Olympic Games were threatened. All the Games are disputed in one way or another and for Rio it was Zika. Should the Games go ahead? The fear was that the virus could spread worldwide. Some competitors withdrew, while the organizers went to great lengths to protect athletes and spectators. The show must go on.

The Zika virus was the least of my worries as I arrived in Rio de Janeiro. I am exceptionally healthy. As I've told you, I have never had any immunization. The risk would have been greater for Iftu, had she been attending and had she been pregnant—the virus was known to cause birth defects.

The couple of days before my race are a blur now. I didn't check out the marathon course or go to the stadium. I used my time training and resting, but I do remember how good it felt to be with the others in the Olympic

Village, talking about performances and experiences. Team Ethiopia had won a few medals, and I sought out a friend of mine, Mare Dibaba, the women's world marathon champion and the favorite for the Olympic title.

'A bronze medal, Feyisa!' she said. 'I hoped for gold. It was very hot, but we all had to get through that.'

'You did well. Quite a few didn't finish the race.' I'd heard that Tigist Tufa had pulled up with cramp, about the 18-kilometer mark.

'You never know what can happen, but that was bad luck for Tigist. Usually I have the confidence to win because my last lap is fast, but I couldn't seem to kick in. It was Jemima's day.'

Jemima Sumgong was the first Kenyan woman to win the Olympic marathon title and I was happy for her. But all eyes were on my hero, Mo Farah, running for his 'double double'—four Olympic gold medals—in the 5,000-meter race the evening before my race. He had already won the gold medal in the 10,000-meter race a week before, as well as those same two distance races in London in 2012. In awe of him, I watched the 5,000-meter race on a television in the Village, wondering if he could win again.

As usual, Mo was content to run at the back for a while, biding his time as he waited for the race to develop. My teammates, Dejen Gebremeskel and Hagos Gebrhiwet, took turns to set a quick pace in the first half. Mo moved through the field to sixth place, monitoring the runners in front of him before going to the lead with four laps to go. The pace was fast but not excessive. At the bell, Mo was leading but he had six athletes on his tail. With 250 to go, Hagos Gebrhiwet headed him but Mo soon headed him and won the race. He crossed the line with his arms outstretched. Then he knelt to kiss the track in celebration.

Everyone laughed and applauded as he performed his mobot act and danced around, barefoot and jubilant. It was Mo's golden moment. Afterwards, he admitted that he hadn't expected the Ethiopians to push it so hard from the gun.

'I was surprised by the first lap,' he said. 'I thought it was going to be a slow race. They had a plan, they wanted to take the sting out of me, but when I hit the front, I wasn't letting anyone past me.'

That night, Rio was Mo Town. I watched an interview with the Rio champion. 'It has been a long journey,' he told the reporters, 'but if you dream of something, have ambitions, and are willing to work hard, then you can get your dreams.'

Another man on a journey.

'I hate to lose,' he went on. 'Even in PE as a kid, I hated losing. I have that drive—it's just in me. I can't quite believe it. I wished for just one medal as a junior.'

Mo had already dedicated his previous three Olympic gold medals to his twins, Amani and Aisha, and his eldest daughter Rihanna. Before this final, he had promised one for his young son, Hussein. Now his son had a medal too. I thought of Soko and my promise to her. 'Tomorrow, Soko,' I had whispered. 'Tomorrow it's our turn.'

I have never been long in a different place without calling my family before a race. I had phoned them as soon as the plane touched down in Rio.

'Iftu, I'm here! How are you? What about Soko and Sora?'

'We all miss you! How was the flight?'

'It was OK. I'm glad to be here preparing for the race at last.'

'Ababa! Have you got the medal yet?' Soko had snatched the phone from her mother.

'Not yet! You will have to wait for three more days. Tell Sora I want to speak to him.'

Sora would not talk to me. Iftu had the speaker phone on and I told him I missed him. I could not say, I will see you soon, like I usually did. I wondered whether Iftu noticed that.

After watching Mo's victory, I had one more thing to do before I went to bed. I scrolled through the photographs on my phone until I found the one I was looking for. It is one of me wearing a white shawl and a perky hat. In my hands I am holding a sheaf of green grass and my *bokkuu*, ceremonial stick. Oromo pray and worship holding wet or green things. This picture signified my prayer to *Waaqaa* before the big race. It was like a good luck wish for me. Then I shared the photograph on Facebook.

5

I am on a pony, bareback, riding across the Jaldu plains. I give the pony its head and we gallop east, towards Finfinne. This is urgent, I have a mission, I am racing against the clock. The sun is coming up and I must be there to deliver the message.

'Feyisa! Wake up! It's time to get ready for your race.'

I was in my bed in the Olympic Village and the coach woke me for the marathon. I was in a deep sleep and the dream was still with me—the Oromo man facing the east and an unknown future. I studied my hands—I clenched them into fists, my hands were dry and thin—I would run well. I felt lighter, stronger, and sharper. I sensed victory that day.

We assembled in a dining room to eat breakfast. There was a schedule to follow: when to eat, when to be at the bus stop, when and where to warm up, when to go to the changing rooms, and when to be on the starting line.

I telephoned Iftu. She answered immediately.

'Iftu, *Washaawwashee*! I am about to leave the Village for the race.'

'Feyisa! All our prayers are for you today! Good luck.' *Carraa gaarii siif haa ta'uu.*

'Are you all there at the house to watch the race on television?'

'Yes, of course! I could hardly sleep last night, thinking of your race today. How do you feel?'

'Confident. Calm. Now I must go. I will speak to you after the race.'

Iftu. Perhaps she wouldn't want to speak to me after the race. She wouldn't sleep tonight either.

Rain was falling as we went through the drill before the last major event at the Rio de Janeiro Olympic Games: the men's marathon. We shed our tracksuits and attached transponders, little devices that measure times and splits, to our shoes.

All of us, in our bright singlets and shorts, a mass of color, moved into position. Some were wearing caps, perhaps to deflect the rain from their eyes. My mop of hair can do that job. Mist was swirling about us. Someone pointed out the huge statue of Christ the Redeemer gazing down from a lofty summit, nearly obscured in the cloud. He was majestic, but eerie.

I looked along the front line of runners about to go into battle. Eliud Kipchoge, the Kenyan, the favorite for the race… Ghirmay Gebreselassie, the Eritrean, the reigning world champion… Stephen Kiprotich, the Ugandan, defending Olympic champion… Galen Rupp, the American, running his second marathon after winning at the Los Angeles trials… Lemi Berhanu and Tesfaye Abera, the Ethiopians, ready to repeat previous marathon wins.

I was not a favorite for the race. My time in Tokyo was 2:06:56, only the 31st fastest time of the year. I knew Eliud Kipchoge was very strong, but sometimes strong athletes do not perform well in a big competition when they represent their country and not just themselves. The pressure is too much. Anyway, a different unrehearsed script is played out in every marathon. There will be unexpected performances and unpredictable tensions. This is what makes the race what it is, a drama with a running time of more than two hours, with all of us, veterans and novices, wanting to play the lead role, to be center stage at the medal awards, and to exit triumphantly to loud applause.

The camera scanned us as we toed the starting line. When it focused on me, I stared into the lens and tapped the tattoo on my right shoulder and pointed to it. Other athletes wear lucky charms; I had the *odaa* tree to remind me of my purpose for running this race. Perhaps some people among the millions watching were already asking. 'What is that? What does it mean?'

We surged forward in response to the gun. The competitors, 155 of us, from 80 different nations, remained compacted for the first few kilometers, before a front group of about thirty asserted itself, running military fashion in almost straight lines about four deep, arms pumping, legs propelling us forward. I saw Lemi Berhanu take the lead; I was content to stay in the middle of the pack. You must maintain a constant pace and regular rhythm. Already some runners were jostling for position, changing their speed, exhausting their precious energy. Soon they would start to feel numbness in the body.

The rain was heavier. It was not cold like rain in Ethiopia, but warm and soothing. The sensation when it splashed on my legs was relaxing, pleasing to me. I could not risk feeling too comfortable—I had to stay alert for sharp corners and potholes in the road. Watch out for that hairpin bend that one runner had trouble with—he had to correct his stride. I was on the side at the back of the group, but I never positioned myself in no-man's land between this group and the one that followed. I never run alone until I hit the front.

I was vaguely conscious of what was going on around me—the feet hitting the ground, the motors of the escort vehicles, the chatter of the helicopter hovering overhead, the spectators waving flags and pointing cameras. The rain eased and the reflections on the road were mesmeric. Look ahead, keep the rhythm, control your mind, control your body. The pace was slow. We were testing each other's nerve to see who dared to increase speed.

The pack splintered at about the 15-kilometer mark. I saw Kipchoge make an early move, signalling his intention to take control of the race. He was in the front line the whole time, with others beside him changing places. Stephen Kiprotich moved to the front, then someone else took over the lead. Later, when I watched a replay, I saw that it was Callum Hawkins, a British runner. The lead place at this stage was just as dangerous and lonely as no man's land.

The humidity taxed our strength. Some train in heat chambers to prepare for this, the slow killer of marathon competitors. I paused once at a drink station; others grabbed saturated sponges to squeeze over their heads. Some were running just within their comfort zone; some were going beyond it and fell back. You could see them wobbling about, their shoulders rolling and their hands flailing.

An hour or so passed. I started to move forward. This is the time to close in on your opponents and put the pressure on. This is a race of attrition, wearing each other down, using tactics to best advantage. Tesfaye Abera was struggling. At 23 kilometers he dropped out. The group was thinning. Lemi Berhanu joined Kipchoge and briefly took the lead again. At the 30-kilometer mark, we were down to eight runners.

Lemi Birhanu asked Eliud Kipchoge to run beside him! I don't know what he was thinking. When Eliud moved to run beside him, Lemi could not keep up. I would have advised Lemi not to do that, but I must run my own race, not his.

Within two more kilometers, the lead pack was down to four—Eliud Kipchoge, Galen Rupp, Lemi Berhanu, and me. In the next kilometer, Lemi fell behind. The three of us left in medal contention ran Indian file: Eliud,

Galen, Feyisa. The numbers on their bibs were imprinted on my mind—2680, 3097. I wanted them to see mine—2398—although running behind them benefited me with the windbreak they provided. They must work harder.

Galen Rupp lost contact with us at a water station. Now I was very close behind Eliud Kipchoge and some commentators accused me of clipping his heels. Kipchoge was angry, they said, motioning me to run next to him, to use the rest of the street. I didn't respond to his signal. This was a psychological battle now between the two of us. He accelerated, and he dropped me around the 35-kilometer mark. From this point, as the course snaked around buildings, the three of us lost sight of each other as the gaps between us increased.

Soko will not get her gold medal. I had no resources left to challenge Eliud. I concentrated on beating Galen Rupp or any other runner coming from behind, desperate for a medal. I could have felt deflated at that point, seeing the Kenyan disappear in the distance, a sure winner, but then a wonderful thing happened.

The sky cleared, and I was running in an easterly direction. The sun shone gently on me, the Oromo son so far from home. Early in the morning, across Oromia, prayers of thanksgiving were being offered to God for the new day. Perhaps this day they thanked God for me, Feyisa Lilesa Gemechu, about to meet the expectations associated with my name. I was about to fulfil my destiny for them.

My legs ran steadily, but in my mind I heard cries for help and saw the tears of the oppressed. No longer should all power remain on the side of the oppressors. I would finish the race well for my Oromo brothers and sisters.

Eliud was gone—he had the gold medal. I focused on Galen Rupp. I was not that concerned about him, running behind me, but I had to be careful. He ran the 5,000-meter race at these Games, the one that Mo Farah won. Galen trained with Mo and came in fifth in that race. The marathon is a difficult race, and even at this point I could become totally exhausted in the last 200 meters. If Galen increased speed, I had to be ready to do the same. I believed I had enough in reserve to sprint to the finish line. I glanced back several times, just to be sure, but he was not challenging. The silver medal was mine.

My time had come, and I would be on the podium. I felt the hairs rising on the back of my neck as I approached the finish line. There was no stopping me now. I flexed my fists and raised my arms above my head, crossed at the wrists. Many people said later that it was a sign of jubilation, as if to shout, 'It is finished!' They were right, in a way, because I felt relieved of a weight greater than that of many Olympic medals around my neck. My plan for the race was finished, but not my life or my purpose. Journalists called it the race of my life or the race for my life. It was both.

I was supposed to feel elated at this triumphant end to an Olympic race. I had beaten many other elite athletes who coveted the trophies. All I could think about were the people dying back home. I saw flashbacks of the enormous tragedy. I wanted the world to know and act and share my burden. I repeated the protest sign four times, arms raised, wrists crossed, clenched fists facing out.

VI

I

gave a little skip as I left the track. My task was complete. Eliud was walking around, smiling broadly for the cameras, the Kenyan flag draped over his shoulders. Someone in the stands offered me an Ethiopian flag to hold high, but I refused it. 'I cannot do it for a country where I have no rights; where my people have no rights.' I hugged Eliud, the Olympic hero of the day. He ran a magnificent race. I watched Galen Rupp come in and make the Catholic sign of the cross. He immediately accepted an American flag to show the world his patriotic allegiance.

A BBC camera focused on me and I pointed again to the *odaa* tree on my shoulder. I was solemn, unsmiling, so different to the happy faces around me. I was thinking about my next strategy. My body was slick with sweat. I pulled off the drenched singlet and sat down, leaning forward, hands between my knees. I can't explain exactly how I felt just then in the midst of all the euphoria. I was free of a great burden and weary from carrying it for so long, yet I was wondering if I might have won the gold had I not been so heavily laden for many months before and during the race. I was also in some suspense, questioning where and how this day would end. Would the world get the message? Time would soon tell.

I told you that the marathon is a great spectacle and I heard about some of the scenes behind me out on the road. One athlete had trouble with his shoelaces and stopped midway a couple of times to tie them before leaving the race. He will have DNF beside his name, with fourteen others who could not stay the distance. Had that happened to me…I can't imagine how bad that would have been.

I watched as others came in. Ghirmay Gebreselassie trotted in fourth; Stephen Kiprotich was in fourteenth place, just behind Lemi Berhanu. Callum Hawkins, who'd led us for some distance, managed ninth position. They will all have their own stories about the race. Some athletes finished in dramatic ways. One slipped as he approached the end, fell and performed a couple of push-ups before finally crossing the line. Another, crippled with cramp, crawled across the line, while another determined to finish by running sidewise. Some fell to the ground, exhausted, and were lifted up by teammates. Others cried, from exhaustion, relief, or disappointment. A couple left the scene in wheelchairs. It's always an emotional finish.

After the ceremony of giving flowers to the medalists, it was time for the post-race press conference and I prepared to make a statement. Usually Ethiopian interpreters rush around to interpret when the press interview us; they want to be seen on stages among elite athletes. I couldn't find anyone who would interpret for me that day. They vanished. I had to put things right as the spectators and the press were thinking that the gesture I showed meant 'the second place is mine, it is over, you won't catch me'.

This was the time to speak. I stepped up to the conference area podium with my jacket unzipped—to divide the block text bearing Ethiopia's name. I raised my arms once again and crossed my wrists above my head. My wristband in Oromo colors—black, white, and red—was visible for all to see. The journalists asked what I had meant by the gesture.

'I have relatives and friends in prison back home,' I said. 'If you talk about democracy, they kill you. If I go back to Ethiopia, maybe they will kill me or put me in prison. It is very dangerous in my country. Maybe I will move country. I was protesting for people everywhere who have no freedom.'

Questions were coming fast. I had to ask the journalists to speak slowly and clearly, as it was hard for me to follow their English and their accent. No one helped me in translation, but I wanted them to report accurately. It was difficult for me to understand what they said and difficult for them to understand me. 'The Ethiopian government is killing the Oromo people and taking their land and resources,' I said clearly but awkwardly. 'So the Oromo people are protesting, and I support the protest as I am Oromo. Oromo are my people...Oromo people now protest what is right, for peace, for a place.'

I glanced at Eliud Kipchoge. His face was shocked; his body started as if electrified when I said that about the government killing my people. Whether he was alarmed because of my daring to speak so or because this was news to him, I did not know.

I was criticized because I took Kipchoge's credit. His victory and Rupp's, they complained, were overshadowed by my story. As I saw it, we were three men making history that day. For once, times and tactics were not the main topics.

This was a great triumph for Eliud, although it was the slowest marathon of his career, 2:08:44. There was a bigger issue for him. 'Everyone wants a medal,' he said in his pleasant, modest way. 'I was coming for gold. This is history, the first time the winners in the men's and women's marathons are from the same country at the same Olympics. This is the best moment of my life.'

Galen Rupp couldn't stop smiling! The marathon was only the second he'd run, and he was the first American-born athlete in forty years to win a marathon medal. Commentators speculated about the significance of this, as it sent a signal to the world that East African runners would no longer dominate the marathon event.

I don't think Eliud and Galen felt cheated of their moment with the media. They were given the best coverage in the televised version of the race, watched by millions. Later, when I spoke to others, they said that one commentator talking his big audience through the marathon hardly mentioned my progress and made no mention of my protest at the end. His attention was focused on Eliud Kipchoge, exclaiming, 'This race from the start has been about one man!' He also devoted a lot of commentary to Galen Rupp, who did run a good race. Perhaps the man was against me because he did not approve of the exclusion of Kenenisa Bekele from selection, and he more or less said so.

I had just proved that my selection was justified—I had crossed the line in 2:09:54, eleven seconds ahead of Rupp. The government officials in Ethiopia were probably wishing I had trailed in last. I heard that some of them were watching the race at Elilly Hotel in Finfinne while having drinks. A peaceful demonstration was planned in Finfinne that day, but did not take place because troops had dispersed the protesters. The officials in the hotel were cheering as I approached the finishing line. When I showed the protest gesture, they started spilling their drinks and breaking their glasses in anger! I felt proud when I heard that.

Kipchoge came up to me after the press conference.

'Feyisa, I had no idea what your protest sign meant. I feel very sorry for you and sad for your country.'

'I am sad too, Eliud. This is a big competition and we should all be happy just to be here, chosen to participate. I am a medalist, but I don't have any desire to celebrate. Why is this? The medal means nothing when they are killing pregnant women in Oromia. I have this strange thought that if they had killed my mother while I was in her womb, I wouldn't exist. Instead, here I am today, telling the world about the killers. It is my destiny.'

Eliud nodded sympathetically and moved away as a journalist approached me. Chris Chavez, a journalist with *Sports Illustrated*, was curious about me.

'Tell me more,' he said.

'In the last nine months, more than 1,000 people died,' I told him. 'And others charged with treason. It's a very bad situation among Oromo people in Ethiopia. This sign is to stop the killing. We need peace, we need to respect humanity in every way. This sign is a symbol of peace, to stop the killing. I wish peace for the world, not only Ethiopia.'

'What are you going to do now? What's going to happen?"

'Whatever happens to me, I have to get this message out. So many people are suffering. I am a witness to what has happened, and I must testify. There are too many false witnesses, inside and outside the court rooms of Ethiopia.'

I should have lingered, explaining all that had motivated me, but I could no longer find the words. I was so tired, from the race and its aftermath, and from the struggle to follow and to speak English. Iftu was right—I should have had a better grasp of it for international events, especially this one. I went back to the Village.

Chris Chavez was contacted by Mohammed Ademo, Oromo activist and founder of *OPride*, a multimedia website in Washington DC. The site had been blocked, hacked, and targeted at various times over the past decade. Mohammed saw news of my protest on Twitter, but he did not believe it. He telephoned Chris and asked, 'Is it real? I am in media and I know about activism. I am looking at a photo of this athlete's protest, but I must have it confirmed.'

'Yes,' Chris assured him. 'It was real. I watched the end of the race. I have just spoken to Feyisa Lilesa.'

'Can you ask him to contact me? Can you talk more to him? He has done an extraordinary thing for the Oromo people. You will have a big story for your magazine. This is important, and it will be remembered for many, many years.'

'He has gone back to the Village. I can't go there to speak to him.'

Mohammed was disappointed, but he responded on Twitter to a tweet from BBC journalist Piers Edwards, who said, 'Extraordinary moment. Feyisa Lilesa: "If not kill me, they will put me in prison. Maybe I will move country.""

Mohammed tweeted: 'His name will be mentioned next to US athletes Tommie Smith and John Carlos, who displayed the Black Power Salute at the 1968 Olympics…. Feyisa Lilesa used the biggest stage of his life to express a muzzled generational cry for freedom. He spoke without words.'

2

I don't know who was in charge of the entire Ethiopian Olympic team, but Alebachew Nigusse was in charge of the athletics team. He is an Amhara, but he can speak *Afaan Oromoo*. I don't know where he learned to speak my language. His attitude to me was hard to gauge. He didn't hate me or like me. Actually, he didn't say anything to me. I knew the Oromo athletes and coaches, even though we were not close friends. Except for two from Southern Ethiopia, all the coaches were Oromo. They were well known because they had trained elite runners like Kenenisa and Tirunesh. The coaches have a special regard for all Oromo.

They were happy that I won the medal, because the team was undermined before that. There were mutterings that this Olympics was the worst that Ethiopia had recorded in twenty years, so the coaches didn't care about my protest. There was a person who works in the EAF who furtively cheered me by showing the thumbs-up when I made that protest gesture.

Most of the athletes applauded me for what I did—they were elated and crying. Some were afraid. You must realize that other Oromo athletes there were not in good spirits about the situation back home, even though I was the only one who protested. Their feelings were not good, they didn't have happiness. There were other athletes who held the Ethiopian flag reluctantly. I knew one athlete who deliberately failed to pick up the flag after her race, pretending she hadn't seen it when thrown to her. Our feelings were those of stateless athletes.

I didn't even take a shower that day, but I was hungry and I ate my lunch as usual in the dining area. My mind was quiet, as if the turmoil was over. I went to the medal ceremony.

I may have been stripped of my medal if the International Olympic Committee took a grim view of my protest. Other athletes have been sent home in disgrace before me. Stories were already circulating about Tommie Smith and John Carlos who were ordered to leave the Mexico City Olympic Stadium after their Black Power Salute. They were not stripped of their medals and neither was I. Rule 50 of the IOC bans political statements of any kind, so there was a risk. An official reminded me of the Olympic Charter after my race, but no further action was taken. I am thankful for that.

Eliud Kipchoge and Galen Rupp were so happy at the ceremony as the spotlight beamed down on us, standing on the podium. For the first time that day, I smiled, when the medal was placed around my neck. It stood for something important and it belonged to my people, not me. I watched the flags raised and heard Eliud behind me, softly singing the Kenyan national anthem. I was thinking that perhaps it was better for Eliud to have the gold and me the silver. I could not have honored the Ethiopian flag fluttering above the crowd. The day will come when a new flag for Oromia flies high in Ethiopia and I will gaze at it with joy. Oromo sons and daughters, and their descendants, will possess their land again and live in peace. I believe this.

The three of us linked arms for the photograph finish. We will all remember this day for the rest of our lives, for very different reasons. The

Maracanã Stadium was alive with laughter and festivity as I left. The multitude was there to celebrate before they went home, but I had left my home, my family, my country and my people. I had never intended going back with the rest of the team, yet there was that stubborn streak in me that wanted to go home and defy the government. What would they do to me? Should I be spared the punishments of Oromo martyrs?

It was clear that I was not going to be welcome back home. EBC, the Ethiopian state-owned broadcaster, showed the race live on television on Sunday afternoon, unable to avoid airing my protest as it happened the first time. Afterwards, it refused to broadcast footage of me crossing the finishing line or receiving my medal.

The Ethiopian government said publicly and deceptively that I was in no danger. 'He is always welcome,' Getachew Reda, the Ethiopian communications minister, assured the media. 'Feyisa Lilesa is an Ethiopian hero.' Before that, Oromia TV had posted on Facebook, 'Feyisa Lelisa has successfully accomplished terrorists' and Jawar Mohammed's mission.' They took down that message and changed it to a more positive one, echoing Reda's statement. I kept a copy of that first post. Jawar was a prominent Oromo activist-in-exile and he believed the Ethiopian government would kill him if he returned to his homeland.

In the Village, the athletes were anxious for me. I knew some of them had family histories of enslavement and mistreatment.

'We have to go back to Ethiopia tomorrow!' they wailed. 'How can we leave Feyisa alone here?'

Friends in Minnesota quickly found and reserved a hotel room for me and sent the details of the La Costa Hotel. The coach saw to my departure. 'Don't worry,' he said. 'This is our brother. We will get him safely from the Village.'

The other athletes were crying and urging me to leave the Village. 'Get away. You are not safe here.' I don't usually cry, but this was an emotional moment. 'I make you cry while I am alive,' I joked. 'Meles Zenawi made us cry when he was dead!' We had all cried tears of joy when that tyrant died. He was chairman of the TPLF, head of the EPRDF, head of the Transitional Government of Ethiopia, then prime minister before Hailemariam Desalegn. He has an ugly human rights record. I despise him, alive or dead.

Some of the athletes gave me money. Others pressed small gifts on me. They were going back to Ethiopia. They could be punished for having anything to do with me, yet they supported me. I left in a taxi. I was alone.

3

At the La Costa Hotel, I was shown to a small room with two beds. I put down the bag that I had packed with Iftu, a long time ago, or so it seemed. Iftu! I would not think about her just now. She had phoned me after the race, but I didn't answer at first. I answered the third time.

'Feyisa!' she spoke gently. 'Are you alright?'

I muttered something. I knew she must be terribly upset.

'Why didn't you tell us? Why didn't you let me know?'

I could not answer her. Not yet. I was close to tears and I hung up on Iftu. I turned off the phone.

There, at the end of the longest day of my life, I seemed to forget all the worries about my wife, my children, and my mother. I miss my family when I am away in a foreign country. Not even a week had passed since I last said goodbye to them and I felt nothing yet. I was numb.

Athletes in the Village sent me clips of what was being reported in the media about me. Someone in the *Washington Post*'s Africa Bureau described my protest as 'the bravest act at the 2016 Olympics'. Another journalist said, 'Lilesa's is a brave, defiant and revolutionary act—one for the ages.'

I wasn't thinking of myself as a hero, just a messenger. Only international intervention, I believed, could change the situation in Ethiopia for the better. I would have regretted it for the rest of my life if I hadn't made that gesture.

'Have you always been this brave?' one reporter asked me. I must have looked puzzled. He wrote, 'Lilesa's English is fairly good, yet he could not comprehend the word "brave". For now, he embodies it.'

I do understand the word, but I can't remember what I said to that reporter. I didn't think that I was brave or bold. I don't know what made my heart as strong as an ox. I have argued with myself from many angles and one way I justified my action was to think of myself as the soldier I wanted to be. 'When a soldier enlists, he knows the risks and because he has sworn to defend his country or its laws, he doesn't think of the consequences.' That is how I thought.

I showered and lay down, wondering if this room would be my prison cell for many weeks to come. I slept, still hearing the clamor of many voices. It was not a restful sleep.

Monday. I was cautioned to stay at the hotel. 'You won't understand the language, Portuguese. The hotel is not in the best part of town. You could be attacked. We don't know if you are being watched.'

I looked at posts and pictures on social media. I saw Oromo elders weeping in the province of Hararghe, where its people struggled and sacrificed for the Oromo cause for years. One elder was crying, 'Behold Oromo, we love our boy! Please protect our boy wherever he is!' It seemed that everybody was crying, and I started to cry too. There were so many posts on my Facebook page, I could hardly bear to read them. 'Feyisa you just made the biggest sacrifice by showing the sign of resistance. Our Hero….'

The hero was about to have his nerve tested. Someone knocked on the door. When you hear that sound, you suspect the worst—especially then, when I felt at my most vulnerable. Who could it be? The desk staff had been instructed not to tell anyone I was there and not permit anyone to get as far as my room. I had been served breakfast there. I opened the door to the extent of the safety chain and looked out. Two uniformed men stood there. I thought at once they were there to take me away. Who had sent them? The Ethiopian government or the Brazilian government?

'Who are you?' I asked in English.

Their English was even more limited than mine, but they were smiling and saying with gestures, 'You are safe with us. We are the federal police. We will help you get a visa to stay here until final arrangements are made.'

I did not know if I should trust them or not. No one had told me they would be coming. If I refused, they might force me. There might be other officers outside ready to help them. This was one of those decisive moments and I chose to go with them. I said I was prepared to die for my people or go to prison. It might be about to happen. I really was not worried about the outcome, but I wanted to know what was going to happen. I had already learned many lessons about who to trust and who to doubt.

The streets of the city were strangely quiet and deserted. I did not know that it was a national holiday and the shops were closed. I looked out the window and saw familiar signs to the airport. I phoned friends who were helping behind the scenes. Perhaps I should have done that before I left the safety of my hotel room.

'I am in a car!' I whispered. 'They say they are the police. They are taking me to the airport! Am I about to be deported?'

My friends were alarmed but tried to reassure me. They would check with friends in the US and Brazil, whose names I did not know then, already at work on my behalf.

We arrived at the airport and I was sure I was about to leave the country. Then the police officers offered me coffee! They went to buy it. I phoned my friends again.

'They can't be bad. They are buying me coffee! What is going on?'

'It's OK, Feyisa! You can relax. Because of the holiday in Brazil the only immigration office open is there at the airport. There are people in Brazil who are helping you; they have arranged this for you. You need a temporary visa to stay in Brazil.'

So the policemen and I sat down together drinking our coffee. Brazilian coffee is good, but not as good as Ethiopian! I did not think I should tell them that, even if we had a common language. We sipped and smiled, sipped and smiled. Then they took me to the immigration office, where the paperwork to protect me was processed. I'll tell you something else. My surname should be spelt 'Lelisa'. Someone made a mistake on my passport, it was never changed, and I am stuck with 'Lilesa'. Now that my name is so widely known as 'Lilesa', I won't try to make the correction. It is so often misspelt anyway.

The official behind the desk was speaking to me. 'These men will take you back to the hotel. They are going to look after you. Enjoy your stay in Brazil!'

Back we went to the hotel. I longed to be outside, running, refreshing my brain, and tuning in to the rhythm of my body. I knew then, confined in the small room, that being shut up in a prison cell would be the worst torture anyone could inflict on me. Every night while I was there, security guards checked to make sure I was safe. During the day I was told, 'We are close by at all time. Call us immediately if you need us.' I was a known face, a wanted man. There were other faces, unknown to me, working hard for me.

4

Tuesday. I remained in the hotel room, doing a few exercises, checking Faccbook and thinking about the next move. The streets below were alive again. Perhaps among them were dangerous men watching the hotel, waiting for an opportunity to confront me. You soon become paranoid on your own. I did not want to be afraid to go out alone in future, wherever I was.

Phone calls from friends helped me.

'Feyisa, you are in so many hearts! Oromo social media lit up immediately and now there are many people committed to helping you in very selfless ways. You are on the world stage right now and there are others working hard behind the scenes to support you and get you to the US.'

I had been thinking that I could have gone anywhere I wanted to after Rio. I had thought of extending my visa in Brazil. My agent could have sent me an invitation. I had been to the US many times and I had already said in one interview that I might go to Kenya if the government there gave me a work permit. 'There they are friendly,' I suggested to others. They all thought it was a bad idea.

'Don't you realize how vulnerable you are? The Ethiopian government could easily extradite you from Kenya. Your experience with the federal police yesterday must have shown that you are potentially in hostile territory. We've been warned of a strong presence of the Ethiopia regime's agents in Brazil. If it weren't for the fast work of others, you might not be talking to us.'

One of those people working on my behalf was Qabbanee, in Washington DC. She wanted me to keep a careful record of all the things discussed and decided with me. Tolcha Wagi and many others assured me that the Oromo know Qabbanee, the anthropologist. *Qabbanee* means 'someone with a cool head and a calm, peaceful nature'. It comes from the words for 'shade' or 'cooling'. She has already given about forty years of study, history, writing, conferences, and advocacy on our behalf. She is a devoted and trustworthy advocate. She worked with Oromos and non-Oromos to help me in what lay ahead. She was in church when her husband sent her a photo on her phone of me crossing the finish line in the marathon. She started to cry.

So many people were shedding tears because of me. As the days went on, Qabbanee consulted me.

'The visa and the protection you have are thanks to Sergio and Dyacy Moreira in Brazilia, who are friends of mine and Carol Simon,' she explained. 'Sergio is a former elected government official with contacts in high places. He has friends in the US and contacted them on your behalf, asking these Brazilians and Americans to help you. Some of Sergio's friends were the federal police knocking on your door.'

I grinned, remembering that knock on the door that made me jump.

'In the US you will meet Carol, a friend of the Oromo,' Qabbanee continued. 'Carol and I connected you with this Brazilia couple. Carol helped them to improve their English while they were in the US. After your protest, we explained your situation to Sergio and Dyacy and they immediately talked to the right people here.'

'What do they know about the Oromo?' I asked. 'Do they understand why I protested?'

'Yes, they do. When they lived in Washington, they visited the Oromo Center and asked lots of questions about our way of life and our history. Sergio is curious and well-travelled. He was intent on getting the story right there, and now he is determined to put things right for you here. "We are here to help him." That's what he said.'

I had become a stranger in a foreign land, but I was soon to learn that many of its people embraced me. Qabbanee told me more.

'Let me tell you about others. You are going to hear many stories about what Oromos were doing when they saw or heard about your protest, and how they reacted. Berhane Kebede, called Iftu, same name as your wife's, is well-known and well-loved in the Oromo diaspora in Washington. She is a successful businesswoman. On Sunday morning, while she was making coffee, her friend called and said, "Get up! Get the TV on! Rio Olympics! An Oromo son is making history!"

'Iftu says that it is not just what you are doing, but what is going to happen to you? Everybody who saw or heard knows that this is momentous and there could be trouble. "This man," they say, "is taking an enormous risk." Iftu (Berhane) started making plans on your behalf too.'

I was silent, thinking about all the activity while I was here in this little room, unable to do much to help myself. I had not counted on others before now. I was always proudly independent, in control of my life, resenting interference or advice. I received many calls from all over the world, offering help. I thanked them, but I planned to just move ahead to sort things out.

Others were also coming to my rescue. Sergio and Dyacy gave Qabbanee the name of a Denver educator, Mary Gershwin, who runs a non-profit exchange programme for students in the United States and Brazil. She agreed to help me once she heard my story. She respected me for my stand against injustice. She was on a hike in California when Qabbanee phoned her and she replied from the top of a mountain! She gave key connections to reach out to in the US Consulate. I certainly did have friends in high places!

'Every Oromo is in some way connected!' one of my friends said. 'You have suddenly opened the way for our voice to be heard. We all had the expectation that an Ethiopian runner would be among the place-getters in the marathon, but your name was not well known till that moment.'

Mohammed Ademo, the Washington DC journalist, knew that a lot of Oromo were writing and sharing photos and celebrating, but in our language; then people started writing in English too. They needed some context for what my gesture actually meant. Mohammed talked to me later about his sense of urgency.

'The sooner we got it out the sooner we were able to control the narrative,' he explained. 'Often what happens is that, when you get a big name, a special story like this, the government officials give their version of the event, and this is what the media runs with. As a journalist, I know this happens a lot in Ethiopia.'

Mohammed published 'Uncommon Courage Made Common in Rio' on his *Opride* website.

I lay back on my bed and read his version of my action at the Games. I have always loved stories. This was the first one I had read about myself.

For a great people who have, after being rendered invisible for centuries, yearned to be heard and to be visible again, who have been forcibly silenced for a quarter of a century, to say nothing of the Oromo people's longstanding economic and political marginalization, this was an extraordinary display of the indomitable human spirit and victory of the undying human thirst for liberty and distaste for tyranny. To witness one of their own using the biggest stage of his life to make a bold and unmistakable statement, is to be inspired, and empowered.

His courage will embolden many an Oromo athlete to break their long-held silence over their own treatment by corrupt Ethiopian Athletics Federation (EAF) officials and the Oromo people's second-class existence in Ethiopia. Oromo athletes are celebrated when they win medals for Ethiopia but never for their heritage. Their glorious victories are forever overshadowing the oppression of the Oromo people.

Ethiopia's glory as the home of the greatest track and field competitors on the world stage was won on the back of the Oromo athletes. From Abebe Bikila to Fatuma Roba and Derartu Tulu, from the Dibaba sisters to Almaz Ayana Eba and Feyisa Lilesa, the most decorated of Ethiopian runners are and have been ethnic Oromos. But their much-celebrated victories did little to improve the lot of their compatriots, who despite their numerical majority, remain the most oppressed and marginalized group in Ethiopia.

The athletes themselves were often abused and exploited. A few years ago, a group of young Ethiopian runners in New York told OPride that EAF officials did not even permit them to speak in their native Oromo language. They were forced to learn Amharic, the language of power in Ethiopia. In exit media interviews, Oromo athletes are often heard struggling to express themselves in broken Amharic, which is then translated to English by the federation staff and their Ethiopian handlers, who themselves spoke in broken English.

The rampant corruption, discrimination and nepotism inside EAF is such that athletes like Lilesa who dare speak out, refuse to join the ruling party and show any sign of dissent or opposition to the ruling party are often disqualified on technical grounds. And as a result Oromo athletes often put up with the federation's implicit and explicit abuses, for the alternative is non-participation in international sporting arena. A handful of Oromo athletes have quit in protest and now live in exile or run for foreign countries.

Lilesa's blossoming career with the EAF may have ended with that simple show of solidarity with his countrymen. But he joins a great company of brave athletes who used the Olympics stage to make a stand against injustice and status quo. In fact, only a few elite athletes have ever put everything on the line the way Lilesa did to speak their conscience and bring political events in their home countries to the Olympics stage.

When Lilesa's story is written, his name will be mentioned alongside two African-American athletes, Tommie Smith and John Carlos, who made history by raising the black power salute during the US national anthem at the 1968 Olympics in Mexico City. It became a defining moment in the history of the Olympics, an inspiration to all oppressed nations and people around the world.

Lilesa's defiant protest may not generate similar attention only because the international media pays little to no attention to Africans and African stories. But for millions of Ethiopians, particularly the Oromo, the symbolic gesture offers hope for a better future. It will serve as yet another inspiration to Oromo protests, which have already shaken the foundations of the Ethiopian state. Through their uncommon courage, the youth, both on the streets and alleys of their homeland and the mother of all global forums, the Olympics, have made courage itself so common.... If there's still any doubt as to whether the budding revolution in Ethiopia has reached a point of no return, Lilesa's protest in Rio is a sign that nothing can stop an idea whose time has come.

I repeated softly, 'The time has come. A time to speak.'

When I met Mohammed in Washington DC, he said his website was about to crash! So many people were reading his article. Others told me that when they Googled my protest, it looked like it was the most talked about topic of the day. I wasn't just trending on Facebook, I was surging! It sounded like a race.

I had a marathon ahead of me to get out of Rio. It could take a long time, but I didn't need to worry about money for a while. An Oromo living in California started an online campaign to assist me. That was amazing. That 'Go Fund Me' soon exceeded its initial $10,000 goal and another $40,000 goal; finally, a total of $163,221 from 2,863 generous donors who gave me help to start a new life. After the deduction of various initial costs, this would cover many expenses.

The time came when I could thank some of these people publicly. I was able to speak to Sergio and Dyacy Moreira on Skype to express my appreciation for their invaluable and strategic help and goodwill when I was most vulnerable. They posted their conversation with me on their Facebook page and provided a statement to be read at a press conference: 'Feyisa should know that he and the Oromo have friends around the world they don't even know.' I was encouraged many times by such words.

I remembered Mo Farah giving me the special shoes dedicated to him at the Olympic Games. I was amazed that a person in such a position had recognized me. 'People like Mo are beside me if I face problems,' I thought. He ran for Great Britain although he is Somalian by birth. He knew what it was like to flee from his home and seek shelter in a refugee camp. He identifies with the oppressed and homeless.

5

'Getting access to the US Embassy will be a little challenging,' I was warned, 'and your security is also concerning. You must not leave the hotel late at night.'

I thought the Brazilians were very helpful, remembering my coffee-drinking friends at the airport. They seemed to be doing everything they could to keep me safe. The security men told the hotel not to disclose my location to anyone.

Brazil is not a war-torn Middle Eastern country, but the Ethiopian security forces did kidnap Andargachew Tsige, an Ethiopian-born British citizen in Yemen, and paid millions of dollars for his capture. I promoted and advocated for peaceful nonviolent resistance against citizens, but because of that I was potentially a target.

Andargachew Tsige was a prominent Ethiopian politician and critic of the Ethiopian government, who had been outspoken about the country's human rights record. In June of 2014, he was abducted by Ethiopian security forces while in transit at Yemen's Sana'a International Airport. He was married to a British citizen, and for years efforts to have him released were not successful. Several Oromos have been abducted from Kenya, Djibouti, and Somalia and inevitably jailed, tortured, and killed.

Wednesday and Thursday. I had an appointment at the US Embassy. With a long waiting list of applicants, they normally will not see anyone unless it is a special case. The embassy appointments and actions taken on my case were set up by consulate officers whose names had been given to Qabbanee and the process was fast-tracked. I had only days to wait.

Friday. I visited the United States' Consulate, where I met several officials, including Consular Chief Michael Yoder. The service was excellent and I seemed to make good progress. Contact was made with James Story, the US Consulate General in Rio, and the National Visa Service.

I was astonished at the staff's interest in me.

'Where is your medal? When you come next time, bring your medal with you!'

When I showed the medal, they were so happy and delighted. They wanted to touch it and hold it. There was a moment when everybody stopped working and lined up to look at the medal! I admit to a lingering regret that it wasn't gold. I was not really satisfied with second best. When they liked my medal, I liked my medal! After that experience with those officials, I took pride in that silver medal.

I had to have a medical examination, which was a new experience! I'd had drug testing, as recently as the Olympic marathon, but nothing so thorough as a full examination. The others thought this was funny—an elite runner, in top physical condition, never immunized, rarely sick. The longest wait we had was at the clinic where the medical examination was conducted. Yes, I passed the fitness test.

6

Saturday. I went out to eat lunch and dinner, although not Ethiopian meals. Brazilian food is good. I liked a chicken and rice stew called *Galinhada,* tasting of many spices and herbs that I had first tried in São Paulo. When I walked down the streets of Rio, many people recognized me.

'Feyisa! We saw you on the television! Where is your medal?'

Others raised their arms and crossed their wrists.

'Oromoo!' they shouted. Then they'd approach to give me a high-five!

They heralded me as a champion of resistance. I was in a country, far away from my own, that had suffered oppression.

I knew about the local protests against government corruption and scandals. The costs and problems of preparing for the Olympic Games had caused grievances too. Many favelas, the sort of shanty towns or slums I was used to in Finfinne, had been removed and the residents forced to relocate, not all happily. I liked the city very much, but it was not that clean. I saw men urinate in public, wherever they were, just as they did in Finfinne; and beggars holding out their hands. We have them too in our country. I stopped beside a blind beggar and gave him some coins.

'*Obrigada, obrigada.*' he said. Thank you, thank you. He said something else that I could not understand.

'What did he say?' I asked one of the group tagging along with me.

'And may you have good health.'

This is a common Brazilian greeting.

People on the street wanted to do 'selfies' with me. I was surrounded by goodwill, but I had to be watchful. It was possible that Ethiopian agents would conspire with sympathizers here and harm me, even on a crowded street.

The Brazilian foreign ministry official, Paulo Torrcz, had advised me to change my hotel and move to a different location. My security was a high concern for them and I was in daily communication with the officials. I didn't change hotels.

Sunday. A week had gone by since the marathon and I was enclosed in the hotel room for most of that time. I had to get out. I must always keep up my training for the next race. I joined a gym a couple of blocks away from the hotel and every morning I ran for a short while in a field close by.

Tuesday. I planned to run from our hotel to the Copacabana Beach and back; a total of about eighteen miles. I had taken a taxi to enjoy the beach the day before and I wanted to run there, have a swim, and run back. I told security of my plans.

I got lost and could not remember the name of the hotel for a taxi driver.

'Take me to the US Consulate,' I instructed him. He must have understood me because he drove me straight there. I could remember the way from there to the hotel and by signs and gestures we got back safely to the Hotel La Costa on Rua Francisco Muratori. I memorized the name after that little adventure.

Wednesday. I started regular training runs in a beautiful park called Praça Paris. We don't have anything like it in Finfinne. I was not afraid there, but there was one place that frightened me.

Thursday. It was the first day of September. I went on the cog train to look at the big figure of the Christ that dominates Rio de Janeiro. The train takes you nearly to the top of Corcovado Mountain through a large forest, the Tijuca National Park, which I loved. The statue stands on a very steep slope, reached by climbing many stairs. I am very fit and used to high altitude, but most tourists struggled with the steep climb.

They swarmed around the statue, taking photos, kissing, laughing, shouting. Some people prostrated themselves before the huge Christ figure, while others carried their babies close to touch it, or reverently placed flowers at its base.

I started to worry about how I would get down. I forgot about the stairs and the train. Where were the trails like the ones I used at home? The huge statue intimidated me, and I wanted to get away.

'We go back on the train,' someone reassured me. 'What's wrong? Look at the amazing views!'

The view over that sprawling city of many millions did not impress me at all. Such dense smog hung over it, making it difficult to breathe. I thought of the view over Finfinne from Mount Entoto and I felt sick. That statue really frightened me.

'I'm scared it will fall on me!' I muttered. 'I must get out of here.'

Friday. I missed Iftu, Soko and Sora so much. I had put my wife in this position and I didn't know what to say to her. We had started talking again, but now it was time for a long phone call home.

7

While I was at risk of harassment, arrest, detention, or deportation, Iftu was equally in danger. My thinking had been that at least my family was alive. Leaving them behind was insignificant compared to what other Oromo people were going through. I didn't want to look at my children as any different to others in my country, who were being killed or orphaned. Soko and Sora faced the same fate and the same destiny as all other children in Ethiopia.

'Many in Ethiopia have lost their brothers, sisters, mothers, fathers, sons and daughters,' I reasoned. 'I love my country and my family; I don't want to leave them. I want to change the situation, so I can return and live with them in peace.'

I made my decision to protest and to face the consequences, but Iftu had not shared in that decision, which equally affected her safety and well-being. Had I heartlessly assumed that she would support me and understand that we should not put our personal comfort above that of other Oromos? She was entitled to feel hurt and angry. Over various stilted conversations we talked about what had happened.

Iftu and other family and friends watched the race on television at our home, commenting on every move I made. They were on their feet cheering and urging me on as I went to the front and warded off Galen Rupp. Then they saw me lift my arms above my head.

'The room went completely quiet,' Iftu told me. 'I wondered if I was dreaming. There was shock and sadness. Not a sound. Then everyone was talking at once, asking how is he going to come home after this?'

'What do you think, Iftu?' I asked carefully.

'I understand you have been pained for years, Feyisa. You often said you felt stifled, that you kept quiet for fear of reprisal.'

'The time to speak had come.'

'Why didn't you tell us what you were doing?' she demanded. This was the hardest thing for her to understand. She saw my action as a betrayal.

'You would have tried to stop me. I would have weakened because of you and the children.'

'You gave us this good life, and now our lives aren't so good. What plan do you have? You've changed everything.'

'Iftu, I can come back. I will come and see you at least. Let them kill me. I am willing to come back and die.'

'No! You must stay there! Now you have done this, it is better to stay there. You will be killed if you come home.'

'Let them kill me.'

'This is foolish talk. You are alive and perhaps we can come and join you. You are a hero to everyone here.'

'The one who leaves isn't a hero. Heroes are the ones who stay and fight alongside the people.'

'Don't come back! You won't be able to fight now. You will be put in prison, tortured, and killed.'

This was as far as we got, and I proceeded to make all the necessary moves in Rio. I was confident that it would all work out in time, but it was hard to reassure Iftu of this.

Saturday. When I was missing them all so badly, nearly two weeks after the marathon, I yearned to talk for longer, to be calm and consoling. Iftu was always waiting for my call and wanting to talk.

'Even people who don't know me have asked others for my number and are phoning,' Iftu reported. '"You don't know me," they begin, "but I am Feyisa's friend…" Some are upset for me, others cry with happiness, others can't eat. Some are worried that they will be hurt because of you. "What's going to happen to us?" they ask.'

"Iftu, what do you say to them?'

'I am still in a state of shock, Feyisa. I have a shortage of words to speak. I do not always answer the phone. Volumes of calls….'

'Have you been threatened?'

'No. You have to prepare yourself though—if they come. You don't have any other option. I worry but I can't do anything if they come. I am in their hands. I won't escape by running from them.'

She had been advised to move from place to place and to let the children live somewhere else.

'Perhaps you should do what they suggest, Iftu.' I was very anxious for her now.

'I am not going anywhere. I didn't do anything wrong.' She can be stubborn like me. 'If they are going to hurt me because I'm your wife, let them do it. I won't change my heart, Feyisa. People are advising me because they are afraid, not me.'

'How is Tokuma?'

'I go to Qilinto, to the prison, every day to visit him. Nothing has changed for my poor brother. The security guards ask me why I am still going there. I say, "*Why*? I haven't done anything wrong. I haven't committed any crime!" If they are going to hurt me, it doesn't matter if I am here or where I am. They know where I live.'

'You are a brave girl, Iftu. How is Hadhaa?'

Iftu chuckled and it was lovely to hear.

'A few days ago, we were interviewed by a journalist from BBC Africa. Your mother, Biritu Fulasa Sanbata, told him she does not want you to come home.'

'What did she say?' I was trying to imagine Hadhaa talking to the media.

'She was answering the journalist when he talked about the government's assurance that you would be welcome back in Ethiopia. "Do you really believe what the government is saying?" she demanded. "I was crying too much the other day but now I am feeling better. I want him to stay there. I wish him well." That's what she said.'

To think of Hadhaa crying for me brought the tears to my own eyes. Later I found out that she was in shock after the race. 'When I heard you weren't coming home, I could not eat and I could not sleep for many days. I pleaded with God, "Please don't let me die before I see my son one more time." I expected you to come home as usual after Rio.'

Hadhaa got better when others fussed over her, hugging and comforting her. They came up to her in the marketplace and congratulated her because she was my mother! 'He did this for his people,' they told her. Then she understood. I wondered how Iftu felt.

'Iftu,' I asked hesitantly. 'Do you understand why I had to do this?'

'I am not surprised that you did it, Feyisa.' She sounded teary too. 'I understand the problems in the country as well as you do. And I know you. Once you make up your mind you won't back down. But don't come home.'

Soko was begging to speak to me. Iftu handed her the phone.

'Ababa, Ababa, when are you coming home?'

Tears ran down my face. 'Not yet.'

A time for tears. So many tears. Many more would flow this day and the next and many more to come.

Sunday. Two weeks since the race. I had been gripped by a dream during the night about being thirsty. I was in a very hot place and I tried to find something wet. I wanted to reach the spring near my village which offers the water I love.

I began the day in my usual way, checking Facebook. My friends were posting messages about Kebede Fayissa, mourning his death. Surely not! They were saying he had died in a fire in Qilinto prison. Qilinto? What about Tokuma? What about Bekele Gerba? Had they survived? I must phone Iftu, regardless of the time in Finfinne.

'Is it true? About the fire? What do you know?'

'Kebede is believed to be dead, Feyisa. It's hard to get accurate information. We don't know for sure about Tokuma or anyone else.'

'Why didn't you tell me Kebede was in prison?'

'Feyisa, we were all trying to protect you. We didn't want you upset for the Olympics. What could you have done?'

I could have been there for my friend. I felt sick and fell to the floor, my chest heaving. Why should this upset me so much when so many others I knew had been killed? This was no surprise really. But I loved Kebede like my own brother. My worst thought was that the fire had been started and prisoners killed as revenge against me. They would know that Kebede was my friend, that Tokuma was my brother-in-law.

Family members who were waiting at the gates to visit on that day, before the fire started, were told to leave. 'No visitors today.' I wept in despair for my friend and for the others who were in the fire that broke out in the morning and continued for a long time before a fire brigade arrived. At first the government claimed that only one person was killed in the 'accident'. Soon they were blaming the prisoners for starting the fire as part of an attempted jail break. More lies.

I followed the stories and pictures all day and the next and the next. Gunfire had been heard coming from the prison and then plumes of smoke rose from the prison compound. Mattresses were burning. The prisoners could not see each other due to the smoke and were running around shouting and crying. Prisoners from other parts of the compound who tried to reach the burning section were kept back at gunpoint. Those fleeing to escape the blaze and leave the prison compound were shot.

The Agazi soldiers, or whoever it was with the weapons, shot dead more than twenty. Some reported as many as sixty dying from gunshots or suffocation; and many others were badly wounded from bullets or burns.

'Some shot dead were those who had mental illness,' Iftu told me. It was well known that some prisoners became deranged after torture and mistreatment in the prison.

The guards started to shoot each other. There was exchange of fire between Oromo and Tigre guards—when the Oromo guards tried to move the prisoners who were shot, the Tigre shot them. Several guards were killed.

Let me tell you about another case from that day of murder. The badly burned body of a prisoner was taken to his parents' home near Hana Mariam. The parents held a funeral ceremony for their son and buried him. Meanwhile, prisoners who survived the fire were taken to other prisons, Shoa Robit north of Finfinne and Ziway in the south. The man who they had thought was dead called his family from Shoa Robit. Imagine their shock at knowing their son was alive! And their horror at learning they had cried over and buried an unknown person. Whose body did they bury? When would the family whose son was buried learn that he was missing, presumed dead, but no body? How would they feel when they found out that he was already buried in another place? Would they ever find out?

The stories were shocking. Kebede's body was returned to his home, accompanied by armed federal police officers who told the family not to open the body bag. Of course they opened it. Their son's body was burnt and violated with gunshot wounds. His abdomen had been opened and organs removed. Why did they remove the organs? What was going on? We didn't want to believe such horror, but we had already witnessed and heard many terrible things. The prison fire was, in the opinion of many well-respected observers, a deliberate mass killing carried out by government security forces to scare and silence the opposition and the populace.

Kebede was buried in his birthplace of Shukute in Jaldu, in a place called Orga Eri. Sometime later, I phoned one of his relatives.

'He was shot by bullets and his belly was torn,' the relative told me, in the voice of grief. 'Then he was thrown in the fire.'

Nagaa dhaan haboqtuu, my dear friend. Rest in peace. *Biyyeen isaa sablatinna.* May the soil be light for him. No more crying, no more pain for you. You will not be forgotten. I miss your presence in my life, I mourn your death, and I will do all I can to avenge it.

For weeks we did not know whether Bekele Gerba and Tokuma were alive or not, whether harmed or unharmed physically by the fire. We thought it was possible that the whole fire was a ruse to 'disappear' Bekele because he was unaccounted for and the authorities taunted the concerned public for two weeks by refusing to release information about him. Finally, he was seen.

Bekele made eye contact with his daughter, Bontu, across the prison yard. She took food regularly for him, like Iftu did for Tokuma.

Tokuma was sent to Shoa Robit prison. They tortured him and others, accusing them of burning the prison.

'How would prisoners burn the place?' cried Iftu. 'How could they smuggle in the materials through tight security to start a fire? Even when a menstruating woman goes to the prison to visit, she must show the guards that she is wearing a pad. The searches are humiliating and thorough. There is no way you can smuggle in anything. Remember, Feyisa, when we begged them to give the *rigaa*, that very small wooden toothbrush, to Tokuma and it was not permitted?'

I remembered.

Yet Tokuma and his friends were charged with burning the prison.

8

Wednesday. It was September 7th, seventeen days since the marathon, one month since I left Finfinne. Departure and defiance, danger and death, now the sadness of distance from everything I held dear. My story at this point had it all—a real-life drama. I had been assessed as physically fit. How, people asked, was I mentally? Many things weighed heavily on my mind, but I am disciplined. An elite athlete trains his mind and his body to meet every obstacle, every turn in the road. I was ready for whatever lay ahead of me, just as I am in a race.

I worried about my training and my fitness in Rio. I gained nearly a kilo in weight, which shows you that my appetite was good and I was not wasting away with anxiety. I had commercial contracts with Nike for the next three years and I wanted to meet them. I needed that sponsorship to satisfy the authorities that I had the means to live in the US and to satisfy myself that I could continue supporting my family.

I was so rich compared to other Ethiopians. I gave some of my share of the GoFund Me donations to the Demisse, Tasisa & Angasu Support Fund. Tamiru Kefeyalew Demisse is a paralympian, who won two gold medals in the Africa Championship in Tunisia and a silver medal in the 1,500-meter contest at the Rio Paralympic Games. Megersa Tasisa Bati, another paralympian, has won many gold medals. At the Rio 2016 Olympics, they showed the same protest sign that I gave. They knew that if they went back to Ethiopia, they would be killed or otherwise mistreated.

Adugna Anigasu Yigezu was a journalist, stranded in Brazil, facing a similar fate as the two athletes. This brave journalist, father of two, had been reporting on the brutal nature of the corrupt Ethiopian government, with its reputation for jailing journalists who dared criticize its policies. Their situation was dire, and I was leaving them behind in Rio.

Thanks to a dedicated network of people, the US Consulate opened the door to my future in record time. My case was cleared in a couple of weeks and I was on my way, visa in hand. I departed for Washington.

I left the hotel in a taxi, directing my driver to the airport where I'd been entertained with coffee and smiles. My first flight was to Houston, Texas, where I connected with a flight to Washington DC.

VII

I

Airports are foreign lands, unnatural places full of strangers and unexpected sights. I have been in many different ones, waiting and watching. At the Houston airport, I studied the big screen listing departures, working out which flight would take me closest to Finfinne. Since that day, at every airport, I scanned the faces in the crowd for the dear familiar faces of Ethiopians and I yearned to be on that plane going the way of my heart, back to my homeland. I imagined Iftu waiting for me outside the Bole airport, ready to hug me and drive me back to Sululta and our children.

I arrived at the Ronald Reagan National Airport in Washington DC about two o'clock in the afternoon to a quiet reception area. There had been talk of a hero's welcome from the large diaspora in the city, a red carpet rolled out, and a throng of well-wishers with cameras and flowers. The place appeared to be deserted, except for my good friend, Tolcha Wagi, accompanied by another man.

Tolcha hugged me tightly. 'Feyisa! Oromia's son! Welcome to Washington.' He held me at arm's length and studied me.

'Feyisa, we struggle for fifty years and no one knows what is happening in our country. You do it alone, no one advises you, a young guy! You are in my heart, the one who does a good job for our people.'

I grinned at this OLF warrior, now fighting a different war with demonstrations and placards to draw attention to the plight of our people.

'No one listens or believes us! No media interest, none, for all our demonstrations. You, Feyisa, in one gesture, start the questions being asked.

Oromo? Who is Oromo? Questions! I am glad to have lived another fifty years to see this day.'

He led me out to a big black Lincoln car. I have always liked black cars and this one was long and large and comfortable. I sat in the front—I wanted to see the city sights.

Mohammed Ademo and Qabbanee were arranging a press conference for me with the international media. This would provide me with my own platform as I arrived in the US. I accepted the proposal, but realized that making the event enticing to international journalists would come at some cost in relation to the Oromo and Ethiopian community preparing to greet me at the airport in the US. The rules of the press highly valued 'exclusive access' to a breaking story. If I allowed an airport welcome prior to my press conference, any person, let alone a journalist who attended or posted on social media, could 'scoop' the story and make it uninteresting to the major media outlets. Our big challenge was to reach the public that was largely unaware of the Oromo plight.

Mohammed and Qabbanee explained that a big airport welcome would kill the story and undermine my purpose of getting the story of suffering of Oromo and other Ethiopians to a wider and more general public—the Olympics watchers, the sports fans, others attracted by the human-interest aspects.

I understood what my Washington supporters were doing and why, but I needed to get out and run. I'll talk to the important journalists, I decided, but I had my job too. I didn't want to lag behind. I have never understood the life of those who sit at a desk all day. I often joked with them about their confined lives. 'We would love to be out there running like you!' This is what they say. 'We are prisoners of our own desks.' I was bound to a life on the road and I could not spare precious days of training.

'I'll give this two days,' I said to the advocates who supported my arrival.

'We won't even start this if you can only give it two days.' They were firm and determined. 'We understand that this is a sacrifice for you to be sedentary for one week, but your cause will benefit enormously. You will see.'

They gave me the choice and waited until I agreed to keep my arrival secret until the day of the press conference, September 13, 2016. They planned the event and set up international attention to my story.

'We will do this in such a way to maximize exposure.' Mohammed, the *OPride* journalist, had professional contacts and acted as my interpreter. 'We will invite reporters I know and reach out to key organizations; we want them to do follow-up stories on your protest in Rio, which some of them already covered.'

Mohammed had started by phoning people in direct contact with Feyisa, wanting everything done properly. He said to Qabbanee, 'Let me talk to Feyisa's handlers.'

'You're talking to them!' Qabbanee shot back. 'We don't need professionals. We would end up paying these "handlers" big bucks, then advising them on every step. We would still be doing all the preparations anyway if we want to give Feyisa—and the current Oromo condition—the best exposure.'

I met my volunteer 'handlers' in a downtown place, an AirBnB it was called. I came to appreciate their very precise ways of explaining our background and customs in a way that others could understand.

'You need to be very private about your whereabouts before the conference,' they insisted. 'If we got you a hotel, you would be immediately recognized by one or other of the many Ethiopians in the area. The word will be out on social media. The journalists who want to break your story would lose interest.'

'If you want to sit at a bar and allow people to take photos, something may come out of that,' added Mohammed. 'But if you wait just a few more days we can make this the most media-intensive event by an Oromo—ever.'

They talked me into staying at least a week. I worked with the group to prepare the agenda and the statements to meet the media.

A single big event. I liked the idea. This is why I did the protest; this is why I was there, to notify the world. This is why I agreed to arrive secretly without fanfare. I hoped that my supporters would understand.

People brought food to my room; otherwise I had intense meetings with those who were helping me to prepare my own press conference. We met at a hotel close by where they had nice seating at the end of an extended lobby. We huddled there.

'Is that Feyisa?' asked passers-by.

'No! Just someone who looks like him!'

We needed Aduna, who does look like me, as a decoy. He was coming to Washington to support me.

Even people who worked in the hotel, waiters and desk staff, were thrilled to see me.

'I must have a photo with him!'

'No, no, we can't allow that.'

'Please take a photo of me with him and send it to me later.'

'If we agree to this you must not tell anyone who he is. Not yet.'

After a couple of days, I issued the following letter, a painstaking translation of my own words that were initially handwritten in *Afaan Oromoo*:

> *On August 21, 2016, I won an Olympic Silver medal in the men's marathon in Rio de Janeiro, Brazil. As I was crossing the line to victory, I crossed my arms above my head to show the sign of peaceful resistance adopted by*

the #OromoProtests movement in Oromia, Ethiopia. In so doing, I took the extraordinary privilege and the distinct honor of expressing solidarity with the predominantly young men and women who perished in hands of the terrorist regime in Ethiopia in the last nine months.

Running the Marathon in Olympic Games is the dream, and the greatest honor, of every athlete. Running it to win a medal, like I did today, is a life-time dream come true. Running it to win is an exceptional honor incomparable to any success as a professional athlete. It was with the awareness of this singular honor and of the solemnity of the Olympic Games that I ran the race and achieved what I could achieve.

But when I ran on August 21, 2016, I ran with a heavy heart. I ran with the thought of the hundreds of men and women, most of whom are of the same age as me more or less, who were brutally murdered by the Ethiopian regime only within the last nine months. I ran with the thoughts of thousands that were shot and maimed, tens of thousands who are languishing in military detention camps, thousands more whose whereabouts are yet unknown, thousands who are tortured, raped, and otherwise violated by a state terror machine. I ran with the memory of close friends, members of family, relatives, and acquaintances who were killed, maimed, arrested, abducted, tortured, and dehumanized just because of who they are as Oromos. I ran with the memory of all the injustice, the repression, and the dehumanization I have witnessed or heard about since my childhood which coincided with the tenure of this regime.

Needless to say, it takes a toll on one's life to run a marathon in the Olympic Games with all this on one's mind. As you can understand, it was under the weight of the suffering of my people in my heart that I ran the race. It was in memory of them that suffered, and keep suffering still, that I chose to show the sign of peaceful resistance in the Olympic tracks today. I am aware of the dire consequences this has for me and for my family in Ethiopia. The regime that sought to silence every dissenting voice would use this as an occasion to silence me, my family, and anyone related to me.

I am aware that from now on other athletes may face pressures the severity of which I cannot even imagine. But I am equally aware that just to be alive as an Oromo person in Ethiopia today has a dire consequence anyway, as that alone would make you a target of violence routinely meted out on Oromos by this ethnocratic regime, thoroughly biased in favor of the elites from Tigray.

Back in Finfinne, I have a young family—a wife and two small children. Along with other relatives including my mother, they still live there. While there, I had the comfortable life that one leads as a professional athlete. Contrary to what the regime is saying, I have not done what I did just to create a justification for seeking asylum elsewhere. As everyone understands, by so doing I have a lot that I have put on the line: my career, my future, and above all, the safety and wellbeing of my family. My act was a response to the call of conscience as an Oromo person whose close relatives, friends, and contemporaries suffered and are suffering a lot in the hands of the repressive regime.

I would like to confirm to the IOC, the IAAF, and the world of professional athletics and beyond that I uphold all their principles in everything I do. But I would also like them to appreciate the extremely difficult circumstances of our people that I needed to bring to this platform if only I could express, with gratitude and humility, the pain I share with those who suffer under a brutal regime in my country.

For those of you who expressed concern about my safety, I would like to say that I am doing well at the moment. But from where I stand now, the future is uncertain both for me and my family just as the future of the youth at home is uncertain, perhaps much more than mine.

I would like to say thank you to everyone who has reached out to me with your love, prayers, care, and concern. I never felt prouder of my compatriots.

Sincerely, Feyisa.

I exchanged my running gear for a dark suit and white shirt. I was ready to meet the press.

On the big day, September 13, 2016, *The Washington Post* published an op-ed piece paired with a video in my own voice featuring an English translation, longer than the usual letter to the editor. This was an opportunity to reach many readers and start the conversation. This is what I wrote:

'Things are getting worse in Ethiopia. I fear for what could happen in the future. Our grievances have not been heard in the rest of the world because the government has blocked communication. Here is my question: Can nonviolence succeed if no one hears our voices or sees our protests? We all yearn for peace, but the government continues its attacks. I fear that if the killing does not stop, people could abandon nonviolence in self-defense.

My country is an important ally of the United States. We in Ethiopia and people around the world see America as a beacon of democracy and promoter of human rights. Allies should not let allies commit the abuses that happen in Ethiopia every day. I don't think that the United States wants Ethiopia to disintegrate. I am asking the U.S. government to demand an explanation from Ethiopia and to condemn the brutal and unfair actions of the government. The United States needs to push hard for democracy in Ethiopia. I think that is the only thing that will keep my country together.

I have no plans to initiate contact with the Ethiopian government, and no one from the government has reached out to me. If the government desires to have contact with me, it should free all political prisoners. It should also free those who have been arrested without even being involved in politics at all. That includes freeing all Oromo, Amhara and those from other nations and nationalities who have been unjustly detained.

I'm a runner, not a scholar or politician. But I know that all people yearn for fairness and justice. I will continue to race and pursue my career, and I will speak out until the Oromo and others in Ethiopia find justice.'

In the video clip I explain my protest sign. I am shown running, highlighting my life as an athlete; Soko is included, kissing my photograph; and at the end I raise my arms in the now familiar gesture.

My words, like my protest gesture, quietly emphasized non-violence and I wanted my audience to understand this. I was in a country where the most memorable protests had been led by Martin Luther King, in a city where people with the charcoal color of my suit and the chocolate color of my skin were once segregated from those with the white color of my shirt. The US still has much work to do on racial issues and the ill treatment of native Americans.

I had been told about the promise of tightly scheduled 'exclusive' interviews. One journalist, Chris Chavez, the man who spoke to me after the Rio Marathon, had been given first access on the day of the conference, but he had to fit into the day's tight schedule and a last-minute request from a Congressman to appear at the Capitol. I answered Chris's questions in the car taking me to that first public appearance in the city, at a microphone and lectern near the steps of the Capitol. At the same time, the first US House Resolution on Ethiopia was to be introduced.

'There is ethnic conflict escalating in Ethiopia,' I warned my listeners. 'The government is using the power of the gun to silence Oromo protesters who demand economic, political, and land reform.'

People in this country understand all too well the power of the gun in wrong hands, with the massacres at schools and other public places.

'Hundreds of my fellow Ethiopians have been killed by security forces,' I said, my voice trembling, thinking of Kebede, 'only because they peacefully protested against injustice.' Even when they didn't. My poor friend.

'I want to tell the world what is happening in Ethiopia—in Oromia, Amhara, Ogaden, Gambella, and elsewhere. The Oromo are Ethiopia's single largest ethnic group. The Ethiopian coffee that Americans drink comes mostly from my region. We are also well known for our long-distance runners. Please help my people.'

I encouraged American citizens, including Oromos, to use their democratic right and express support for an important Bill that I had been briefed about. Congressman Chris Smith, from New Jersey, a staunch supporter of our cause, was there beside me. He announced House Resolution 861 that day in the House of Representatives. In a few months, this Resolution would be updated and given a new number: H Res 128. It supports respect for human rights and encourages inclusive governance in Ethiopia. It has strong bipartisan support.

'Once passed,' Rep. Smith said, 'the resolution will be a strong statement of policy that will see funding to the Ethiopian government conditional on respect for the rule of law and for human rights.'

Ethiopia received a lot of US aid—more than any other country in sub-Sahara Africa. It was, ironically, a partner in counter-terrorism efforts in the region.

I said in my op-ed that I was not a politician, and I did not want to get involved in US politics, but I understood that the Resolution would send an important signal of support to peaceful protesters who sought justice and demanded human and civil rights in Ethiopia. It urged protesters to refrain from violence and to reject all aggression in demonstrations. My fear was that my people, who had mostly exercised restraint, would start to retaliate if the killing continued, and civil war would break out.

After we had spoken, Chairman Chris Smith and other co-sponsors, Republicans and Democrats, made the protest sign with me. Pictures taken on the day show us there, white and black men and women, some Oromos in ethnic dress, against a deep blue sky and the stark white of the beautiful Capitol building. Now was the time to build strong international support and to tear down the structures of tyranny and corruption.

My own press conference was scheduled to begin within the hour at the Phoenix Park Hotel and progress to it was slow by car. Some walked the short distance from the Capitol. I wouldn't have minded running, suit and all.

My first words for the journalists assembled in the hotel's conference room were about freedom of speech, a right that I do not take lightly.

'We Oromo have not had access to you who are in the media,' I told them. 'We have been cut off from you. We do not have a free press in our country. The urgency of our protests has been suppressed by the state-run Ethiopian media and largely ignored by the West.'

Some of them would know, through organizations such as the Committee to Protect Journalists, of bloggers and journalists charged with terrorism and imprisoned in Ethiopia. The Committee to Protect Journalists described Ethiopia as the third worst jailer of journalists in Africa after Eritrea and Egypt. The journalists listened intently to me.

'My legs were running,' I told them, 'but my mind was preoccupied by all the suffering that was going on around me. More athletes are likely to follow in my footsteps.'

I thought of the paralympians in Rio. I also heard that Ebisa Ejigu had won the Quebec City Marathon a couple of weeks ago and made the protest sign. How good it was to see my friend Demssew Tsega Abebe, the athlete whose feet were deliberately damaged to prevent him running. He had been in the US for several months and he told his story at the press conference. He talked about the Torture Abolition and Survivors Support Group (TASSC).

'When I arrived in Washington,' Demssew said, 'I found TASSC, which has helped me in so many ways, including finding a doctor for me, providing me with psychological counselling, a case manager, and giving me medical evaluation. The doctor who works with TASSC referred me to a foot doctor who has been treating my feet and now I feel better. I hope I will be able to run again because running is my life.'

I nodded, understanding better than anyone in the room how much running means when it is your life. Others told me that Demssew reached out at TASSC. He was a community builder supporting fellow exiles as they all went through the long process of asylum and work permits. Mostly they relied on the kindness of others.

He came up to me afterwards, still limping, but beaming and hugging me. I asked him about his family in Ethiopia. Our shared pain for our wives and children bonded us even more now.

'My son does not speak, Feyisa. I am much worried about him. I am working here at a hospital, some night shifts, taking food to patients and feeding some of them, also cooking. I try to send money home. Last year my wife did not have any income.'

'This is hard, Demssew.'

'The boy he is crying and kisses my picture. After they arrest me, he hides under the bed and runs away when I Skype. My wife is expecting our second child. Last year I borrowed money from a friend to help them. Now I have a job I can repay this guy—he is my best friend.'

The last words of my speech were for people like Demssew. 'People are saying from now on we want to live in peace, we are tired of being killed, we don't want to be in prison, we don't want to be forced into exile, we want to decide on our own resources and shape the destiny of our country. We've had enough.'

My press conference was well attended, with a lot of excellent, penetrating questions from some of the best sports journalists out there. The positive reports that came out generated dozens of responses in print, digital, and video stories. I was pleased that readers would know that I am the way I am because of my upbringing. My Oromo culture shapes my being. I have faced the media in post-race interviews many times, not always understanding the questions, but prepared to answer if I can. I am more animated when I can speak in my own language, but I did answer some interviewers in Amharic, softly and self-consciously.

In the following days, I was interviewed on VOA and ESAT radio in Washington, responding in Amharic, which many Oromo refuse to do. I speak Amharic badly, which pleased Oromos, and tried my best, which pleased Amharas! I think I made many new friends because I focused attention on people rather than politics. 'I miss my family,' I admitted. 'I am miserable at what I am putting them through, but I remind myself that my family is not suffering any more that others in Oromia and my kids are no better or worse that other children. It's not about my family. I am not just doing this for Oromos, but for all people in Ethiopia.'

My friends showed me later some of the reports that came out of that concentrated week of interviews. These described me as a committed young person, who exuded energy… he seemed to have a good sense of humour although exhausted and anxious… he was articulate and broad thinking in his position and in his understanding of the problems… he was tenacious and focused.

'People are deeply moved because of what you have done, Feyisa,' my new friends said after the press conference. 'You are a good agent for political change.'

2

The next stop was a welcome reception at a hotel in Silver Springs, located in Montgomery County, Maryland. I was transported in style to the event.

'There is nothing that a struggle cannot bring,' I said aloud to no one in particular in the car. 'Think of our Oromo expression, "*in turra malee in urra jette boombiin*".'

'It may take time, but we will eventually pierce,' said the wood piercing beetles. This is what the saying means. I hoped a lot of things would be successfully accomplished in the future to justify the cost of so much human suffering.

The welcome event organized by the Oromo community was huge and very exciting. They had invited guests from the wider Ethiopian and American communities. More than 1,000 people attended. Tolcha Wagi opened the ceremony. He and Oromo community organizations had arranged a lot of security, bodyguards with bullet-proof vests, to protect me.

'We want you to be safe, Feyisa,' he told me. 'We say you are like our prime minister!'

'I do hope I am not like the Ethiopian prime minister!'

The protection, along with many other gestures, arranged from a modest budget, was touching to me. They were showing me respect. I liked this being an interfaith celebration, with blessings from a priest of the Orthodox Church and a Muslim imam as well as elders of the Oromo traditional faith, *Waqeefaanaa*. Oromo people are the first to recognize others as human beings and give them citizenship in the form of the traditional process, *guddifachaa*, which means adoption or the process of adopting others to themselves. Oromos respect God's creation. Since they believe other peoples are also God's creation, they respect and love them. We are tolerant and patient.

The feast prepared in my honor smelt wonderful and I was very hungry. They were disappointed when I ate a small helping of rice and not much more.

'I'm not running just now,' I explained when I refused dishes. 'I have gained weight and I must eat very little.'

Hundreds of people lined up to have their photographs taken with me.

The celebration in my honor was overwhelming, with songs and poems about me. No trouble had been spared to make it my day, a long and unforgettable day. I was thankful to be given my own platform, to tell my own story, and to be honored so warmly by people from my own country, and many expatriates as well.

One of the best things was having Aduna, my brother, there to enjoy it all with me. Once the feasting, dancing, talking, and singing were all over, we ran together along some of Washington's paths, past big monuments and waterways. There was no cherry blossom at this time of year, but I had garlands of flowers to spare.

Aduna was just twenty-two then and he liked to run. I worried about his returning to Ethiopia after the visit, but he insisted, like Iftu, that he had done nothing wrong. Not long after, though, when he was training in Burayu, outside Finfinne, soldiers approached him. They hit him on the head with the butt of a rifle, kicked him, and threatened to shoot him, demanding information about me. He was detained for hours. Fearing for his life, Aduna lied and told the soldiers what they wanted to hear about his brother: 'He is a terrorist; he is no good.' After the Olympics, his wife was suspended from her job with the Ethiopian government radio.

I didn't hear about it for weeks. My family kept the news from me, worried again that it would devastate me, like the news about Kebede. People were beaten and arrested in Finfinne because they had pictures of me on their phones. If they were caught listening to songs about me, they were beaten. When I pressed for details, Iftu told me one story but wouldn't give me his name for fear that officials were listening to our conversations.

'Feyisa, one of your relatives, the farmer, the one who only studied until eighth grade. He knows how to use Facebook and he downloaded a picture of you and made it his screen saver. The police are even going to houses and interviewing people. They saw the picture on his phone and beat him badly and left him for dead.'

Remember the boy who used sticks to draw a likeness of Abebe Bikila in the dirt on his legs? I thought of how, before mobile phones, I cut out pictures of athletes like Kenenisa Bekele and Haile Gebresilassie and pasted them in my exercise books or stuck them on the walls of our house using thorns as paper pins. Having athlete heroes wasn't a crime back then.

I heard about a runner called Bonsa Didha who rode a motorcycle from place to place. When he was riding his bike in Burayu, west of Finfinne, he was stopped by a police officer, searched and questioned. They found a few US dollars in his pocket. Bonsa went abroad to run – the money would have been change from a recent trip. They took him to jail and beat him.

'Where did you get this US money?' they shouted. 'Feyisa Lilesa gave you this money, didn't he?'

He was detained for a couple of months because of me. How hard it was to be feted as a hero when I heard how others paid for my action.

After Washington I flew to Minneapolis, home to a large, active Oromo expatriate community, where I was met by a motorcade at the airport and celebrated in an event similar to Washington, only this time in a Convention Center. Once again, I was overwhelmed by the reception and the huge crowd that attended.

'You need to do something to reach out for our people,' I told the assembled crowd. 'They are waiting for you.'

Ethiopia was presumably an essential partner in the US 'war on terrorism', but the US government was unwilling to apply meaningful pressure on the Ethiopian government over its human rights record. In Ethiopia, if you were not a supporter of the ruling party EPRDF, you were a 'terrorist'. If you were a supporter of a lawful opposition party, you were a 'terrorist'. If you repeatedly questioned things, you were a 'terrorist'. I didn't know persons who detonated bombs that much. If there were real terrorists in that country, a lot of bad things could have happened. Ethiopian security is not so technologically sophisticated to avert terrorist attack.

Many people did not have enough food to eat, let alone the resources or knowledge to terrorize the country. Nobody thought about committing acts of terrorism except a dishonest government, which used the 'terrorist' threat to get the attention of the US and attract bilateral aid. They were cheating and getting a lot of dollars in the name of the war against terrorism. I feared that the Resolution explained to me so optimistically will be blocked by the Ethiopian government terrorists.

3

While all that was going on in the places of power, I was about to start my new life in a strange land. I had chosen to leave my own country to alert the Western world. The publicity died down and I wondered if it was worth it. Meanwhile, I had to find a place where I could train and make a home for Iftu and the children. When Demssew and others talked about their families waiting long months for the word to come to America, I felt disheartened. I had to stay positive for Iftu's sake, believing that we would be together again one day.

The best options seemed to be in Colorado or Oregon or Arizona, places with the high altitude I needed to be like Finfinne. Snow bothered me, but I wouldn't be able to avoid it altogether in a northern country. Through a connection with an Ethiopian friend, I made contact with Yonas Mebrahtu, an Eritrean, one of several East African runners who lived and trained in the thin air of Flagstaff, Arizona, nearly 7,000 feet above sea level.

'You will like it here in our community,' Yonas assured me. 'Some of us train together and we will help you settle in.'

Do you remember my telling you about Teklu Deneke, a friend in the Armed Forces Club in Finfinne? He moved to the US in 2008 and lived in Flagstaff. Imagine his surprise when he went out training one day and saw me with Yonas and Abdi Abdirahman, a Somalian-born runner!

'Feyisa!' he called. 'I have been worried about you! I thought to myself it would be good for you to come to Flagstaff and here you are!'

I was among friends, committed athletes who shared their lives and their homes with me. I unpacked my bags in Yonas's apartment in Oakwood Village on S. Yaqui Drive. In this complex of wooden homes, I watched the children riding their bikes and scooters and heard them chattering in the playground outside my bedroom window. My room was small and bare, but I did not have much to put in it anyway. All I needed was a temporary place to eat and sleep and train.

Soon my shoes were added to the pile beside the front door. I studied the Eritrean flag hanging in the lounge room. Eritrea fought bitterly for its independence from Ethiopia for thirty long years before winning it in 1991. What was gained in the battle? The country was governed by a single-party, presidential, totalitarian dictatorship, no different to Ethiopia. Yonas told me about his family's suffering during the war. Sometimes I talked politics with him and Teklu, but our focus was on our running. We communicated in Amharic.

There were no Ethiopian restaurants or grocery stores in Flagstaff. Iftu had looked after me so completely, and now I had to learn to shop and cook and wash the pile of sweaty clothes that grew bigger and smellier after each training session. Sometimes I was too tired to be bothered cooking and ate just one or two meals a day. That's the way it was when I was a kid, going off to mind animals or run to school without breakfast. Instead of *buddeena* (*injera*), I bought wheat bread from Wal-Mart. If I wasn't careful, I'd be getting fat like that little boy, Bogia.

Yonas took pity on me and prepared omelettes, pancakes, and vegetables. He made it look easy.

'Let's buy some goat meat,' he suggested when a visitor was expected. 'We can buy it at the Native American Reservation.'

We paid $100 for the carcass of a half-butchered goat and attacked the hindquarters with dull knives. My knife got stuck and I grinned at the others.

'This was a tough old goat!'

We ate the tough old goat, seasoned with chilli powder. Teklu knew about an Ethiopian store in Phoenix, a couple of hours drive away from Flagstaff, but he did not own a car. I was determined to get my driver's licence as soon as I could and buy a car. I needed it for when Iftu arrived.

'Where do I get my licence?' I asked Teklu.

'We need to go to the Department of Motor Vehicles. You'll have to pass a written exam and a driving test.'

We applied for a permit and looked through the manual together. I can read and write English much more easily than I can speak it and I was pretty confident I could do the written test.

'It's all done on a computer,' Teklu warned.

I failed the first time. Back we went, and I was sure I'd pass this time. I was too hurried and excited—I failed again.

'It's not a race!' Teklu's patience with me was wearing thin.

I succeeded on the third attempt. Then came the driving test with two women watching every move I made. If you can drive in Finfinne, I reasoned, you can drive anywhere. The traffic was not heavy in Flagstaff and there were no goats or donkeys to avoid, no mad intersections or impossibly congested roundabouts. This was easy. I understood all their instructions—turn here, go straight ahead there. I pulled in to the Department of Motor Vehicles with a flourish and gave the women my most charming smile. I passed.

Now I had wheels, a black Lexus, to fill with runners or, one day soon, my family. I explored Flagstaff—its mountain trails, its Coconino State Forest, its Lake Mary Meadows, its grazing elk. I thought it was a good place to be. They are very good people in Flagstaff. When I went to the gym or the swimming pool, they invited me to dinner and asked about my country and my family.

The stands of aspen trees with their quaking leaves were turning gold as autumn advanced and I thought of little Soko, my golden girl. Would she be here to see these yellow leaves next year? Winter worried me, but Teklu and Yonas reassured me.

'When it snows here we go south to Sedona or east to Winona. These places are not so high up and there is not as much snow.'

The scenery around Sedona is truly amazing. The strange shapes of the red buttes are like nothing I had ever seen before in my travels. Runners are privileged to be out on the roads early and late with eyes to see and marvel.

I felt energized once my training was underway in earnest. I stepped outside each morning and breathed in the clean, cool air. Too many weeks had passed without a proper schedule. I thought of runners at home whose focus must be affected by the turmoil and crackdown.

'If this continues without any change,' I predicted gloomily to Yonas and Teklu, 'Ethiopia may not win as many medals as it used to. How can they perform with all the stress?'

I did not compete in the New York Marathon in November. Ghirmay Gebreselassie, fourth in Rio, claimed that one. I ran in the Honolulu Marathon in December, but I did not do well, coming in fourth. The city was so lovely, with its beaches and Christmas decorations and fireworks, but my feet were following my uphill thoughts rather than the road ahead of them. I fretted after the race that, if my running results faltered, I would disappoint thousands of supporters watching me and would please the Ethiopian government.

'They want me to fail,' I told a journalist after the race. 'I cannot let them see me fail.'

At the Houston Half Marathon in January of 2017, I was defeated in the narrowest of margins, fighting it out, elbows and all, with a Kenyan, Leonard Korir. I raised my arms in a clenched-fist cross as we reached the finish line, almost as one man. A photo of the finish was beamed around the world and shared on social media. I wanted to win, but, even if not in first place, I said with a smile for the press, I had to show my people that I was still defiant. 'Next time I will win!'

I ran with a new determination after the events of October 2nd in Ethiopia. I cannot use them as an excuse for my disappointing result in Honolulu, but they certainly affected all Oromo, wherever they lived in the world.

4

There are times when the black clouds above are matched by the ominous dark events below. I have told you about *Irreecha*, the annual thanksgiving holiday that marks the end of the rainy season and the beginning of the warmth and bounty of the dry months. The festivities are filled with color and tranquillity, with happy greetings, as friends and family—separated for months by rivers overflowing from heavy rain or by grievances—reconnect and reconcile.

In recent years the traditional festival had become an opportunity for Oromo people to openly express their identity as a unified nation, bound by history, culture, and family. The youth, the *Qeerroo*, have also used the occasion to express their disillusion with the government and their suppressed anger at its vicious treatment of Oromo.

The festival draws crowds of up to four million from across Ethiopia to the town of Bishoftu, about forty kilometers southeast of Finfinne, to pray and sing alongside the crater lake we call *Hora Arsadi*. *Irreecha* is a sacred event and the site is a hallowed ground for all Oromo. I would not miss going to *Irreecha* if I was in the country, but recently a threatening cloud had overshadowed the *Booqa Birra* (meaning a shining day when light replaces the dark).

At the last festival I attended, soldiers grabbed my *bokkuu*, my ceremonial staff.

'Why are you holding this?' they demanded.

They turned on Tokuma, Iftu's brother, who was holding his own staff tightly. He was not willing to let it go.

'Why should we let them take them?' he hissed at me.

'Give it to them,' I ordered. 'We don't want trouble. Let us enjoy the day.'

Soldiers were confronting those wearing clothes that were completely red or green, accusing them of flaunting the OLF flag.

'What are you thinking of?' they blustered. 'What is your motive for wearing this color?'

Our *Irreecha* costumes are mostly white, but that didn't stop the outrage. They tore off necklaces with *Odaa* tree shapes from people's necks. They insisted that people wearing clothes imprinted with the *Odaa* tree remove them. They confiscated or damaged books for sale at the festival if the colors on the covers resembled the OLF flag.

Signs of trouble before Sunday, October 2, 2016 included the blocking of the road to the office of the *Abba Gadaas*, the council of traditional leaders who were supposed to preside over *Irreecha* the next day. The government and the *Abba Gadaas* had already engaged in long negotiations about the arrangements for the festival.

The government deployed thousands of soldiers in preparation for a showdown if those attending the festival used it for voicing dissent. State forces surrounded festival-goers. Several armoured vehicles were pointed at them. Tensions within the massive crowd built when government officials appeared on stage and intensified when the current *Abba Gadaas* were not present on stage. Instead, a retired *Abba Gadaa*, believed to be closely aligned with the government, appeared.

A military helicopter flying low overhead increased public concern about the government's intentions. Eventually, one defiant young man, Gemeda Wario Wotiy, jumped onto the stage, grabbed a microphone, and led the crowd in chants associated with the #OromoProtests movement as they raised their arms with crossed wrists. They were chanting, 'Down, down Wayane!' Wayane is a derisive term for the dominant TPLF. When Gemeda was thrown off the stage, a group of youngsters, including a young woman, replaced him, kneeled down between the police forces, and defiantly displayed the protest sign. The crowd cheered them on. When the young woman left the stage, a young man lifted her onto his shoulder and she was given the black, red, and white *Abba Gadaa*'s flag.

The masses of people grew restless as events escalated and suddenly security forces threw tear-gas cannisters. They had a history of using live ammunition while confronting and dispersing other public gatherings in Oromia, with tear gas preceding the bullets. When the pattern seemed as if it were about to be repeated at *Irreecha*, panic quickly set in.

People ran and fell into ditches, while others were trampled in the ensuring chaos. The exits are narrow, and the safest, widest exit road was blocked by military vehicles. Nearby there is a dangerous deep gorge. Since the gunfire came from the opposite direction, the people ran towards the gorge, not knowing the danger it presented. Did the military know that those who ran away to escape bullets being fired from behind would be finished in the gorge and ditches? I think so.

Many believe the *Irreechaa* massacre was deliberately executed. The police knew exactly where the deadly cliff was. In previous years, some were assigned to guard the gorge and protect the crowd from approaching the area. They even prevented the youth from climbing trees near the gorge as a precaution to avoid accidental falls. The police knew the safe exits and in what direction to let out or disperse the crowd. This year, there were no police guarding the cliff, no rope or tape to mark off the dangerous hole. The closing of the wider exit road and firing on a panicked crowd from that direction cannot be dismissed as a mistake. It was a cold, calculated, and inhumane military decision.

Survivors were eventually escorted out by heavily armed police on top of several pickup trucks, with machine guns pointed at them. Others pulled people out of the ditches, including those who were buried alive and died from suffocation.

At Bishoftu Hospital, the corpses were placed in three different centers—female victims in one and males in the other two. Witnesses and hospital staff insist that the number of dead was much higher than the government estimate. I have heard figures of 600 or more. The media could not gain access to morgues, and bereaved families were unwilling to speak for fear of reprisals, so we don't know how many died. Some hospital staff indicated high numbers in the hundreds, but they were under pressure to keep silent.

There were numerous reports of medical staff not being permitted to speak or being pressured to under-report deaths. They may also have had limited access to the bodies. It is widely known that during the previous twelve months several medical staff were arrested for speaking out about killings and beatings by security forces or, in some cases, for treating injured protesters.

What more can I say about this tragedy? The crowds were not violent, but they were clearly protesting against the government. The response of the security forces was disproportionate and triggered the stampede that resulted in many deaths.

The massacre reached international attention, as awful images of the butchery and bloodbath were seen around the world. Then came the usual expressions of disbelief and condemnation.

'Why is nothing done?' Yonas asked me, but we all knew the answer.

'Those responsible for the massacre,' I predicted to Yonas, 'will face justice from the Oromo nation. We will rise up against those guilty of firing on innocent people.'

I wept for those who were mourning and burying their dead. I feared that the cycle of death… funeral… demonstration… more death would go on and on. Protests would continue. 'We have nothing else to lose,' the young ones said. 'Better to go down standing up for our rights than ending up dead, disappeared, or in jail.'

Accusing and punishing those who advocated or engaged in non-violent acts as criminals or terrorists sent a very dangerous message. Remember Skip Marley's song, *Lions*? 'We are the lions, we are the chosen, we gonna shine out the dark, we are the movement, this generation, you better know who we are….'

Immediately after the bloodshed at *Irreecha*, there were angry reprisals against the property of those who had taken Oromo land, but no deaths during the assault on businesses. The government declared a three-day period of mourning. One week later it went further, announcing a six-month 'state of emergency'. This meant the army was deployed nationwide, military command posts were established in resistant districts, and access to social media and mobile Internet was indefinitely suspended.

'They have laid their actions bare,' I said. 'But there's nothing new here.'

My cross-armed protest was banned, punishable by detention or worse, and could only be used with official permission. For days after the massacre I was haunted by an image from another *Irreecha* when I sprinted ahead of Hadhaa, Mother, teasing and calling for her to catch up. She accepted the challenge. She clutched her long white skirt with one hand and held her headdress in place with the other. She could run fast, my Hadhaa, and I danced in front, encouraging her, till she joined me. We ran together, laughing and happy to be there. There was no blood on our white clothes or fear in our hearts that day. We were not among bodies trampled underfoot or gunned down or limp at the bottom of a gorge.

5

After the state of emergency was declared, I could not always reach Iftu by phone. All I could do was hope and pray that my current celebrity status protected her, but when days passed without hearing her voice or seeing new pictures of the children, I was restless and anxious.

When Iftu described Sora's behavior, I was very troubled. At home, as I was ready to leave in my big car, the V8 with the loud engine, Sora could hear it starting up and he ran out to wave goodbye. When I returned, he heard the car coming and he was out the door, to welcome me home. In my absence others drove the car and Sora ran out, excited and hopeful, calling 'Ababa!'

'At first, I tried to hide him when I knew the car was about to leave,' Iftu explained, 'but he knew, and he struggled to get free. Then I decided that the car cannot go out. It is too upsetting.'

The little one, Sora, did not understand. He didn't ask, 'Where is Ababa?' I heard his plaintive voice crying for me as he did before I left. Soko was persistent in her demands.

'She asks, "When is Ababa coming home?" all the time,' her mother said to me. 'I say "Tomorrow" and repeat that many days.'

'You are lying to me!' screamed Soko. 'Call him and ask him.'

Iftu relented until it was too hard for all of us. After a while I could hardly bear to hear Soko's babbling talk and her questions.

'This is no good for you, Feyisa,' Iftu decided. 'She has to wait for the day we come to you.'

When the child sobbed and sobbed, I said, 'Let me talk to her.'

'Ababa, when are you coming home?' Always the same question.

'It is not me coming to you,' I explained. 'You are the one who is coming to me!'

Soko had seen movies and she liked what she saw of America.

'I want to see where the children play!'

'You shall see those places, Soko. I am going to find you a beautiful place to live.'

I longed for Iftu and the children. I watched other families in Flagstaff preparing for Christmas—such times are always hard for separated families.

'I know the process is going to be successful, Feyisa.' Iftu was calm and reassuring again. 'I have a peace about it all and we will be ready to come. I have started sorting our things and packing our bags.'

She didn't tell me that her main anxiety was her reception at the airport when she was ready to board the plane. She feared that government officials would be waiting to detain her.

In Flagstaff, the other runners and I were leaving the comfort of our heated apartments for the stinging cold conditions outside. We had to rug up, warm up, and prepare for icy winds. I was in constant fear that I might slip on the frozen ground and injure myself. Snow lay on the mountains and in the branches of the ponderosa pine trees around our apartment. I tried to imagine Iftu and the children there, marvelling at the snow and shivering in unfamiliar weather.

'They will come. I know they will come,' I told others repeatedly. 'All they need is final clearance from the US Embassy in Finfinne and for the Ethiopian government to let them go.'

One evening in late January of 2017, we were sitting in the lounge room watching news reports on CNN. Newly elected President Donald Trump was giving an executive order to temporarily close America's doors to immigrants from seven predominantly Muslim countries. Ethiopia wasn't one of the countries, but Sudan and Somalia were on the list.

The President's decision gave his administration time to develop more stringent screening procedures for refugees, immigrants, and visitors.

'I'm establishing new vetting measures to keep radical Islamic terrorists out of the United States of America. Don't want them here,' Trump announced. 'We only want to admit those into our country who will support our country and love deeply our people.'

The bans took effect immediately, causing havoc and confusion for travellers with passports from Iran, Iraq, Libya, Somalia, Sudan, Syria, and Yemen. CNN showed sad scenes at airports, some passengers forced to return to their own countries. Even Green Card holders were advised to consult immigration lawyers before travelling outside the country or trying to return. I turned off the television. We were all silent.

'What does this mean?' I asked.

It did not affect Iftu's arrival, but debate about the order occupied Americans for many days, some denouncing it as 'un-American'. What does *that* mean? I can't imagine that term applied to my country. 'Un-Ethiopian'! I smiled at the thought. There was a controversial President in the White House.

Iftu visited the US embassy in Finfinne to collect her invitation to the US and to have a medical examination. She was given the visas. Ethiopian bureaucracy involves multiple stamping and signing of documents, and the family took their visas to the Post Office for final clearance. You can never be absolutely sure that you have all the right stamps, that you are there on the right day, and that the queues waiting will be cleared that day. You expect to be told of another stamp required and to have more money ready. Iftu had never travelled outside the country before. Everything was new and challenging. She managed it all efficiently.

Our wider family was worried about me, not about Iftu and the children. They knew she had to join me, but the separation from the children was going to be hard. They were all crying as the day of departure approached.

'I am going to bring the children back to see you,' Iftu promised. 'Feyisa is the only one who cannot come back.'

She made one more visit to Tokuma in prison. That was the hardest goodbye of all, except the last visit to her grandmother, who was in poor health. Family and friends were there at our house, advising on what to take and what not to take. Everyone had a story about life in America. I could picture the scene—the overcrowded rooms, the preparation of food, the loud excited voices, the children running around, calling out, getting in the way.

Iftu was worried about how Soko and Sora would manage American food. She included all sorts of groceries for them and coffee for me. I had given her a list of things to bring. The bags were packed to capacity.

Iftu dreaded the airport. She tried to explain that day to a journalist in one of the interviews we gave after her arrival in the US.

'They can do anything and not let you leave the country. It is a big thing for them to have to connect us with Feyisa. As we were going out to the plane I was thinking, Can they come and take us from the plane? Maybe they mistakenly let us pass through the airport. The people who took us to the airport waited till the plane was off the ground. They were worried too. I was relieved when that plane took off!'

'How did you feel as you were on the plane? Did you have any stops along the way?'

'I was not like a new person on the plane. My family was saying I'd be frightened. I talked to the people around me. My son was disturbing me, from Finfinne to Miami! He was not happy; he did not want to buckle up. "Take me out of the airplane! I want to get out." That's what he was shouting.'

Sora probably had earache like his mother and sister. They were not prepared for that or the huge airports in Jeddah and Frankfurt, where the sound of foreign voices and the push of packed crowds were overwhelming. It was difficult, moving from one end of the airport to the other, with little children, carry-on bags, and tickets to work out.

I was waiting for them at Miami International Airport on Tuesday, February 14, 2017, six months after I left Finfinne for Rio de Janeiro. I wanted them to see big cities like New York or Chicago on their first trip to America, but those places are very cold in February. 'They won't believe they are in the US if they come straight to Flagstaff!' I said to Yonas, laughing. I was in a light mood as I planned for my family. 'They will think it's like going to Ginchi from Finfinne!'

Miami was a good choice. I went there the day before they flew in to arrange a hotel and a car.

I bought a bunch of red roses for Iftu.

There they were, running towards me! Soko and Sora leapt into my arms and held on to me tightly. I put them down and they clung to my legs as I turned to embrace Iftu. With both hands I wiped tears from her eyes.

'Hi,' she said awkwardly. There were journalists watching us and cameras flashing. 'I did not think I would see you again so soon!'

I wanted to be alone with my family as soon as possible, but I had prepared a statement for the press:

'First, I want to thank Wuuqu (God) for reuniting me with my family. I also am grateful to the US consular staff at the embassy in Addis Ababa, Ethiopia.

'Second, I would like to thank my family for their patience and understanding during more than six months of my absence. And my friends and everyone who supported us during this time.

'I am really happy to see my family. But I am also filled with mixed emotions. That's because it's always been my wish to live in my country, with my entire family, and among my people. In fact, I have never imagined I would be exiled from my country and be separated from my people.

'Regardless of whether I had enough to eat or I went hungry, whether I had a pair of clothes or not, in times of happiness and sorrow, it was my wish to live among my great people, who raised me with a sense of Oromumma (Oromo identity) and who taught me about love, respect, history, and courage.

'But despite my physical safety here in the US and now a family reunion, the Ethiopian government's ongoing abuse of the Oromo people gives me no rest.

'No one builds a family with the intention of going into exile. Instead, to live in one's own country and ensure familial continuity. Unfortunately, exile, however dreadful, has become my fate and the fate of many Oromos.

'As I celebrate this small personal victory, I want to make sure that we don't forget the plight of millions of Oromo and other Ethiopians who are still being killed, beaten, imprisoned, dispossessed, and kept in poverty.

'Toward that end, I renew my call to the US government and the international community to re-evaluate their foreign aid and other dealings with the Ethiopian government in light of the worsening human rights situation in the country. I urge them to stand with the Oromo and all oppressed nations in Ethiopia.

'The struggle continues. The Oromo people will win their freedom. Until victory is achieved and justice is served for those who shed their blood in the merciless killings, I will continue to resist and stand with my people. My commitment to this cause is not simply raising my crossed wrists over my head after every race. I am prepared to do all it takes to help my people win their freedom.

'I will continue to speak out against injustice and its perpetrators using my platform. My biggest wish is to see the freedom of my people—all people, in every country.

'Thank you!

'Feyisa Lilesa Gemechu'

6

We stayed in Miami for a few days. Iftu loved it there in the sunshine near the sea. This place was a wonderland to her and our children, who had never seen waves breaking on the shore or walked along a beautiful beach, barefoot, feeling the sand between their toes and capering away from the water.

'I wish we could stay here,' Iftu said wistfully. She was still thinking about Miami months later.

'For a holiday,' I suggested. 'We must go to Flagstaff now, so I can keep up my training. I have a half-marathon in New York soon. You will come with me and see one of the most amazing cities in the world.'

Even as we walked from the plane at the Flagstaff airport, Iftu was exclaiming about the cold.

'It's burning me!'

She was wearing thin-soled shoes and a light jacket.

Some days later, when I entered our apartment, I could hear Iftu talking to someone at home about what it was like.

'I am thinking, *How am I going to live like this?* I have never been so cold in my life. I don't say anything to Feyisa to upset him. Then I am saying to myself, "Why did I come here?"'

This was a very heavy time for Iftu. Being alone was difficult when you came from a big family that was always around you in your house or in theirs. In Flagstaff we closed the door and we stayed indoors. We were still alert for the unexpected knock on the door. We were used to the US Anti-Doping Association (USADA) sending one of its control officers to collect blood and urine samples from me. They test me and elite athletes around the world for prohibited substances. We never know when this will happen, but I know I have nothing to worry about. I run to win on my own merit and ability.

I don't think Iftu was afraid to go outside in a foreign place or to meet strangers, yet I had trouble encouraging her to leave the apartment. When we went out she ran to the car and when we came home she ran straight to the front door. Iftu can move fast when she wants to.

'Come outside and get some fresh air,' I pleaded. 'It helps you forget many things when you walk briskly.'

'It's the time of snow,' she argued. 'I will wait till it is not so cold and then I will go outside.'

I had rented an apartment for my family, on East Pine Knoll Drive, in another big wooden complex among the trees. Iftu brought the Oromia flag with her at my request and we hung it on the wall in the lounge room with a wood cutting of an *Odaa* tree below it. We had very little to remind us of home, except in our minds, where we lived too much of the time.

Soko started school at the nearby Kinsey School. She had been learning English at the Dandi Boru School in Finfinne and she settled into our new life very quickly. Iftu sometimes told her that we would go back to Ethiopia one day. She cried.

'I don't want to go back! I like it here!'

A few months after we arrived, Iftu showed her photographs of her cousins. She flounced away.

'I do not know them.'

Internet and phone connections had improved in Ethiopia. Iftu called her family once a month and kept in touch through social media.

'Nothing has changed, Feyisa,' she informed me. 'People are still dying. Tokuma is still in jail.'

I wondered, was she really saying, *What are we doing here? What have we done? What have I done?* I had my routine of training, eating, resting, but Iftu was home all day with Sora, a silent child, not as ready to engage with others. When I returned home from training or trips, sometimes he took no notice at all. Soko was constantly in motion, while her brother was still, except when we had Oromo DVDs playing. A protest scene grabbed his attention, and he mimed the dissent using a stick as a spear and the lid of a pot as a shield. Sometimes he stood in front of the television staring at song and dance celebrations, then joining in, running on the spot for ages, trance-like.

'We will tell them about the traditions,' I said to Iftu when she expressed concern about his behavior. 'He is hearing and seeing Oromo. It's a start.'

'It would be better if the little ones live in the place of our traditions to learn,' she replied stubbornly. 'If you simply try to teach them about traditions, they may not hear you. Children believe what they see rather than what you talk to them.'

I knew that Iftu would go back home immediately if she could. I did not blame her for that, alone all day. I am not much company with my rigid schedule, but she is there always, waiting for me to come home and wanting to meet my every need. I longed for her to be happy, this woman who chose to share my exile and my fate. I remembered her once saying, *Badiin biyyaa wajjinii badhaadha*, which means 'Sharing burdens with everyone is a blessing.' She was sharing a very big burden, carrying the heavier load.

7

Our apartment was close to the campus of the Northern Arizona University. Sport is a big part of its life and much of it happens in a huge stadium called the Skydome. Teklu and I and others are glad of its facilities, like the weights room, especially in the cold months. We used the running track at the Coconino High School too. We were not an unusual sight in a city where many runners and cyclists share the roads and where, in the warmer months, the locals live more outside than in.

Each day when I watched the day dawn beyond the mountains of Arizona, I recalled the same scene over the hills of Jaldu or the peaks of Finfinne. My often-repeated prayer was that a new day of change and freedom would soon dawn in Ethiopia and that all the runners in exile could return to their own land. 'It won't be like this forever,' I promised Iftu. 'One day we will all go home together.'

My family flew with me to New York City in March for its annual half-marathon, with a course from Central Park to downtown. Iftu suffered her usual pre-race nerves and a sleepless night, but I woke fresh and confident. I had a really good run, overtaking Callum Hawkins in the last few meters to win the race and raise my arms again as I crossed the finish line. Soko darted out from the crowd and ran to me. I hugged her, so happy that I had won and that I could give her another medal to add to the collection which came with the family from home. She was satisfied with the Olympic silver medal and showed it off at every opportunity.

That evening we went to the Sea Shore Restaurant in the Bronx, where Oromo expatriates honored us. The children pointed and exclaimed about the lights when we went back to the hotel in midtown Manhattan. Iftu stroked Sora's head as he drifted into asleep and I held Soko close. I wondered if she ever thought of her home city, Finfinne, as I did, and Iftu, all the time.

Back we went to Flagstaff, where I was going to train in earnest for the London Marathon on April 23rd. I nearly didn't make it to that race. I ran out of pages in my Ethiopian passport and needed a special travel document to fly to London. I applied for it in November, but the weeks went by and I had no reply from the United States Citizenship and Immigration Services. I showed a local official my invitation to the marathon and explained what was at stake, but he said I might have to wait many weeks for the documents to be cleared. This was beginning to sound like Ethiopia's signing and stamping.

The London Marathon pays an appearance fee of at least $200,000 and much more if you place in the top ten competitors. The money is very good, and I wanted another chance to confront the world with my message. I got the document in time.

The media was making much of the confrontation between me and Kenenisa Bekele, who made a decisive statement winning the Berlin Marathon a month after the Olympic race. That was the time he was asked about the protest gesture and he answered that sport should be separate from politics, that everyone had a right to protest in Ethiopia, and that the government was trying to 'solve things in a democratic way'. I still couldn't believe he actually said that.

For the thousands of Oromo watching their elite athletes compete around the world, I was seen as the dissident athlete living in exile, while Kenenisa was seen as submissive in his refusal to criticize our country's regime, despite its ongoing persecution of our Oromo people. 'The blood is still flowing,' I said in an interview with BBC Africa. A spokesman for Ethiopia's embassy in London called my comments 'fairy tales'.

One journalist claimed that many diaspora-based activists regarded Kenenisa as a regime apologist. Another said, 'Lilesa is running the London Marathon representing the Oromo voice in exile while Bekele represents the silenced Oromo population back home in Ethiopia. Bekele is a face that represents a forced narrative of the regime as imposed on the people back home while Lilesa's protest performance in its entirety is a counter-narrative that negates authoritarianism to its core.'

The media love newsworthy stories of conflict and personal clashes. Kenenisa and I posed obediently for photographs in London, reluctantly standing closer to each other when instructed to do so by the large group of photographers. Then we joined other favorites for the marathon in a pre-race jog. I was pleased to see my Kenyan friend, Abel Kirui, among them. I could gladly look him in the eye and talk naturally to him in a way that I could not with Kenenisa. Abel had won the silver medal at the London Olympics and we talked about our Olympic experiences.

'Then I had a dry spell,' he said. 'I am back on the scene now after winning Chicago last year.'

I have run the Chicago Marathon three times, with a place in two of them. Ethiopia ran first, second, and third in 2012. I was in second place and scored my PB (Personal Best)—2:04.52—just under the time that many regard as the benchmark for the elite runner's marathon, 2:05. Like all of us, I want to edge closer to the two-hour time.

'Perhaps we will compete at Chicago in October!' I said to Abel. 'Good luck today, my friend.'

My supporters wanted me to win in London and have another prominent platform on which to protest, but it was not to be. I went there confident of winning, and I thought that even second place would not make me happy. I prepared myself very well for this race, as I knew the Oromo people were eagerly waiting for me to win. I dreamed the night before that I was watching the winners come in at the end of the race and I was not among them. This was a bad omen, but I had assured the journalists that I was not in the least bit nervous. Too much confidence and pride are not good. I was cautious in my tactics and they did not work on the day. After I ran thirty kilometers my legs got fatigued and cramped. I just couldn't run as I should have in a sure rhythm and regular stride, timing my splits.

My rival, Kenenisa, came in second. A Kenyan, Daniel Wanjiru, was the winner, with my friend Abel in fourth place. I trotted over the finish line in twelfth position. I was sad and disappointed with that unexpected result. I can only say that the interrupted training and the distractions of eight difficult months must have been factors and the old leg injury flared up again. It didn't feel right to let my people down.

I returned to Flagstaff while Kenenisa took the shorter route to Finfinne. We would always go our separate ways. For the first time in my career I knew discouragement and for about three weeks I neglected my training.

The spring days were lengthening, and the sun was shining in May. Flagstaff was blooming with wildflowers and the leaves were back on the aspen. Iftu and I took the children for walks and soon their bikes and scooters were lined up with the shoes at our apartment. We visited the famous Grand Canyon, which is very grand indeed. I have been told that the Simien Mountains in northern Ethiopia, with deep ravines and gorges, and tall sharp peaks, are comparable. One day we will go there to see for ourselves.

I was scheduled to run a half-marathon in South America at the end of July—the Bogotá Media Maratón—and instructed to think about Chicago. I had competed in Bogotá a few years before, coming in second after Peter Kirui from Kenya. This time our positions were reversed.

'I feel wonderful because five years ago I was in second position,' I told the waiting media. 'I like Bogotá a lot. If everything is really good next year, I will try to come again.'

I had made my gesture of defiance and explained it again to a new audience.

'This crossing of my arms means stop killing, stop jailing, stop land grabbing in Oromia. While the Ethiopian government is killing the Oromo, Amhara, and Gambela people, there can be no peace.'

Bogotá was good for my diminished confidence. There was one more race before my first year of exile in the US was over. This was the Great North Run, the largest half-marathon in the world, with participants running between Newcastle upon Tyne and South Shields in North-East England. The date was September 10, 2017 and I knew I had a big contest ahead of me with Mo Farah running as the favorite. Sure enough, he won, with Jake Robertson from New Zealand coming in second and me third. This was Mo's fourth successive victory in the Great North Run. Kenenisa Bekele had beaten him to the finish line in 2013, the first time Mo had attempted the race. Haile Gebreselassie came third that year.

Mo was stretched out on the track afterwards, exhausted. I went over to him and he flashed his marvellous grin.

'That was really really tough, Feyisa. I'm sore everywhere—I have never been this sore.'

He scrambled up.

'With four miles to go I was just hanging on, gritting my teeth. As we got closer, I managed to believe in myself and dig, and I was thinking, *If I can just sit on Robertson, at the end I can sprint.*'

'Maybe a marathon next?' I suggested. 'How about the next Olympics in Tokyo?'

'I'm not so good at marathons. I have struggled so far.'
'Mo, I'll race you there in 2020!'

8

The dream of running in the 2020 Olympic marathon is like the dream of a poor farm boy watching Sydney Olympic athletes running in the television. The words of my friend that long-ago day come back to me: 'Feyisa, if you train for even a week you will fly like the birds.' I dreamed of flying back to Oromia, running for my country once again. I was racing with the country code ETH beside my name on the lists of competitors, for Ethiopia is my place of birth, my nationality, but not my location. I have not applied for American citizenship. I was very grateful to this country for giving me and my family a refuge, but it was not our home.

I had the thought that in Tokyo I might run with "ROT" beside my name. The Refugee Olympic Team took part in Rio de Janeiro as independent participants under the Olympic flag. An Ethiopian, Yonas Kinde, was in the team of ten athletes and competed in the men's marathon. He left our land because of political problems and lived in Luxembourg. He ran in 90th place at Rio.

The IAAF, the governing body for track and field, requires athletes to be citizens of a country to represent it in competition. If the athlete changes citizenship, there's typically a one-year waiting period. The runners who've been granted asylum fall into a grey area and must wait for five years before they can apply for US citizenship, a lifetime for an elite athlete. This is hard for runners like those I met in Washington.

I was surprised when some critics accused me of using the protest sign as a ploy to gain asylum. 'He is not doing it for the people in Ethiopia,' they said. 'He is doing it for himself.' You learn to live with such comments, part of the price for taking a stand. On the other hand, I did not expect the outpouring of global support that I received and the impact my gesture had in creating awareness. I've been told that my protest in Rio and the press conference in Washington DC, when I spoke to about thirty journalists from twenty-five media organizations, opened the way for more press coverage of recent protests in which over 1,000 of my people died.

I won international recognition with my defiant protest. The *Foreign Policy* magazine named me among the top 100 global thinkers of 2016. I was applauded as a challenger, 'for breaking the rules of the game in order to call attention to the brutal actions of his country's security forces'. I emphasized again that I wanted to be a voice for a story that hadn't been getting any coverage. *Deutsche Welle* featured me in its 'Year in Review: The Stories That Moved Africa in 2016'.

I was included in the *Huffington Post*'s list of inspirational athletes, who 'flexed their muscles off the field on a wide range of social and political issues in 2016.' That's what the article said about us. I follow other sports and I heard about the American football player Colin Kaepernick, whose name was also on the list. He refused to stand during the national anthem. Instead, he knelt in protest. Reporters called it 'taking the knee'. Colin wouldn't honor a country that didn't honor its own people. He made statements that sounded like mine. 'I am not going to stand up to show pride in a flag for a country that oppresses black people and people of color. To me, this is bigger than football, and it would be selfish on my part to look the other way. There are bodies in the street and people getting paid leave and getting away with murder.'

In their Western democracy, African Americans are often the victims of racial violence and police brutality. In Africa, the totalitarian Ethiopian government got away with murder every day. President Obama was still in power while I ran the Rio Marathon. I hoped that he saw me make the protest sign. When he visited Ethiopia, he said that it is a democratic country. I showed him that he was wrong. Galen Rupp, the athlete who was behind me in the marathon, is an American and I believe Obama watched that race. I hope that he regretted giving credibility to the Ethiopian government.

I was once a barefoot shepherd boy and a grubby day laborer, now an elite runner with unexpected opportunities to meet with influential people. In early November, barely two months after I raised my arms in Rio, I was invited to Brussels, where Merera Gudina, chairman of the opposition Oromo Federalist Congress, and other Ethiopian activists were meeting with members of the European Parliament. We were there to discuss the human rights situation in our country.

I went back safely to the US, but Merera Gudina was arrested when he returned home, on the charge of communicating with a banned terrorist organization. Berhanu Nega, the leader of the outlawed "Patriotic Ginbot 7" armed group, attended the meetings with us in Brussels. This was enough for the Ethiopian government to accuse and imprison Merera. At the same time Prime Minister Hailemariam Desalegn gave a briefing to foreign diplomats declaring that the country had largely returned to calm since the state of emergency was declared. He dared to say that, knowing that Merera's arrest would increase anger and frustration in the Oromo community.

When my mind turned, as it often did, to the protesters, one image stood out. On Facebook I saw a picture of this older woman and I added it to my own page. She was like so many Oromo women, scratching out a bare existence, wearing a shabby shapeless dress and shawl. Her feet, in plastic sandals, were planted firmly on the ground and her thin brown arms were taut. She clutched a stone in each hand. She was the face of the Oromo matriarch, protecting her young, claiming her space, defying authority. I had no doubt that she was ready to throw those stones at the enemy. I called her the Stone Thrower.

The youth of Ethiopia, her sons and daughter among them perhaps, were protesting. A generation was protesting. I was just their known face from a country that idolizes athletes. I saw Oromo youth back home as my own children when I heard what they were doing. I was proud of them and I'm glad that *OPride*'s Oromo Person(s) of the Year 2016 was the *Qubee* Generation, often referred to as the *Qeerroo*.

The citation read: 'For inspiring and moving the world with their disciplined courage and bravery in the face of relentless state brutality, for bringing the dream of freedom ever closer to being realized, for their bold commitment to a cause greater than self, for finally forcing the world to pay attention to the plight of Oromo people and for rejuvenating and energizing the Oromo movement and bringing it to the cusp of victory—the *Qubee* Generation.'

OPride made special mention of Oromo musicians who released more than 100 #OromoProtest singles in 2016. 'The Oromo singer is at once a provocateur, social critic, and an inspiration and outlet to a generation suffocated by a deep state hell-bent on clinging to power through the barrel of the gun.' Many of our artists have been in and out of prison or forced into exile. I knew many of them.

'Feyisa, there are many songs about you at home,' Iftu told me. 'Athletes, teenagers, farmers with those big cheap Chinese mobile phones! Even Hadhaa has songs written about her because she is your mother!'

'She'll love that!'

'I have heard people say to each other, "Get rid of that playlist! There is no Feyisa Lilesa among the songs!" They dare to wear shirts with your face printed on them. You are their hero.'

My supporters were on the streets where I once ran. They were the heroes. Many times I wished that I was back there among them, but I had made up my mind to live in Flagstaff as long as my career as a runner continued. I didn't know what would happen after that, but I hoped the story of my life would end in Ethiopia. Since my family depends on my running, I thought I would not be successful if I moved to somewhere else. This place suited my training. This was a good place to raise my family. My English slowly improved as I helped Soko with homework and watched YouTube cartoons with her.

I know that I speak only a half-truth about our situation as it was then. I had trouble concentrating on my training, and my performance was suffering. I was aware that my family was also suffering, because I was not giving them the attention they deserved. I was too far away in my thoughts, in Oromia, following on social media all that was happening there. Homesick and sad, I desperately wanted to return to Ethiopia. Iftu must have felt the same way. I was neglecting the family when they needed me. One day, I promised myself, I will make it up to them.

After six months, Iftu, Soko, Sora, and I moved to another apartment, located on Lake Mary Road. This one was modern and spacious, and it smelt like home when Iftu made *buddeena* and the spicy sauces we like so much. She was never far from Oromia in her own thoughts. She often walked over to the large window in our lounge room and stared out into the gathering dusk. She often marvelled at the long twilight here, unlike Finfinne where the day closes abruptly, giving way to the dark.

We were surrounded by forests, and the smell of the trees at certain times took me home to the forest where I played as a boy. I've been told that in the past large areas of ponderosa pine were cleared and sent east by train. The Jaldu people have that harsh fact in common with the inhabitants of Flagstaff. I was interested in the local Native Americans, for the Oromo share some cultural practices with them. There is a large Navajo Reservation near where we lived and I saw one of their traditional homes, their *hogan*, with fire-pit in the middle and the door facing east. I was reminded of the humble home where my life began.

Each day I left the apartment for my morning run, often remembering the little boy who left his house to run to school. When I returned, Iftu was waiting, ready to serve my breakfast. I do not go without breakfast as I once did. I put on expensive jeans with holes and patches and frayed cuffs, a designer version of the tattered ones I wore as a teenager. I pulled on the latest Nike shoes, while Soko and Sora danced around me, barefoot.

VIII

I

As I packed my bag for the October 2017 Chicago Marathon, I told Soko and Sora about my athlete friend who dances after he wins a race.

'Abel Kirui dances for joy! He is so happy when he wins that he dances around. The crowd loves it. He dances more with his arms because his legs are tired. I could see him when I ran in behind him in Daegu. He got the gold medal that year at the World Championships.'

'Will you win the gold medal in Chicago?' asked Soko, tucking my socks into the bag.

'My golden girl, you'll have to wait and see!' I lifted her up and twirled her around. 'See if I dance like this at the end like Abel!'

Abel and I have talked about our plans and strategies. Unlike me, he has trouble sleeping before a race.

'I often have very little sleep, maybe only three hours.' He held up his long thin fingers. 'From about three o'clock I am awake and I usually put the radio on to listen to music.'

Abel is a Christian and he always prays to God on race day. 'I ask him for energy.' He grinned at me. 'And also for him to place me higher than my opponents, like you!'

We reminisced about our childhood running days. He lived close to the Nandi Escarpment, a rugged, long, steep slope in Kenya which drops many meters to the valley below. He ran and played on that escarpment. He always visited his grandmother to receive her blessings before any race, but she died a few years ago.

'That does not stop me from winning now!' he warned me, with the same cheeky grin. I thought of Geti, wishing that she had lived to see her favorite race against the world's best. Mo Farah was also very close to his grandmother.

Abel is a great admirer of Eliud Kipchoge, so he changed his training base, motivated to be around and learn from Eliud.

'I wanted to steal some good ideas from Eliud.' Kirui looked at me half-defiantly. 'He is trying to run under two hours and I knew it would be amazing to be around him. Eliud is very smart, far smarter than me. He is so organized. If he says dinner is at 7 pm, dinner will be at 7 pm. If it is time for sleeping, it is time for sleeping. He is always on time.'

'His discipline is his strength,' I said. 'Eliud is serious, but he is simply focused on winning.'

'Well, he has made me a better athlete. He is a man fighting with time.'

Eliud wasn't on the starting line in Chicago for the October 2017 marathon. But Galen Rupp was there, making the sign of the cross before the crack of the gun sent us on our way. I glanced at Abel, the defending champion. He'd explained his starting practice to me.

'I prepare my mind for the battle ahead. I say to myself, "I need to win today" and, if I can't win, to at least finish in the top three. Training has been too painful to waste it all on a bad performance.'

My training was wasted on that day in Chicago. I lost sight of the leaders and I was in 14th place when I crossed the finish line. I looked for Abel. He ran in second, behind Galen Rupp, who was talking up America's future in the marathon.

I've never won Chicago, but I've been part of its dramas. On the plane from Flagstaff to Phoenix, taking me on the first leg of that last journey to Chicago, I was sitting beside a local runner, also on his way to compete in the marathon.

'Your epic battle with Sammy Wanjiru in the 2010 Chicago Marathon was one of the greatest races I'd ever seen,' he enthused.

My English was still not the best, but I was puzzled. The battle for first place was fought out between Sammy Wanjiru of Kenya and Tsegaye Kebede of Ethiopia. I came in third. My manager, Federico Rosa, agreed with my fellow passenger. He called it the greatest marathon race he had ever seen and the biggest surprise.

'Ah, Wanjiru!' I said to my fellow passenger on the plane, shaking my head. 'He was crazy!'

Sammy's brilliant short career and controversial life came to a tragic end a few months after the Chicago race that fans still talk about. He died from a fall off a balcony at his home in Kenya. I remember that my manager, Federico Rosa, mourned his death.

'He had the special gift of the champion.' That's what Federico said. 'Besides a big talent, champions have what I could call an arrogance. They know they are stronger than the others. He was so focused on winning, not to be famous or get a lot of money, but just to show that he was the best.'

We all want to be the best. I have endurance, but perhaps not the arrogance of that colorful character, Sammy Wanjiru. I desperately wanted to keep the message out there, to repeat the protest sign for the Oromo cause at every opportunity. I went home from Chicago, questioning, 'What existence is mine?'

2

Maalan Jira—What existence is mine? It's the name of a song that became the soundtrack of a revolution, the marching music of Oromo youth—the *Qeerroo*. The song was released about a year before the Rio Olympics—a spur to the legs to take me there and a pulse to the protest I had conceived.

'Haacaaluu Hundeessaa voices our cause.' Kebede's quiet assertion came back to me. 'He is our generation's Ali Birra.'

'Remember what his father kept saying to Haacaaluu when he was in prison?'

'*Jabaadhu gurbaa, hidhaan qoraasuma dhiiraati.*' Kebede and I said it together.

The words mean 'prison is the crucible of manhood'.

When he was still a high school boy, Haacaaluu was arrested and imprisoned for nearly five years at Karchale, Ambo, a prison dreaded for torture and mistreatment of Oromo dissidents. His jailers tried to break Haacaaluu and force him to give up singing, but they did not succeed. He wrote songs in jail and when he was released, he fearlessly sang about torment and the intolerable Oromo situation.

In some of his songs, he called attention to prisoners of conscience in the Maekelawi and Kaliti prisons, the Qilinto remand center, and Karchale Ambo, which stole his youth. He was forced into exile at some point, but he went back to Ethiopia more determined than ever. 'I am not a fugitive,' he declared. 'As an artist I sing about what I feel and think. I will continue to sing in the future too. The run to exile must end with this generation.'

Haacaaluu Hundeessaa's protest ballad, *Maalan Jira*, is about the dispossession of the Oromos' heartland, Finfinne, denouncing the evil of a so-called Master Plan for the city that I have told you about. Haacaaluu wept for Finfinne, crying out the original names of localities.

Maalan Jira became my song, *full* of anguish and hope. I have run to its challenging words and danced to its strident beat. By now you will understand that we Oromo use storytelling to explain our proud past and our present pain, but often our stories linger only in the minds of those who heard them around the village fireplaces. We knew that our narrative was at odds with that of our oppressors, cut short by the gun or denied in the place of torture. Too often fear silenced our voice.

The *Qeerroo* found a way in music to reject the wrong version and to resist oppression. Their freedom songs called for unity among a people divided by the colonizers. Their bold expression was destined to bring us out of darkness into the light of a new day and a new order. Where their politicians had failed, they would succeed.December 9, 2017. Haacaaluu rallied the *Qeerroo* at the biggest Oromo concert ever seen in Finfinne. He was on a stage no less public than mine in Rio, the lead singer in an event broadcast live by Oromia Broadcasting Network (OBN). '*Ashamaa, ashamaa, ashamaa!*' he called. 'I salute you! How are you?'

The audience watched him stride around the stage, calling repeatedly, 'Where are you? Are you here?' Then he started singing *Jirra*, 'We Are Here!', the defiant message of the *Qeerroo*. 'Our needs are deep-rooted. We speak for the whole people. We will not be dismissed. We are not going away.' Haacaaluu repeatedly demanded, *Jirtuu*? "Are we here?' The crowd roared, 'Yes!'

I was not there, not physically, but among the Oromo leaders sitting in the gallery was a man called Abiy Ahmed, observing the ecstatic crowd and hearing the urgent message: 'We are here, closer to Arat Kilo.' Arat Kilo is a liberty monument, symbolic of government, four kilometers from the main palace in Finfinne.

When he was a child, Abiy Ahmed's mother predicted, 'You will end up in the palace. So when you go to school, bear in mind that one day you'll be someone who will serve the nation.' As he listened to a challenging young singer, I wonder if Abiy also heard again his mother's words? Transformation and victory for the Oromo were within reach and this man Abiy would take a firm hold of both. He understood, as Haacaaluu understood, that the youth of the country were leading the way. We are an old country, but our population is young. Its average age, I've heard, is just eighteen.

3

Without the weapons and battle tactics of their ancestors, the *Qeerroo* were destined to bring down a repressive government by non-violent civil resistance and a youthful Oromo leader was destined to lead the country.

The protests in Ethiopia, about a year after my Olympics moment on August 21, 2016, were not on the streets, which were eerily empty and quiet. Thousands participated in stay-at-home strikes, when businesses were closed and buses were stationary. The *Qeerroo* coordinated the strike through a wide range of tactics, including social media for some participants.

'Will the strikes work?' asked Iftu, as we followed events from faraway Flagstaff.

'Social media is very effective in making things happen,' I said. 'The *Qeerroo* know how to use it to best advantage. The government must make reforms or face anarchy.'

Every time public attention was focused on its wrongdoings, the Ethiopian government shut down social media platforms and the Internet. This was one way they tried to stop the strikes too. As you might expect in one of the most censored countries in the world, Internet and telephone services were controlled by only one provider, state-owned Ethio Telecom.

The strikers protested many injustices, including the wrongful imprisonment of Oromo leaders, Bekele Gerba, Merera Gudina, and many others. At the end of September of 2017, the Federal Supreme Court had announced Bekele's imminent release from prison on bail. We thought he would be able to defend the charges against him from outside the grim walls of Qilinto.

I often thought of Bekele, there in Qilinto when the fire and gunshots ended the life of Kebede. Bekele's daughter, Bontu, led a search for her father when prison authorities refused to provide information to anxious families and friends, and she spoke publicly on their behalf. Bontu was briefly detained by security forces in the town of Mojo, not long after the fire.

'We are relieved that the Supreme Court granted my father the bail,' she said in a statement released when the decision was announced, 'but we are at the same time worried that he is still facing serious criminal charges. We are even more worried because we know all the charges against him were politically motivated. We have to wait and see what happens because sometimes the prison administration acts above the law.'

She hoped to see Bekele walk out of prison the next day, but he did not appear. Prison authorities claimed 'an administrative mix-up' and refused to let him go.

'I wonder if the ruling party is deliberately trying to provoke the *Qeerroo*, who respect Bekele?' I demanded. 'If the young ones oppose the delay for his release, the authorities have an excuse to gun them down and impose a new state of emergency.'

The previous state of emergency, imposed after the *Irreecha* murders, was lifted after about ten months.

'Provoking our people didn't work after the prison fire,' Iftu said. 'We didn't know for ages where Tokuma was, or Bekele. It was a taunt, wasn't it? Protest and we will come after you.'

We soon knew where Kebede was. I didn't say this aloud to Iftu. She knew where Tokuna was, but she lived in daily dread of hearing that he had died in prison.

We were following the fate of another prison inmate, Merera Gudina, arrested after his visit to those meetings in Brussels that I attended. He was silenced and isolated, but a good man called Lemma Megersa was elected by the Council of the State of Oromia as President of the regional government, the Oromia National Regional State. His deputy was Abiy Ahmed.

I remembered Merera Gudina declaring in Brussels, 'Until the Oromos get their proper place in our country, I don't think it can function effectively. The problem is the government wants to rule in the old way and people are resisting being ruled in the old way.'

I had much to occupy my thoughts as I trained around the streets and nature trails of Flagstaff. My second winter in a foreign land was approaching and I watched the aspens drop their leaves. If only Ethiopia could shed its corrupt regime so easily. The EPRDF insisted that Ethiopia was an island of stability in a troubled region and a vision of 'Ethiopia rising' was on the horizon.

I wondered why the US, the country that gave me sanctuary, an ally of Ethiopia, was not responding to an island of stability about to sink under the weight of its corrupt deeds and human rights abuse. The *Qeerroo* were rising, however. In October, US House Resolution 128 was pulled in apparent response to threats by the Ethiopian government that it would withdraw as a partner in America's counter-terrorism efforts. A big lobbying firm in Washington DC was paid $150,000 a month ($1.8 million annually) to influence America's policy makers largely to oppose this legislation calling for reform in Ethiopia.

As the American Christmas approached in 2017, clashes in Ethiopia intensified. Attention was increasingly focused on conflicts instigated by an armed force known as Liyu Police at the border between the Somali and Oromia regional states within Ethiopia. Thousands of Oromos and a large number of Somalis were dispossessed of their homes, herds, and businesses in a large-scale displacement that once again was scarcely noticed in the Western world.

The Oromo and the Somali. I thought of Mo Farah, my rival on the track and my brother off it. Mo was born in a Somali town not far from the border where all the conflict was occurring. He was separated from his twin brother when the family suddenly left their war-torn country. He didn't see his twin again for ten years. I thought of Aduna, who looks so much like me we could be mistaken for twins. He sometimes visited me in the US, but at each parting he became distressed at leaving me behind. *Kan booyee nu raasu garaa garaa…*What cries and trembles is the heart, the heart….

4

The people I met on my training runs called 'Happy New Year!' as they passed me on January 1, 2018. I grinned and raised my hand. It was destined to be a revolutionary year in Ethiopia, starting with an announcement by the prime minister, Hailemariam Desalegn, that the notorious Maekelawi detention center in Finfinne would be closed! The unspeakably awful place was used by Mengistu Hailemariam as a headquarters for 'police investigation' for seventeen years. The EPDRF used it for the same purpose for the next twenty-seven years.

The closure was good news, but it meant nothing if prisoners were just relocated to another prison to face the same abuses. Those responsible for torture at Maekelawi should be held to account. The Maekelawi prison was destined to be 'a state-of-the-art museum'. What a sick joke. Who would want to remember the grisly horrors of that dreadful place? Anyway, Maekelawi didn't close until after other amazing changes occurred.

I went to Houston to run the half-marathon. It was a bitterly cold day and I thought of my hero, Abebe Bikila, struggling with the icy conditions in Boston all those years ago. I also thought of Demssew Tsega Abebe, who had run well in Houston before his captors savaged his feet. I ran in 3rd place in January of 2018. Then I went home to the good news that Merera Gudina had been released from prison.

Before I left for Houston, I read about Hailemariam's Desalegn's decision to have the cases of jailed politicians annulled or pardoned 'in order to improve the national consensus and widen the democratic space'. I didn't really believe it, but the man was getting desperate. That much was clear. His government was disintegrating.

'It feels good to be out of prison.' Merera was replying to questions after his release from Qilinto. 'I call on the government to hold honest negotiations with political organizations to create a democratic Ethiopia that accommodates everyone equally. I have never violated the law. I was a former member of parliament. I know the constitution and the law. I have been always respecting that.'

About 1,000 supporters gathered in Merera's hometown of Burayu to welcome him. They held banners that read Hidhaa fi shirri gabsoo Oromoo duubatti hin deebisu (Incarceration and intrigue will not reverse the Oromo struggle).

Iftu longed to hear that Tokuma was free. Thousands of others were being released. Iftu and the children had been with me for nearly a year. In 2018, on the same day, February 14th , that we were reunited in Miami, I heard that Demssew Tsega Abebe's family had arrived in Washington DC! They had won a humanitarian immigration petition. Tears came to our eyes as we read his press statement.

'I miss my family, my children. My son, he knows he waits a long time, but I am coming back to him. This is the first time I see my daughter. Valentine's Day isn't much of a holiday in Ethiopia, but I am proud to be reuniting with my family on a day that celebrates love, in a nation where I am free to express myself. I am so happy. I thank God.'

What about Bekele Gerba? We were all anxious about Bekele because of reports that he was in poor health. The diaspora rallied to his support.

'Bekele is a principled and visionary leader who has become a defiant symbol of freedom and justice in Ethiopia, a symbolism that came to represent a mortal threat to the EPRDF regime,' wrote Mohammed Ademo in *OPride*. 'His message of hope and redemption resonates far and wide among the young generation whose energy continues to fuel the relentless anti-government protests. That is why in calling for his release, activists and protesters throughout Oromia and Amhara, see themselves in Bekele's ordeal, thus their individual moral duty.'

A social media campaign urged medical care for Bekele and more general strikes called for his immediate release. Finally Bekele walked free in February. In Adama, he was given a hero's welcome by tens of thousands who gathered at the stadium, and Oromo everywhere celebrated. I agreed with those who saw Bekele as a giant but gentle champion of our nonviolent struggle for justice. Someone in the social media said that he represented the moral clarity of Martin Luther King, Jr. and the defiance and steadfastness of Nelson Mandela.

Soon similar big claims would be made for another Oromo man, but not before the astounding news that Hailemariam Desalegn had resigned as Ethiopia's prime minister and as chairman of the EPRDF. In a televised address, he said his resignation was 'vital in the bid to carry out reforms that would lead to sustainable peace and democracy. Unrest and a political crisis have led to the loss of lives and displacement of many.'

That was an understatement. By the time he finally stepped down, Desalegn had no power and no control over the streets. His resignation was an unspoken acknowledgement of the strength of relentless opposition to his government.

This was a crucial moment in our history and all eyes were on the palace in Finfinne. Who would take Desalegn's place and what difference would he make?

Then, before the ink had dried on Desalegn's resignation signature, another state of emergency was declared.

Iftu and I stared at each other in disbelief.

'What now?' she asked. 'Why now?'

'I suppose it's in response to the resignation.' That's the only thing I could think of. 'They'll want to make the transfer of power without too much more disruption.'

I also thought to myself later, as I ran along one of my favorite routes near Sedona, that the EPRDF had not learnt much from its past mistakes. Denying basic rights under another state of emergency wasn't going to work. I had to concentrate on my next big race, the Tokyo Marathon on February 25th. So much was happening in a short time and I could not afford to be distracted. I had to stay focused. My training was disrupted in so many ways. The sun was shining and the red buttes stood out tall and strong against the blue sky. I ran on with renewed purpose.

My race in Tokyo was better than the one in Chicago, but the day belonged to the Kenyans and the Japanese runners. I was in 6th place. I flew out of Tokyo, with the silent prayer that I would return for the 2020 Olympics in the city where Abebe Bikila won gold more than fifty years ago. To think that he rose to the challenge so soon after an appendix operation. There were many challenges ahead for me, on and off the course. I went back to Flagstaff, wondering what would happen next. Just as it was hard to predict a winner in the marathon, it was hard to choose the winner in the choice of a new Ethiopian prime minister.

'The ruling coalition must appoint an Oromo politician as prime minister.' That was the general opinion inside and outside of Oromia.

Many Oromo protesters thought that the only suitable candidates to lead Ethiopia out of this unexpected situation would be Lemma Megersa or Abiy Ahmed. Whoever was elected had to quickly address deeper problems in Ethiopia. Would he heed the protesters on the street crying, 'Self-rule for our region, shared rule for Ethiopia'? The Oromo were calling for greater self-rule at the regional level, as well as the right to control the lands they lived and worked on. They demanded recognition of their ethnic identity and language rights at the national level.

Abiy Ahmed was elected leader of the Oromo People's Democratic Party, a move seen by many as positioning him for election within the ruling EPRDF ruling coalition as the next prime minister of the country. Was Abiy the man for the job?

5

Abiy Ahmed was born in 1976. His childhood name was Abiyot, meaning 'Revolution' in Amharic, a name sometimes given to children in the aftermath of the Derg revolution of 1974. He was born at the right time, destined to become an Oromo revolutionary leader. As a young man, after the death of his oldest brother, he joined the armed struggle against Mengistu. When the Derg fell, he took formal military training—a soldier before he was a politician, like many Ethiopian parliamentarians.

He was one of the central figures in the violent fight against the illegal land-grabbing activities in Oromia, especially around Finfinne. Although the 'Master Plan' at the heart of the land-grabbing was quashed in 2016, the disputes continued for some time, with a rising toll of injuries, imprisonments and deaths. His firm stand against land-grabbing promoted Abiy rapidly in the ranks to commander of the Oromo protesters, mostly *Qeerroo*. He was ready to combat all foes in the political arena.

In late March of 2018, Abiy was elected from among the parties within the EPRDF to become the next prime minister of Ethiopia and was approved by the parliament in early April of 2018. I admit that I was cautious at first. 'I am hopeful he will change things,' I said in a public statement. 'At least some things will be better than the past. However, this won't happen overnight. I think it is better to give him some time and see what he does.'

What he did in a short time in 2018 was truly astonishing. He put an end to the state of emergency, closed Maekelawi, released tens of thousands of political prisoners and journalists, and committed to reform Ethiopia's anti-terrorism and civil society laws. When he acknowledged that torture and state terrorism really did happen, I enlisted as one of his many supporters, thinking of my murdered friend, Kebede, and many others. By admitting that the EPRDF used torture and terrorist tactics to stay in power in the past, Abiy showed that he was serious about changing our country for the better.

This was the first time an Ethiopian prime minister has publicly admitted that torture was taking place and the first time he commented on the poisonous problem of security force abuse.

'Terrorism is not just an act of trying to forcefully overthrow a government,' he said in parliament. 'The government's unconstitutional use of force to stay in power should also be considered terrorism. Does our country's constitution sanction torture?'

After I heard that speech, I suggested to Iftu, 'Let's put something on Facebook to show we are with Abiy Ahmed.'

We included the children and stood as a family group, holding up photographs and a poster, 'I stand by Dr Abiy and support his vision and direction for our country.' About 1,500 of my followers gave the thumbs up for that post. Many of them were in Finfinne, wearing T-shirts with pictures of Abiy and hailing taxis plastered with Abiy stickers. Facebook was bright with 'Abiy-mania' scenes.

We saw footage of a huge crowd of people gathered in Meskel Square, the favored place in Finfinne for public gatherings, to attend an Abiy rally. He addressed the crowd wearing a brightly colored T-shirt with Nelson Mandela and the African continent on it.

'For the past 100 years, hate has done a great deal of damage to us,' he said.

Then a grenade exploded, killing and wounding some in the crowd, but not Abiy. He was escorted from the stage.

'It was [a] well-orchestrated attack, an unsuccessful attempt by forces who do not want to see Ethiopia united.' That was Abiy's response to the incident. 'Love will win. Forgiveness will win. Killing is a sign of defeat. They failed yesterday. They failed today. They will fail tomorrow.'

Abiy's next dramatic move made headlines around the world. He brokered peace with Eritrea, ending a bitter war that dated back many decades. Abiy and Eritrean President Isaias Afwerki signed a declaration, saying that the state of war between the two countries was over.

'What do you make of this?' I asked Yonas Mebrahtu, the Eritrean runner who first invited me to Flagstaff and befriended me.

'It is amazing,' he said cautiously. 'So many people are overjoyed that they are reunited at last with family across the border.'

We were sitting at the table in my apartment. Yonas was fond of the children and kind to Iftu. He was a regular visitor to our home and we shared many meals together. We didn't have to eat a tough old goat while Iftu was in the kitchen!

'It is strange to think,' Yonas went on, 'that in the most recent Ethiopia-Eritrea border war, Abiy led an intelligence team to discover positions of the Eritrean Defence Forces.'

Many strange and unexpected things were happening, but exiled Eritreans were gloomy. It seemed that the Eritrean president was in no hurry to match the reforms in Ethiopia. On his side of the border there was no rule of law, no parliament, no constitution, one-man rule, and many cabinet ministers in prison or dead in detention. The exiles, for the most part, were not in a hurry to go home.

6

Abiy was appearing on many different fronts, meeting his supporters and making new friends and allies. He visited Djibouti, Kenya, Sudan, and Somalia to build better relations. Soon after his meetings with Isaias Afwerki in Asmara and Finfinne, he was in the US to enlist help in his reforms from the diaspora communities. He encouraged Ethiopians to go home and help him in any way they could, as professionals and investors.

He asked us to support '*medemer*', meaning 'to be added to one another'. There he was, hugging and shaking hands in public with former opposition politicians, taking selfies with fans and beaming for the media, but he did not deviate from his reform platform.

'Today, if you all decide, if you commit to healing, then we as Ethiopia will write a new story, like we did during Adwa,' he said. Adwa was a decisive 1896 battle that ended the first Italian-Ethiopian War and ensured that modern Ethiopia would remain free of 'formal' colonial rule.

'If you want to be the pride of your generation,' he went on, adjusting the cuffs on his stylish blazer trimmed with colors identified as Oromo, 'then you must decide that Oromos, Amharas, Wolaytas, Gurages, and Siltes are all equally Ethiopian.'

He addressed the crowds in *Afaan Oromoo*, Amharic, and Tigrinya. He is also fluent in English.

'My ultimate goal is to ensure a democratic election takes place in Ethiopia in 2020.'

We were all thrilled at such optimism and we wanted to join his peaceful march to democracy.

'The level of hope is something we had not seen since the election of Barack Obama,' observed Mohammed Ademo, who acted as a consultant during Abiy's tour to visit the American diaspora. 'People are crying because for the first time they see light at the end of the tunnel. People have finally found the leader they've been waiting for.'

So many tears, but happy tears. Tokuma was out of prison! It wasn't long before he told us that he had returned to university studies.

Then Mohammed called me with exciting news.

'I'm going home, Feyisa! Before Abiy, a return to Ethiopia was too risky. I had freedom here in the US to speak out loudly on behalf of our people and I would almost certainly be arrested had I gone back. But now I am happy to be going home at this hopeful moment for country and people.'

He had been in exile for sixteen years. I was happy for him too. Reading what he said about going home brought more tears to my eyes. This was an emotional time.

'Exile is a deeply lamentable, nostalgic, and at times traumatic existence. You live here and also there but ultimately in neither of the two places. The fond memories of "home" and the struggle to regain it were what kept me going all these years.'

Bekele Gerba visited the US from early May to early August, welcomed wherever he went.

I felt restless, but another race was getting close and I was training for it, the Bogotá Half Marathon at the end of July. I needed a win, but I missed out again, running in behind Betesfa Getahun, an Ethiopian. I had a tussle with the Kenyan, Dickson Chumba, for second place. We clocked identical times, 1:05:23. Bogotá is at 2,600 m above sea level, and the day was hot, sunny, and windy. My heart was in another place of high altitude, where it was almost certainly raining at that time of year. I could almost smell the wet eucalyptus trees. I watched Betesfa board a plane bound for Finfinne and wished I could go with him. I was homesick.

I thought of other things that Abiy said while he was in America. 'This country has beautiful highways, it has beautiful malls. All of you with the means have cars. Lights don't go out. Phones don't cut out. Water doesn't get shut off. So why is it that via Viber, via Facebook, via YouTube, you all spend every night in Ethiopia?'

Why? Many Oromo were ready to go and do what Mohammed said we could do—change the narrative. When Jawar Mohammed, the outspoken activist, returned in August, he was well received. He agitated for years on social media for political change back home. This was the first time he would see his own country since 2008, made possible now after terrorist charges against him were dropped.

'We used social media and formal media so effectively that the state was completely overwhelmed,' Jawar claimed in one interview. 'The only option they had was to face reform or accept full revolution.'

Jawar had promised his supporters among the *Qeerroo* that he would take off his shoes and walk through the streets of Ambo. He did that and planted a tree at the site where a young man was killed by security forces nearly fifteen years ago. I had similar plans to plant a tree for Kebede in Jaldu.

Anything seemed possible in this time to rejoice. Andargachew Tsige, the opposition politician seized in Yemen, was released from jail. Criminal charges against Berhanu Nega, leader of Ginbot 7, were dropped too.

I reflected on all that had happened as I trained. Two years had passed since I left my country. I had been dreaming more and more about home. I had even predicted to myself that I would be back in my beloved Jaldu before another year passed.

One morning, when I returned home, ready to shower and eat, it happened. An invitation for me to return home, offered in an open letter from Haile Gebresilassie, president of the Ethiopian Athletics Federation, and Ashebir Woldegiorgis, head of the Ethiopian Olympic Committee.

'Athlete Feyisa Lilesa has scored great results at the Rio Olympics and other athletics competitions enabling Ethiopia's flag to be hoisted to great heights,' the letter said. 'We want Lilesa to return to his home country to resume his athletics competition and upon his return we are prepared to give him a hero's welcome.'

Iftu was looking over my shoulder and I turned to embrace her. She gave me her best cheeky grin.

'I hope it will be better than the one promised if you returned home after Rio!'

I kissed Iftu and swung her around. It was a time to dance. 'What about Haile Gebresilassie? He might pretend to be nice to me at the welcome!'

I did not respond to the invitation immediately. There was much to think about. The children were settled in school and I had commitments on my racing calendar. By now you understand that I begrudge time, even for a big occasion like this, that interrupts my training schedule. Would we all go home together or would I go alone and gauge the situation before making a final move? Iftu had sold most of our household goods before she left for the US. We would have to start all over again to set up a new home.

The media was buzzing with speculation.

'Lilesa can teach his exemplary ways to other athletes and teach strength to our youngsters,' urged Ashebir Woldegiorgis, speaking to one journalist. 'That's the main call, so he can come back to participate in the sport he loves and pass it on by running and by advising to elevate Ethiopia's sport.'

I decided to go home alone, but only for a visit. I was the risk taker. All of us—Iftu, Soko, Sora, and I—could go back to live in Finfinne later if everything worked out. I could not be sure if the situation in Ethiopia was ready for us and I did not want to put the family in danger. This was hard for Iftu, but in her usual quiet way she accepted it as the best plan for now.

The date for my welcome home was set for 23 September 2018. 'It's going to be grand,' promised Mohammed. He was working on details with the organising committee.

I had a race to run in Philadelphia, the Rock 'n' Roll Philadelphia Half Marathon, a week before my big day in Finfinne. I came in 5th, with my occasional Arizona training mate, Abdi Abdirahman, close behind me.

Qabbanee was there to watch the race. I presented her with the medal I was given for competing in the race, a small gesture of thanks for all she has done for me personally and for Oromos everywhere, most recently in advocacy.

I went back to Flagstaff, my mind on what lay ahead. I allowed myself to dream of attending *Irreecha* with Hadhaa and seeing the *kello* flowers blooming in the countryside. As I thought about our land, I wondered what plans Abiy had for the majority of his people, who live in rural villages dotted across Ethiopia. Too many have been moved off their ancestral land. Too many barely survive in extreme poverty. For Oromo, land is not just a natural resource, but a source of life, spirituality, culture, and identity.

The land will be looking at its best, I imagined, green and fresh as the rainy season eased. Instead of vultures, the yellow-billed kites would be flying in the skies over Finfinne. Oromo flags would also be flying high. I was going home.

7

The big news from Ethiopia was that members of the previously banned Oromo Liberation Front had arrived in Finfinne, just one week before me. About 1,500 OLF fighters returned from Eritrea, where they had established their base of operations. OLF fighters and leaders were welcomed by thousands of Oromo in Finfinne, *handhuura Oromiyaa*, center of Oromia, there to witness this historic moment when the long-banned force came home.

Drone photos showed scenes of huge crowds, estimated at close to four million people, in a sea of Oromo nationalist flags: green and red fields depicting an *odaa* tree on a background of yellow in a sunburst pattern, a design long championed by the OLF and adopted by the youth as a symbol of national identity. *Qeerroo* turned out in force to celebrate their *Oromummaa*.

'I am happy to be here after twenty-six years of struggle from outside of Ethiopia,' said the OLF leader, Dawud Ibsa. 'We have been struggling to bring the changes that we are seeing now, positive signs that include the respect for rule of law. That's why we came here.'

Abiy had adopted a policy of inviting and welcoming various opposition groups back to Ethiopia. The tumultuous 'coming home' was costly. Dawud Ibsa had declared that the OLF would become part of the peaceful struggle towards democracy. But while he claimed a victory of sorts in Meskel Square, clashes erupted that ended in more bloodshed on the streets.

I think that these events were partly symptomatic of 'Oromophobia', an irrational fear of all things Oromo by other ethnic groups who felt threatened by the large gathering in the city, the waving of flags that once would have been seized and the bearers beaten and arrested. But there was also talk of unruly Oromos, a criminal element, on the outskirts of Finfinne, targeting minority groups, attacking homes, and looting businesses, chanting, 'Leave our land'.

The scene had turned ugly. This ought to be a time for peace, not a time for war. Abiy's reforms had to go further to investigate the causes and instigators of this violence and put an end to it.

'Perhaps you should not go,' Iftu said anxiously as we followed the drama. 'You may be targeted. It is too dangerous, Feyisa.'

I had no intention of changing my plans. I was planning to fly to Chicago first, where I would be joined by some of the diaspora accompanying me to Finfinne. It was all arranged.

Then, a couple of days before I was leaving, I got a phone call from an organizer of the event.

'We have to postpone the event.' I could hear the disappointment and weariness in his voice. 'I'm sorry, Feyisa. The Police Commissioner is concerned about the general unrest in the city since the OLF arrived. He has banned all public gatherings until further notice.'

This decree affected not only my return from abroad, but also required the postponement of a huge concert planned by the popular Ethiopian singer, Teddy Afro.

I put on my running shoes and drove to Lake Mary Meadows, outside of Flagstaff, where the *kello* flowers bloomed and the beautiful horses grazed. I left the car to look at them. I thought of the photograph of a horse, shared with thousands on Facebook, when the OLF came to town in Finfinne. Against a grey backdrop of heavy clouds, wet roads, and bleak buildings, a big brown Oromo horse was rearing up on its hind legs, forelegs in the air. A masterful Oromo horseman, wearing a baseball cap, was in the saddle.

I started to run hard and the horses lifted enquiring heads to watch me. I was that Oromo horse, hooves clattering down, charging forward, preparing to clear the last high hurdle.

<h1 style="text-align:center">8</h1>

Two runners well known to me were charging forward on the track, claiming big victories. In Berlin, on September16, 2018, Eliud Kipchoge broke the world record for the men's marathon in a time of 2 hours, 1 minute, and 39 seconds. Dennis Kimetto's record had fallen to 'the boss man', as Eliud was known in his training camp.

'I have run 2.00, 2.01, 2.03, 2.04, and 2.05!' Eliud joked. 'Next time I want to run 2.02!'

We all knew that he really wanted to be the first man to run the sub-two-hour marathon.

Mo Farah won Chicago on October 7, 2018. I saw him on YouTube, grinning hugely, dancing around at the finish line like Abel Kirui, who ran in 7th place.

Eliud and Mo will be the men to beat in the 2020 Olympics men's marathon. What a contest that will be. In a dream I saw them leading the field, first and second, with an Ethiopian runner behind them. Who was he? The image was not clear.

You have now heard a lot about me, 'the dream man'. Dreams are not all wild imaginings. I remember Iftu thinking she must be dreaming when she saw me make the protest sign at the end of the Rio race. Returning to my country seemed like the end of a marathon dream that started when I left Ethiopia on August 17, 2016. There will be a happy ending, I told myself, and I will be smiling as broadly as Eliud Kipchoge or Mo Farah at the end of a race when they claim victory.

My return was rescheduled for October 21, 2018, but once again, the organizers were told to call the event off because of security concerns.

'No,' I said firmly. 'This time I am coming. I will not delay the trip or disrupt my training any more. I don't need a big welcome, I just want to go home.'

Iftu packed one small case for me and I stuffed other things in my Nike sports bag. The family gathered around me at the door to watch me go.

'Remember Spiridon Louis, the winner of the first marathon?' asked Iftu. '"That hour was something unimaginable and it still appears to me in my memory like a dream. Twigs and flowers were raining down on me. Everybody was calling out my name and throwing their hats in the air." This is what it will be like for you, Feyisa.'

'Next time,' I whispered as I hugged her, 'I hope we will all go together.'

I left my little family in a faraway place. They were accustomed to my absences, but this one was different.

Just over two years ago, I left an unhappy home called Ethiopia, where too many of her children were harassed, intimidated, detained, abused, tortured, and disappeared. Those who escaped capture were deprived of the simplest and sweetest things that make a safe and hospitable haven. I was torn between love for the home that nurtured me and despair for those who dared to protest her harsh disciplinary measures.

I was not a prodigal son or a runaway athlete. I had to leave and report on the parent body. I had to warn the world about what was happening in my mother country. I lived in exile, watching from a distance, everything that occurred in my absence. I was allowed to go home because the door was no longer shut against me. I hoped to walk into welcoming arms and to hear reassuring words about the new caretakers.

9

First stop, Chicago, a familiar airport. Then I boarded an Ethiopian Airlines flight, direct to Finfinne, a 14-hour journey. I slept well, with no memorable dream, and when I woke my destination was close. I changed into the grey suit and tie with white shirt that I wore to the Washington DC press conference more than two years ago. I was ready.

I looked out the window, watching as the plane descended into Ethiopia and thinking of all the tragedies that had taken me away and all that had happened since I left—some triumphs, but many more tragedies. I had resigned myself to many years in exile, but here I was, after two years and two months, about to see many things that were dear to me.

When the plane landed, I was taken by car to the VIP section of the domestic terminal. A row of Federal Police in their blue uniforms and forage caps, batons in hand, stood guard, but I scarcely noticed them. I saw my mother and father waiting, proudly clothed in Oromo apparel.

'Feyisa! My son! Feyisa! My son!' The slight figure of *Hadhaa* came towards me, raising her arms and crying. I held her for a long time, as she sobbed my name over and over again.

My father was watching, stern of face and rigid in stance. We hugged each other briefly and walked together to the entrance. A crowd ran to meet me, with garlands and bunches of roses, wrapped in 'Welcome' paper. Smiles, laughter, hugs, tears, television cameras, photos, and more photos.

We moved into the lounge for the first press conference. I was seated in an ornate chair, surrounded by reporters, friends, and family.

'I knew this day was coming,' I told them, 'because I knew the blood spilled by all these people was not going to be in vain.'

I looked around the room. There was Derartu Tulu, the hero of Iftu's grandmother, representing the Ethiopian Athletics Federation. Mohammed Ademo was there, then Director of Oromia Broadcasting Network. Questions were asked and answers given for about an hour. I thought of the sceptical reporters who interviewed me at the airport when I left for the Olympics, and my words to them came back: 'I am going to the Games as an Oromo runner, like many others before me. I love my country....'

I went out to the car waiting, with police escort, to take me to the next venue. We drove off but did not get far.

A jubilant roar from my Oromo supporters, mostly *Qeerroo*, waiting outside the terminal, greeted me. A line of soldiers stood their ground in front of the crowd, who shouted my name. I left the car and thanked them for their courage in keeping up their resistance to wrong. Together we raised our arms to give the protest sign. I spoke hopefully of the changes that were happening and we raised our right arms in the victory salute.

'Feyisa Lilesa! Sinjalada! Feyisa Lilesa! We love you!'

I left them reluctantly. This day belonged to them too. Many of them had done so much more than I had. I heard later that a couple of the police holding them back had tried to provoke them by seizing flags and stamping on them. When the holders of the flags reacted, others in the crowd begged them to remain still and silent. They didn't want trouble on this big occasion.

The next stop was the Elilly Hotel, the same hotel where politicians watching the Olympic race spilled their drinks and broke their glasses in anger as I protested against their regime. Another press conference was held. I thanked the international media who had picked up my story and taken it to the world.

'What sign will you use now that you are home?' That was the final question.

I looked out at the cameras, the microphones, the journalists poised to record my answer.

'I want to give the victory sign, the right arm raised, to acknowledge all the things that have been achieved.' I paused, and the scenes came back to me—the bodies in the street, the tortured in prison, Tokuma and his friends, Bekele Gerba, the *Irreecha* massacre, the prison fire, the murder of Kebede. 'So many have suffered, so many have died. There is still much to be done. The protest sign is a reminder to the world of what has happened in Oromia. I must use it still....'

The tears would not be stopped. I bowed my head and pressed my fingers to my eyes. The room was silent.

*Kan booyee nu raasu garaa garaa…*What cries and trembles is the heart, the heart....

I stood up and left the room. I thought of the press conference after the Rio Marathon, when I tried desperately to find the words that would reach the world. 'The Ethiopian government is killing the Oromo people and taking their land and resources. So the Oromo people are protesting, and I support the protest as I am Oromo. Oromo are my people. Oromo people now protest what is right, for peace, for a place. I cannot go back. If not kill me, they will put me in prison. Maybe I will move country....'

The journalists were day runners, couriers and heralds like Pheidippides, that long-ago Greek hero. Now they hurried to write their versions of my story and to file their copy. Their editors would decide the best headlines.

I thought of Aduna once welcoming me home. 'Feyisa is back! Feyisa is back!'

That's a good headline: Feyisa is back.

Do you remember where I was when he ran to meet me that time? I was back in Jaldu, returning to my village after a very difficult time in the city. I made another memorable return about a month after my 2018 welcome in Finfinne. This was a homecoming like no other, pageantry on a *booqa birra* (shining day). This was one of my best dreams coming true.

As I entered the place of my birth, the villagers came running to meet me. Some were on horseback, surrounding me on all sides. I didn't have to beg for a horse like I did all those years ago at the *gugsi*. A brown horse, every bit as splendid as the one I saw on Facebook, was ready and waiting, decked out in Oromo colors to match the finery worn by many in the cheering crowd. I was presented with a lion headdress and cape to wear, a privilege reserved for someone highly regarded.

There can be no greater honor for an Oromo man than to ride a horse in ceremonial state, on his own land, among his own people. The day proceeded with our traditional greetings and blessings, songs and speeches, food and dance. One older man, overcome by seeing our culture on full display, cried, 'I am reminded of what we have lost in my lifetime!'

My last visit to Jaldu was just before the Olympic Games. I drove away that day feeling so much pain and anger and frustration.

'I am so happy to be home,' I told the crowd who welcomed me back. I stood in front of the modest house where I was born. 'I see here today so much love and respect. We must build our future together. We must be united. I appeal to the *Qeerroo* to work for the good of all. Never reject those of us who come to you with a message of peace and reconciliation.'

My people needed hope; they needed heroes. We have songs and stories about the heroes of old. *Bara Mulata Fayiso*—in the era of Mulata Fayiso... *Bara Alemu Qixessa*—in the era of Alemu Qixessa... For my era people will speak reverently of *Bara Bekele Gerba*—in the era of Bekele Gerba... *Bara Mulata Abiy Ahmed*—in the era of Abiy Ahmed.

My people may weave my part into the story of the Oromo, starting, 'In the era of Feyisa Lilesa, a story is often told. He was born in his family's home, according to tradition, in Tulu Bultuma village, district of Jaldu, West Shoa Zone, Ethiopia. He is Oromo. His birthday, February 1, 1990, was his time to be born. His destiny, decided at his birth and endorsed by his name, Feyisa, was to save or heal his people....'

My story ends here for now. The silver Olympic medal is the symbol of my destiny. It came home with me to Ethiopia. It is a memorial to all those who were tortured and killed in the struggle for *bilisummaa Oromoo*, freedom and peace for the Oromo. When I die, I will be buried in *biyyee Oromoo*, soil of my father's land, Oromia.

Postscripts

I n 1960, a barefoot Abebe Bikila won an Olympic marathon in Rome and became a symbol of the determination and the endurance of the Ethiopian people. Since then the world has watched, awestruck, as the country's long-distance runners have triumphed at the Games time and again.

Poster at the entrance to the VIP lounge at the Bole International Airport, Domestic Terminal, Addis Ababa, under the heading: *Ethiopia: Land of Origins.*

In 2019:

With a symbolic gesture, Feyisa Lilesa and Abiy Ahmed demonstrated publicly that Feyisa's hands are now unshackled. Feyisa gave his medal to the Ethiopian people, announcing: 'Guyyaan gootni oromoo waadaa ummataaf gale dabarsee kennu dhiyatee jira; goota irraa hin hafan (The day an Oromo hero delivers a promise he made for the public is coming up; so do not miss out on the hero's event).' Abiy Ahmed was awarded the Nobel Peace Prize. He is the first Ethiopian Nobel Laureate. Eliud Kipchoge became the first athlete to run a marathon in under two hours, beating the benchmark by 20 seconds. He covered the 26.2 miles (42.2 km) in one hour 59 minutes 40 seconds in Vienna, Austria. Irreecha was celebrated in Finfinne, the sacred center of Oromia, for the first time in 150 years.

Demssew Tsega died from cancer in 2019.

Postscripts 2020:

The killing of Haacaaluu Hundeessaa, the popular outspoken Oromo singer, sparked protests and a police crackdown leaving at least 177 dead and hundreds wounded.

In Addis Ababa and Oromia, police arrested at least 5,000 people, many in incommunicado detention with their whereabouts unknown. Those arrested included Jawar Mohammed and Bekele Gerba.

Author's Note

Feyisa Lilesa's protest gesture gained the attention of the world and the curiosity of one foreign writer living at the time in Addis Ababa. I am that writer, so this book was conceived in Ethiopia, an ancient, enigmatic country associated with famine and poverty, but also famous for its long-distance runners. The country has always intrigued me, especially after writing the authorized biography, *Interestingly Enough: The Life of Thomas Keneally*. Thomas delighted in going to distant places to find his stories. 'I have just visited the most remarkable place on earth,' he claimed, after his first visit to Eritrea. I felt the same way about neighboring Ethiopia.

I went to Ethiopia in August of 2016 as a volunteer teacher, arriving one day after significant protest marches in Addis Ababa. I observed the people, their lifestyle, and their grievances. I followed the deteriorating situation before and after a state of emergency was imposed. I read about Feyisa Lilesa's defiant action at the Olympic Games, started researching the background to it and asked for his permission to write about him. This was a story that begged to be told. Feyisa agreed to my proposal and I interviewed him during a couple of weeks in Flagstaff, Arizona, in September of 2017. I returned to Ethiopia in October of 2018, when he did, to finish the story.

My firsthand (if limited) experience of Ethiopia, my cordial association with Feyisa, the network of contacts I have established, and the interviews I have conducted enabled me to write an unforgettable book. I am the author of several biographies of Australian authors, including internationally famous Colin Thiele (*Storm Boy*) and Thomas Keneally (*Schindler's List*). I have also written family and institutional histories, short stories, numerous feature articles, and conference papers.

Acknowledgements

I am particularly grateful to Feyisa Lelisa Gemechu for sharing his story with me and permitting it to be told to a worldwide readership. I also give thanks for the following people who have helped me in various capacities along the way:

Caalaa Hayiluu Abaataa, Demssew Abebe, Fessehaie Abraham, Mohammed Ademo, Jaalataa Alemu, Reeyot Alemu, Andrea Barron, Lubee Birru, Qumbi Boro, Gianni Demadonna, Teklu Deneke, Roman Dugassa, Bayissa Gemechu, Bekele Gerba, Sendaba Gerba, Sally Gibson, Mohammed Hassen, Lelisa Hika, Bonnie Holcomb, Felix Horne, Mo Farah, Iftu Kebede, Thomas Keneally, Assefa Kitilla, Martha Kuwee Kumsa, Hika Lamu, Iftu Mulisa Lamu, Melaku Makonnen, Yonas Mebrahtu, Sergio and Dyacy Moreira, Ken and Ruth Mortenson, Abdi Nureesa, Ebissa Regassa, Carol Simon, Abera Tefera, Megerssa Tolessa, Jimma Tufa, Tolcha Wagi, Negussie Wako. and Mulugeta Wondimu.

Thank you, Kassahun Checole (publisher) and Frank Blisard (editor) for your excellent work preparing the manuscript for publication.

Select Bibliography

Bartles, Lambert. *Oromo Religion, Myth and Rites of the Western Oromo of Ethiopia: An Attempt to Understand.* Berlin: Dietrich Reimer Verlag, 1990.

Baxter, P.T.W., Hultin, Jan and Triulzi, Alessandro. Eds. *Being and Becoming Oromo: Historical and Anthropological Enquiries.* Lawrenceville, NJ: Red Sea Press, 1996.

'Because I am Oromo: Sweeping Oppression in the Oromia Region of Ethiopia.' *Amnesty International Report*, 2014. https://www.amnesty.org/en/documents/afr25/006/2014/en/

Brokensha, David (ed). *A River of Blessing: Essays in Honour of Paul Baxter.* Syracuse, NY: Maxwell School of Citizenship and Public Affairs, Syracuse University, 1994.

Holcomb, Bonnie K. and Ibsa, Sisai. *The Invention of Ethiopia: The Making of a Dependent State in Northeast Africa.* Trenton, NJ: Red Sea Press, 1990.

Journal of Oromo Studies Vol. 1.1 (1993-). Publication of the Oromo Studies Association. http://www.oromostudies.org/publications/osa-journal

Judah, Tim. *Bikila: Ethiopia's Barefoot Olympian.* London: Reportage Press, 2008.

Kaplan, Robert D. *Surrender or Starve: Travels in Ethiopia, Sudan, Somalia, and Eritrea.* New York: Vintage Books, 1988.

Kumsa, Martha Kuwee. *Songs of Exile.* Kitchener, Ontario: Duudhaa Publishing, 2013.

Maffetone, Philip. *1:59: The Sub-Two-Hour Marathon is Within Reach....* New York: Skyhorse Publishing, 2014.

McCann, James C. *People of the Plow: An Agricultural History of Ethiopia, 1800-1900.* Wisconsin: University of Wisconsin Press, 1995.

Pankhurst, Richard. *The Ethiopians: A History.* Malden, MA: Blackwell Publishing, 1998.

Waugh, Evelyn. *Waugh in Abyssinia.* London: Longmans, Green Co Ltd, 1936.

Smith, Lahra. *Making Citizens of Africa: Ethnicity, Gender & National Identity in Ethiopia.* Africa Studies. Cambridge: Cambridge University Press, 2013.

'Such a Brutal Crackdown: Killings and Arrests in Response to Ethiopia's Oromo Protests'. *Human Rights Watch Report*, 2016. https://www.hrw.org/report/2016/06/15/such-brutal-crackdown/killings-and-arrests-response-ethiopias-oromo-protests

Websites:

http://aims-worldrunning.org/aims.html
https://www.amnesty.org/en/
http://www.europarl.europa.eu/portal/en
http://finfinnetribune.com/
https://www.hrw.org/
https://www.iaaf.org/home
https://www.opride.com/
https://oromoadvocacy.org/
https://www.oromiamedia.org/
https://www.runnersworld.com/
https://www.tassc.org/
https://www.washingtonpost.com/